Canada Through American Eyes

Jennifer Andrews

Canada Through American Eyes

Literature and Canadian Exceptionalism

Jennifer Andrews
Dalhousie University
Halifax, NS, Canada

ISBN 978-3-031-22119-4 ISBN 978-3-031-22120-0 (eBook)
https://doi.org/10.1007/978-3-031-22120-0

© The Editor(s) (if applicable) and The Author(s), under exclusive licence to Springer Nature Switzerland AG 2023
This work is subject to copyright. All rights are solely and exclusively licensed by the Publisher, whether the whole or part of the material is concerned, specifically the rights of translation, reprinting, reuse of illustrations, recitation, broadcasting, reproduction on microfilms or in any other physical way, and transmission or information storage and retrieval, electronic adaptation, computer software, or by similar or dissimilar methodology now known or hereafter developed.
The use of general descriptive names, registered names, trademarks, service marks, etc. in this publication does not imply, even in the absence of a specific statement, that such names are exempt from the relevant protective laws and regulations and therefore free for general use.
The publisher, the authors, and the editors are safe to assume that the advice and information in this book are believed to be true and accurate at the date of publication. Neither the publisher nor the authors or the editors give a warranty, expressed or implied, with respect to the material contained herein or for any errors or omissions that may have been made. The publisher remains neutral with regard to jurisdictional claims in published maps and institutional affiliations.

Cover credit line: ravphotographix / Alamy Stock Photo

This Palgrave Macmillan imprint is published by the registered company Springer Nature Switzerland AG.
The registered company address is: Gewerbestrasse 11, 6330 Cham, Switzerland

This book is dedicated with much love to
Linda Hutcheon

DECLARATION OF PERMISSIONS

"Escape to *Canada*: Richard Ford's Fugitive Novel." 2018. *Canadian Review of American Studies* 48 (1): 38–62.

"The Missionary Position: The American Roots of Northrop Frye's Peaceable Kingdom." 2018. *The Journal of Canadian Studies* 52 (2): 361–380.

"German Internment Camps in the Maritimes: Another Untold Story in P.S. Duffy's *The Cartographer of No Man's Land*." 2021. In *On the Other Side(s) of 150: Untold Stories and Critical Approaches to History, Literature, and Identity in Canada*, ed. Linda Morra and Sarah Henzi, 221–239. Waterloo: Wilfrid Laurier University Press.

"Becoming Bird(ie): Exposing Canadian Government Complicity with Forced Adoptions in Christina Sunley's *The Tricking of Freya*" 2021. In *Exploring Canada: Exploits and Encounters*, ed. Gerd Bjørhovde and Janne Korkka, 121–130. Bruxelles, Belgium: Peter Lang.

Preface: Escape to *Canada*

> *A relation of cruel optimism exists when something you desire is actually an obstacle to your flourishing. ... it might be a fantasy of the good life, or a political project. ... These kinds of optimistic relation[s] are not inherently cruel. They become cruel only when the object that draws your attachment actively impedes the aim that brought you to it initially. (Berlant 2011, 1)*

> *Taking the visual world in is a process of loss: learning to see is training careful blindness. To apprehend and recognize the visible is to eliminate as well as absorb visual data. Just as surely as representational technologies—the camera, the canvas, the theatrical frame, language itself—order visual apprehension to accord with a (constructed) notion of the real so too do human eyes. (Phelan 1993, 13)*

Shortly after his parents rob an out-of-state Midwestern bank to rescue themselves from bankruptcy, the 15-year-old protagonist of American writer Richard Ford's 2012 novel *Canada*, Dell Parsons, is asked by his mother, Neeva, "What do you know about Canada?" (2012, 141–142). Neeva Kamper, the college-educated daughter of Jewish immigrants who came to Canada from Poland to give their only daughter a better life, sees Canada as a potential escape for her children in the aftermath of their parents' unlawful activities. The question she poses is critical to Ford's plot because it foreshadows Dell's future in Canada. By crossing the Canada-US border and settling in Canada, and aided by a family friend, the teen can begin his life again and escape the criminal legacy of his parents who are jailed, lose touch with their children, and ultimately die without being

ix

reunited. The scene illustrates the ways that Canada has functioned as a blank slate on which to project the desires and fantasies of Americans. In particular, Canada becomes an attractive alternative for those who find themselves unable to live the American Dream, which offers the promise of material wealth, mobility with respect to class status, and a better life for subsequent generations of one's family. Yet Dell's answers, as constituted by the narrative that comprises *Canada*, provide a much more nuanced and contradictory set of answers than might be expected.

The story is of the marginalization of a segment of the US population who might be expected to reap the benefits of a post-Second World War economy: a white male who has served his country and his family. Dell Parson's father Bev is a discharged Air Force officer who lacks higher education and is barely able to support his family. His wife Neeva's teaching job is critical to their survival. However, as a "Jewish" woman "having an immigrant look," epitomized by her "unruly brown hair" (Ford 2012, 9, 5), Neeva is vulnerable to racism, despite possessing a college education. Thus, she encourages her children to consider themselves "non-observant" or "deracinated" (2012, 17) to protect their present and future opportunities. Bev, who failed to hold onto multiple jobs following his exit from the military, ultimately decides that, to gain access to the American middle class, he must resort to criminal activity. In *Canada*, Bev becomes the intermediary for "stolen beef transactions" between local Cree residents and a Black American train conductor. These goods are used to feed affluent passengers on trains that travel on the Great Northern Railway, both across the US and northward into Canada (2012, 41). The scheme goes awry when delivered meat rots unexpectedly and is deemed unusable, leaving Bev to cover the rapidly escalating losses.

Bev and his family settle in Great Falls, Montana, in 1956, eager to start a new life. Yet what soon becomes clear is that Bev finds himself in what American literary and cultural theorist Lauren Berlant famously described as "[a] relation of cruel optimism" with America (2011, 1). Bev seeks the "fantasy of the good life," and, while his efforts to forge "[t]hese kinds of optimistic relation[s] are not inherently cruel," it becomes clear that his desire to belong to and be part of the American middle class leads to his downfall and ultimately life in jail (2011, 1). For Bev, his efforts to attain a lifestyle that cannot be accessed without enormous risk reveal the ways in which the American Dream is inaccessible to most, even as it maintains an enormously powerful hold on working-class and marginalized American citizens. Bev may be a proud white Southerner who has served his country, but he is also someone who repeatedly makes bad decisions on behalf of his family. In contrast, Neeva poses a seemingly enigmatic question about Canada to Dell, precisely because she sees Canada as offering a viable alterna(rra)tive[1] to the limits of her family's future in the US, given the crimes she and her husband have committed, by offering her children the opportunity to begin their lives again.

Looking more closely at Neeva's efforts to school Dell about a future beyond the US—and Dell's struggle to alter his perspective in *Canada*—serves as a provocative model, in this book and more broadly, for thinking about what and how Americans see and write about Canada in a literary context and for probing the significance of those observations for both nations. To respond to his mother's query, Dell laments that what he knows about Canada is limited to the subject of his father's favorite jigsaw puzzle: an image painted by nineteenth-century American landscape painter Frederic Church titled "Niagara" (1857) that captures the iconic falls, a natural phenomenon that literally straddles the Canada-US border.[2] The day after the robbery, which the couple has described as an overnight business trip to their children, Bev retrieves the familiar puzzle from a hall closet and spreads the pieces out on the dining room table: "the puzzle ... formed a painting of Niagara Falls, painted by Frederic E. Church. It showed the great, rushing green water melting over low red rocks and turning white and yellow as it fell into the white-aired chasm. ... It was our father's favorite because it was dramatic" (Ford 2012, 122). He urges his family members to help him complete it, a task that embodies Bev's unrelenting faith in and desire to access the American Dream—one that seems to be within reach if one works hard and has the purchasing power as well as the leisure time to build the puzzle by "[f]iguring out the picture every time and searching for the right pieces" (2012, 122), tasks that Dell regards as a waste of time.

For Bev, this image of Niagara Falls provides the solace of fantasy. As he explains to Dell when the teenager gets up to use the toilet in the middle of the night, the retired officer lacks the education to get ahead and has failed to provide for his family using his "native ability" (2012, 144). In an act of whimsy, Bev repeats a childhood trick to amuse the sleepy teen by pretending to swallow one of the last puzzle pieces, leaving Dell baffled and frustrated when his father reveals his empty hands, explaining "[i]t's not a trick *every* time" (2012, 146). In this moment, Dell is confronted by the constructed nature of reality, especially as embodied through the commercialization of Church's iconic image, a lesson that will help him to forge an alternative life to that of his parents. So, when Neeva finally queries Dell about Canada, he is already struggling to make sense of a confusing situation. Dell believes that "Canada was beyond Niagara Falls in my father's puzzle" and regrets this oversight: "I'd never looked it up in the encyclopedia" (2012, 142). This apparent failure to look beyond the framework of nation is juxtaposed with Dell's efforts to compensate for his lack of knowledge. He is aware that Canada is "clearly north of us" (2012, 142) but does not understand why it matters so much to Neeva.

Historically, the Church painting embodied the inevitability of American expansion for contemporary viewers, and potentially, at least in *Canada*, the promise of a blank slate north of the forty-ninth parallel: "Many American chauvinists, who fully expected to see Canada folded eventually under the wings of the American eagle, were cheered by such symbolism" in works of art (Howat 2005, 69). So, while Dell's father, born and raised in the American South, may treat the puzzle as a tool of comfort and nostalgia that allows him to sit "in the living room piecing together Niagara Falls," his wife tries to plan the family's escape from the law and into that blank slate, creating an ironic juxtaposition between the perspectives of his parents that is ultimately instructive for Dell (Ford 2012, 122).

Although Dell believes he cannot see Canada within his father's puzzle, he overlooks a central paradox of Church's American image, a lesson that he learns subsequently, having lived most of his adult life on the Canadian side of the border in Windsor, Ontario, where he sees the shores of Detroit on a daily basis and has easy access to the Ambassador Bridge, "one of North America's busiest international border crossings in terms of ... traffic and trade volume" (Detroit Historical Society). Both Church's image and the puzzle place the viewer squarely on the Canadian side of the falls, looking out over the falls and toward the US. The impact of Church's painting depends on being situated on the northern side of the Canada-US border, with the painting leading the viewer to gaze southward.[3]

Dell develops what may be described as a "careful blindness" when reconciling his own location to Church's canvas in puzzle form (Phelan 1993, 13). As American theater scholar Peggy Phelan explains, visibility may be associated with gaining clarity, but it also involves mediation and a recognition of the selective nature of one's perspective at a particular moment in time. When the Falls and the border upon which it sits are rendered commercially in the form of a mass-produced puzzle, they afford Dell the opportunity to learn to look again—but differently—at his birthplace and his life in Canada.

So, when Dell describes himself to his high-school students as a "Canadian conscript" after 35 years as a naturalized Canadian citizen in response to their queries as to whether he is a "draft dodger" (Ford 2012, 396), he has grown acutely aware of the contradictions inherent in this response. He jokingly informs his students that "Canada saved me from a fate worse than death—which they understand to mean America," yet ultimately argues that his students' desire to see Canada in that role cultivates a false set of truths that bolster a narrative of unwavering Canadian superiority (2012, 396). He concedes that the story he tells is nothing more than a convenient fiction, explaining that "Canada did not save me; I tell them it did only because they want it to be true. If my parents hadn't done what *they* did, ... my sister and I would've both gone along to fine American lives and been happy" (2012, 397). Moreover, he rejects the potential for creating his own cross-border lineage, noting that he and his Canadian wife have no children.

For Dell, the conceit of "crossing a border," which shapes his curricular choices, offers multiple fictional models of the "development from a way of living that doesn't work toward one that does" (2012, 395). As he observes, the "Canadians" he works with and teaches seem both supportive of his decision to become a Canadian citizen, but also "impatient nearly to the point of resentment that I even had to make a choice" (2012, 396), a contradiction that he explains by noting that "Canadians think of themselves as natural accepters, tolerators, understanders" (2012, 396). He strategically conscripts his students' imaginations to explore retrospectively the pervasiveness of national desires for self-validation, whether one is located north or south of the forty-ninth parallel.

Ford's *Canada* offers a timely example of how contemporary American fiction may be read as both reinforcing and challenging American constructions of Canada as a site of virtuosity—and it is this moment that *Canada Through American Eyes* uses as its launching point. Ford's novel portrays Canada as a place of possibility and a geographical locale from which to create an alternative persona for Dell, at least initially as a fugitive from the law. It also reveals the powerful ways in which Canada continues to serve as a backdrop to American narratives of selfhood and exceptionalism, providing a literal and figurative space for writers like Ford to examine the marginalization of Americans who may not be perceived of as worthy of being recognized as US citizens yet who also comprehend the limitations of their lives north of the Canada-US border.

Finally, Dell himself offers a provisional model for thinking about what Charles Lee characterizes in his 2016 book *Ingenious Citizenship: Recrafting Democracy for Social Change* as "ingenious citizenship" (27), a concept that I explore in some of its various manifestations throughout the study that follows. Lee explains that for dissonant and dissenting subjects, "whose identities are not easily melded into the concept of 'ordinary American'" and "remain *othered*" because they are perceived of as endangering the US and of challenging its norms of inclusivity, ingenious citizenship offers a way to challenge and reframe that exclusion (2016, 2). As the child of a visibly Jewish mother, and the offspring of parents who have committed criminal acts that have placed them in jail, Dell is, by proxy, regarded as an "unsafe U.S. citizen" who must be placed in child protection to ensure that he does not follow his parents' path (2016, 2). To escape being stigmatized by the American judicial system, Neeva arranges Dell's illegal migration to Canada.

But as he discovers decades later in Canada, Dell is someone who continues to be defined as an "American, though … [he has] been naturalized and … held a [Canadian] passport for thirty-five years" (Ford 2012, 396). When asked by his colleagues about his "forsaken Americanness" and whether he "long[s] to 'go back'," Dell cheekily replies, "Not at all. It's right there across the river. I can see it" (2012, 396), noting that Windsor looks directly onto Detroit, Michigan. Dell argues that "it's not hard to be a Canadian," particularly because he "had so little training to be American anyway" (2012, 396). Canada remains for Dell a place where, when he crosses the border to his adopted home country, he "always feels at peace" (2012, 397), precisely because it has allowed him to "discriminate" between the very things that seem alike but are different and yet so very much the same (2012, 238)—at least when it comes to claims of exceptionality. Dell's complex connections to his birth country and his adopted home foreground the intricacies that shape how recent American authors engage with their neighbor to the north.

It is at this point, on this line and in making this claim, that *Canada Through American Eyes* begins: the importance of context, both geographically and temporally, in relation to perspective and the narratives of exceptionality that are, in fact, just that—narratives. The chapters that follow thus explore how Canada is imagined by US writers in the post-9/11 period when that viewpoint has shifted and what readers and scholars on both sides of the border can learn from these too often neglected depictions.

Jennifer Andrews

NOTES

1. I am grateful to Percy Walton for allowing me to use this term, which she first coined for use in our co-authored 2003 book with Arnold Davidson, *Border Crossings: Thomas King's Cultural Inversions*; the term usefully brings together the idea of alternative narratives.
2. See Roberts 2018 for a comparable reading of *Canada* through the iconic image of Niagara Falls pictured on the jigsaw puzzle. See also Andrews 2018 for a more fulsome exploration of the concept of the fugitive in Ford's *Canada*.
3. See Hughes who states, "Church was not stepping on virgin territory when he undertook to paint the view from the Canadian side of that foaming horseshoe" (1997, 159).

REFERENCES

Andrews, Jennifer. 2018. Escape to *Canada*: Richard Ford's Fugitive Novel. *Canadian Review of American Studies* 48 (1): 38–62.
Berlant, Lauren. 2011. *Cruel Optimism*. Durham: Duke University Press.
Davidson, Arnold, Priscilla Walton, and Jennifer Andrews. 2003. *Border Crossings: Thomas King's Cultural Inversions*. Toronto: University of Toronto Press.
Detroit Historical Society. 2022. Ambassador Bridge. *Detroit Historical Society*. https://detroithistorical.org/learn/encyclopedia-of-detroit/ambassador-bridge.
Ford, Richard. 2012. *Canada: A Novel*. Toronto: HarperCollins.
Howat, John K. 2005. *Frederic Church*. New Haven, CT: Yale University Press.
Hughes, Robert. 1997. *American Visions: The Epic History of Art in America*. New York: Knopf.
Lee, Charles T. 2016. *Ingenious Citizenship: Recrafting Democracy for Social Change*. Durham: Duke University Press.
Phelan, Peggy. 1993. *Unmarked: The Politics of Performance*. New York: Routledge.
Roberts, Katherine Ann. 2018. *West/Border/Road: Nation and Genre in Contemporary Canadian Narratives*. Montreal & Kingston: McGill-Queen's University Press.

Acknowledgments

I have often described the writing of a book as akin to climbing an ever-growing mountain or giving birth to a baby, albeit with a much longer gestation period. No baby is born or mountain is climbed without a village of people to help you get there. This monograph first took shape during an exchange I did as an undergraduate student, spending the Fall 1991 semester at Duke University as a McGill student; there I met the late Arnold (Ted) Davidson who prompted me to start to examine Canada-US literary relations. I owe a great debt of thanks to the many colleagues and friends from that point onward who supported and nurtured my interest in border crossings of various kinds, most prominently Linda Hutcheon, who co-supervised my doctoral dissertation and has been an incredible mentor throughout my career.

I am grateful to a huge network of professional and personal relationships that have inspired me to continue researching and writing, many nurtured through my presentation of parts of this book at the following conferences and the discussions that followed: the Canadian Association of American Studies (CAAS) 2008, 2014, 2015, 2017, 2018, and 2021; the British Association for Canadian Studies (BACS) 2012; the Atlantic Canadian Studies Conference (ACSS) 2014 and 2018; the British Association for American Studies (BAAS)/the Irish Association for American Studies (IAAS) 2016; Culture and the Canada-U.S. Border (CCUSB) 2013, 2014, and 2015; the Nordic Association for Canadian Studies (NACS) 2018; the Modern Languages Association (MLA) 2020; *Untold Stories: Canada at 150* 2017; the Association of Canadian College and University Teachers of English (ACCUTE) 2019, 2021, and 2022; and the Canadian-American Studies Center at University of Maine, Orono in 2021.

Thank you to a wonderful cohort of Canadianists and Americanists for your engagement with my work, the challenges you have posed, and the generous suggestions that you have offered. They include Gillian Roberts, Zalfa Feghali, David Stirrup, Manina Jones, Stephen Schryer, Alyssa MacLean, Brenna Clarke Gray, Jason Haslam, Hollie Adams, Heidi Darroch, Cynthia Sugars, Rachel Bryant, Lily Cho, Elizabeth Mancke, Karina Vernon, Eleanor Ty, Lorraine York, Neta Gordon, Mary Chapman, Bryce Traister, Percy Walton, Jennifer Harris, Jo Van Every, Erin Morton, Maggie Ward, Claire Hoffman, Michael Jessome, Laura Moss, Robert Zacharias, Erin Wunker, Kit Dobson, Triny Finlay, Bart Vautour, the late (and dearly missed) Herb Wyile, and the amazing Linda Morra. Linda Morra has been a fabulous support with her editorial prowess and brilliant scholarly mind; the book would not have gotten finished without her encouragement. I am lucky to have had excellent undergraduate and graduate students at the University of New Brunswick; a special thanks to the members of the ENGL 6748 seminar in the Fall of 2016. Rich Cole proved to be a stellar research assistant and a wonderful interlocutor during the early days of researching the beginnings of this book. Of course, any errors and omissions are my own.

I have also been surrounded by an amazing group of close friends (many colleagues) who remind me every day of how important it is to nurture these intellectual and emotional connections. I am grateful to Sameera Yusuf, Ince, Bilal, and Viqar Husain, Sue Sinclair, Fran Holoyke, Chantal Richard, Kasey Thomas, Ghadeer Anan, Garda Milne, and all of my workout buddies for your endless enthusiasm and support. Knowing when to ask for help is critical to self-care. I owe an enormous debt to Claire Roussel, Wasif Habib, Krista MacMillan, and Rice Fuller for getting me to the finish line. Finally, I have an incredible family who keep me grounded: my husband, Chris Butler, and my children, Alex and Gillian. They are my rock.

I have previously published sections of the Introduction and Chaps. 2, 3, and 4 in various venues. Thank you to Wilfrid Laurier University Press, the *Journal of Canadian Studies*, Peter Lang, and the *Canadian Review of American Studies* for granting permission for republication. I am grateful to the staff of the Cumberland County Museum & Archives and the Nova Scotia Highlanders Regimental Museum in Amherst, Nova Scotia, for allowing me to include photographs I took of objects held at these two museums. I also owe a debt of thanks to the Social Sciences and Humanities Research Council of Canada and the University of New Brunswick for providing generous research funds for this project. I moved as I was finishing this book and was very lucky to find a supportive team in my new position as Dean in the Faculty of Arts and Social Sciences at Dalhousie University. Natalie Wood, Lisa Matthews, and Lindsay DuBois made it possible for me to take some much-needed writing time; thank you for doing so! Joanna Henry was a wonderful developmental editor; Jane Boyes proved to be a terrific research assistant in the book's final stages.

The writing of this book took place on the ancestral and unceded territory of the Mi'kma'ki and the Wolastoqiyik (Maliseet). I am grateful to be a guest on these lands. I also recognize that African Nova Scotians are a distinct people whose histories, legacies, and contributions have enriched that part of Mi'kma'ki known as Nova Scotia for over 400 years.

Contents

1 Introduction: Laying the Groundwork: Canada's
   (In)visibility   1
   References   21

2 The Missionary Position: The American Roots of Northrop
   Frye's Peaceable Kingdom   27
   Frye's Missionary Zeal   28
   Canada's Conversion Narratives   31
   Narrating Images   33
   The Quaker Schism   36
   *Shifting Representations of Animals in the "Peaceable Kingdom"
   Series*   37
   Changing Versions of the Peaceable Kingdom   38
   Cross-Border Schism   42
   Returning to Frye's "Conclusion" to his Literary History of
   Canada   45
   References   49

3 *Evangeline's* Revisioning: Reading Ben Farmer's Post-9/11
   Evangeline: A Novel   53
   Acknowledging Traumatic Histories   55
   Longfellow's Version of Evangeline *and Its Legacy*   57
   Marketing Acadie: Longfellow and Evangeline's *Canadian
   Legacy*   62

xxi

Farmer's Revisioning of Evangeline 67
Evangeline and Gabriel as Refugees 72
Shifting Depictions of Gabriel 74
Ingenious Citizenship: Challenging Canadian and American
Paradigms 76
References 79

4 German Internment Camps in the Maritimes: Another
   Untold Story in P.S. Duffy's *The Cartographer of No Man's
   Land* 83
History of the Amherst Interment Camp 85
Comparing German Immigration in Canada and the US 92
Canadian Multiculturalism and the Story of Heist 95
The Role of Simon 97
An Alternative Voice of Reason and Resistance 98
The Lessons of The Cartographer of No Man's Land 101
References 106

5 Becoming Bird(ie): Exposing Canadian Government
   Complicity with Forced Adoptions in Christina Sunley's
   The Tricking of Freya 109
Babies and Borders 111
Unwed Mothers 113
The Shame Is Ours 115
Becoming Animal 118
Animal Transformations 122
What Is in a Name? 124
The Hidden Costs of Forced Adoption 127
Exposing Secrets and Accessing the Power to Heal 130
References 137

6 Escaping to Canada: Gambling on Northern Salvation
   in Stewart O'Nan's *The Odds* 141
The White Experience of the US-to-Canada Border Crossings 143
Indigenous Border Crossings 146
Cross-Border Criminal Financial Activities and Canadian
Immigration Policies 148
Race, Immigration, and Wealth (for Some) 149

The Sheltering of White Privilege	151
The Recession, Housing Costs, and Racism on Both Sides of the Canada-US Border	154
Moral Failure or Economic Miscalculation?	155
Fixed Versus Speculative Asset	161
Sexual Betrayal and Debt	163
Access to Credit	164
Financial Precarity: Nowhere to Run	166
References	169

7 Turning Away, Going West and South: The Receding Promise of Canada in *Future Home of the Living God* and *The Underground Railroad* 173
Canada as a Safe Haven 178
Places to Hide 181
The Promise of the Underground Railroad 185
Canada as (An)other Lie 191
References 195

8 The Limits of Canadian Exceptionalism: *Bowling for Columbine*, *Come From Away*, and *Nîpawistamâsowin: We Will Stand Up* 199
Canadian Virtuosity in Bowling for Columbine 201
Celebrating Canadian Exceptionality in Come From Away 203
Welcoming the (Queer or Black) Stranger 205
Debunking Canadian Exceptionality in Nîpawistamâsowin: We Will Stand Up 211
The Reality of Gun Violence in Canada 216
Searching for "Justice for Colten" 218
Going South to Seek Justice 220
References 225

Index 229

ABOUT THE AUTHOR

Jennifer Andrews is the Dean of Arts and Social Sciences and a member of the Department of English at Dalhousie University. This book was written while living and working in the ancestral and unceded territory of the Mi'kma'ki and the Wolastoqiyik (Maliseet).

She has written two books previously: *Border Crossings: Thomas King's Cultural Inversions*, co-authored with Arnold Davidson and Percy Walton (UTP, 2003), and *In the Belly of a Laughing God: Humour and Irony in Native Women's Poetry* (UTP, 2011).

List of Figures

Fig. 2.1　Erastus Salisbury Field's "Historical Monument of the American Republic" (1867). (D'Armour Museum of Fine Art, Springfield, MA. Image available in the public domain: https://upload.wikimedia.org/wikipedia/commons/9/9d/Erastus_Salisbury_Field_-_Historical_Monument_of_the_American_Republic.jpg. Source: http://www.the-athenaeum.org)　35

Fig. 2.2　Edward Hicks' "The Peaceable Kingdom" (1829–1832), oil on canvas. (Brooklyn Museum of Art, Brooklyn, NY. Image available in the public domain: https://www.brooklynmuseum.org/opencollection/objects/610)　41

Fig. 2.3　"The Peaceable Kingdom" by Edward Hicks (1829–1832), oil on canvas. (Formerly owned by the Maier Museum of Art, Randolph-Macon Women's College, Lynchburg, VA, auctioned off by Christie's in New York after 2007 to pay the college's mounting debts, and was bought by a private collector　42

Fig. 4.1　Miniature spinning wheel. Cumberland County Museum Archives in Amherst, Nova Scotia. (Photo courtesy of Jennifer Andrews, March 16, 2017)　89

Fig. 4.2　Cello housed in the public exhibition about the regiment and community at the Nova Scotia Highlanders Regimental Museum in Amherst, Nova Scotia. (Photo courtesy of Jennifer Andrews, March 17, 2017)　90

Fig. 4.3　Cello head housed in the public exhibition about the regiment and community at the Nova Scotia Highlanders Regimental Museum in Amherst, Nova Scotia. (Photo courtesy of Jennifer Andrews, March 17, 2017)　91

CHAPTER 1

Introduction: Laying the Groundwork: Canada's (In)visibility

> *[W]hen we ask "Where is American literature?" we can no longer overlook a central dimension of American literature itself—namely that American literature is not "in" or reducible to any one particular location, or to a collection of the various locales that iconic authors call home. Rather, we come to see that it forms part of an unwieldy network that spreads over multiple places—some within current US territory and some not.*
>
> *Attending seriously to the locations in which American literature can be found highlights the significance of multiple centers and peripheries to the constitution of the field—it draws our attention to the dissonances of the term itself. (Levander 2013, 7)*
>
> *A number of questions emerge from these ruminations: Can Canada afford to be subsumed within the category of hemispheric, inter-American studies? ... Yet can Canada afford not to be included within these discussions? To opt out of the discussion of inter-American studies altogether [sic] may be to segregate Canadian literary study even further, to contribute to its hemispheric invisibility. (Sugars 2010, 45)*
>
> *Canada [has] proved to be a remarkably flexible space in the minds of American authors. (MacLean 2010, 7)*

American constructions of Canada as a place of refuge are not new, nor are Canada's efforts to articulate its uniqueness and superiority to the US. There is a long tradition of both Americans and Canadians positioning Canada as better than its American neighbor, from the Loyalists who fled the US in the wake of the American Revolution and the enslaved Black people who sought refuge from bondage in British North America, to draft dodgers and war resisters during the Vietnam, Afghanistan, and Iraq wars, to, most recently, the refugees seeking asylum outside of official border-crossing stations at the Canada-US border, despite the Safe Third Country Agreement instituted in the aftermath of 9/11. Notably, both the US and Canada rely on and continually reconfigure this narrative of refuge as a fundamental feature of their relationship. Canada functions as a convenient ally and point of contrast to the US, given its proximity and similar physical size, the common widespread use of the English language, a comparable standard of living, and analogous histories of colonialism. Moreover, the two countries have a long history of violently displacing Indigenous peoples, which, paradoxically, has enabled their global recognition as "classic immigration countries" (Nischik 2016, 22).

Canada and the US have deep economic and political links and are partners in the largest bilateral trade agreement in the world. Unlike the heavily militarized Mexican-American border, the border between Canada and the US remains, even post-9/11, remarkably porous. While the Trump presidency (2016–2020) did initiate a visible hardening of the border, paradoxically leading to increased traffic northward, "Canadian immigration programs … [remain] much more relaxed as compared to other developed countries" (Satbir Grover, qtd. in Ghatak 2020). Nonetheless, Canada also continues to experience "an influx of irregular migration," with most of these "crossings" going "northbound" as "migrants … [try] to cross into Canada from the US" (Honderich and Gagdekar 2022): this journey can be perilous or even deadly, especially in the winter months.[1] The continued depictions of Canada as more virtuous and inclusive overlook both the uncertain future of recently detained asylum seekers and Canada's long history of discrimination and racism against Black, Indigenous, and people of colour (BIPOC) populations.[2]

Using the contemporary political moment (and some of its previous iterations) as a point of departure, this monograph explores Americans' long-standing imaginative perceptions of Canada and how Canadians have borrowed from, refashioned, and cultivated these portraits to serve their own goals. In particular, this book dialogues with and intervenes in four different but overlapping strands of scholarship that have shaped American and Canadian literary relations over the past three decades in the humanities: American border, hemispheric, Canadian, and transnational studies. A key shortcoming of much of the work done in American border, hemispheric, and transnational studies, despite its ostensible efforts to "view the nation beyond the terms of its own exceptionalist self-imaginings" (Levander and Levine 2008, 7), is its innate "tendencies to [continue to] privilege the United States as primary interlocutor" (Sadowski-Smith and Fox 2004, 7). In turn, this approach tends to ignore Canada altogether because of its seeming similarities.

For instance, Caroline Levander's 2013 *Where Is American Literature?* considers "where American literature can be found" by focusing on locations and contexts around the globe precisely because it "thrives in unlikely places" (4). Rather than attending to regional or area differences within the borders of the US, she broadens her inquiry to think about a variety of "habitats," which extend "beyond the comfortable geographic, political, infrastructural, and subjective containers," by examining the circulation of American texts throughout a variety of "terrains and locales" that exceed the nation's literal borders (2013, 4, 7, 5). Using this approach, Levander emphasizes the contradictory nature of trying to frame and contain American literature, a perspective that I would argue could also apply to Canadian literature, but escapes attention because of the centrality of the US to her argument. Despite her book's ostensibly global reach, her prior engagement with new ways of approaching hemispheric studies that include Canada,[3] and Levander's claim in her introduction that "American literature [is built out of] … borders and vanishing points," her study never references Canada (2013, 27). Nor does she examine American texts that portray Canada in any substantive way. Her monograph captures a larger phenomenon. Too often, Canada remains a kind of "afterthought" with American scholars straining to find ways to include its northern neighbor within these new conceptual frameworks or ignoring Canada altogether (Roberts 2015, 17).

This book, by contrast, explores how Canada is imagined primarily by US writers, and what readers and scholars on both sides of the Canada-US border can learn from these recent depictions. As the "Preface" demonstrates, Neeva's provocation in Richard Ford's *Canada* may be intended as a teaching tool for her son in a moment of desperation. But it also functions as a springboard for the study that follows, which examines a selection of US-authored fiction from 9/11 to the present. These works offer a broad range of test cases for thinking differently about how Americans and Canadians portray and read themselves and each other. While I was born and raised in Toronto, I have spent most of my academic life on the east coast of Canada, teaching at the University of New Brunswick for 23 years and, more recently, at Dalhousie University. My research has been fundamentally influenced by my location and my realization that much of the attention paid to literature about Canada is tied to the economic and political dominance of large urban centers, such as Toronto, Montreal, and Vancouver. In this monograph, I look at texts that explore a combination of rural and smaller urban centers in Canada and the US, and I make a point of not revisiting recent works that explore Canada from a US perspective, like Jim Lynch's novel, *Border Songs*, and have already received considerable attention.[4] As a result, the study orients itself primarily toward eastern and central Canada, with occasional forays into Manitoba and Saskatchewan. Depictions of Canada are found in the novels of the following seven American authors—Richard Ford's *Canada* (2012), *Evangeline* by Ben Farmer (2010), P.S. Duffy's *The Cartographer of No Man's Land* (2013), *The Tricking of Freya* by Christina Sunley (2009), Stewart O'Nan's *The Odds* (2012), *The Underground Railroad* by Colson Whitehead (2016), and Louise Erdrich's *Future Home of the Living God* (2017). These novels represent a diverse array of viewpoints, each of which enriches readers' understanding of these two countries and their complex relationship. This clustering of texts also reveals how many US writers over the past two decades have used Canada to probe their own contradictory perspectives about both their nation and its neighbor to the north.

This monograph grows fruitfully out of but also crucially expands upon existing theoretical work, such as John Carlos Rowe's "Post-Nationalism, Globalism, and the New American Studies," in which he describes the recent critical shift in American Studies. According to Rowe, American Studies moves from a nationalist approach founded on the assumption that "the United States constitutes a model for democratic nationality" through its self-construction as exceptional to current efforts that foreground the examination of the many cultures that have been marginalized by "traditional American Studies or subordinated to an overarching nationalist mythology" (1998, 11, 12). The result is an increased interest in "the cultural, political, and economic boundaries" dividing these populations from both "the dominant social order and from each other" (1998, 12). But he also concedes that to "take into account at the very least the different nationalities, cultures, and languages of the Western Hemisphere, including Canada" may create a field of study that is "too large and challenging" (1998, 13).[5]

Other critics take a different approach. In "The Transnational Turn," English Canadian literary scholar Robert Zacharias contends that "much of the work in what is ostensibly a hemispheric-wide approach" leads to the adoption of "continental perspectives—almost always in the Americas" (2016, 110). The result is that "the hemispheric turn" may be read as "itself an imperializing move" (Siemerling and Casteel 2010, 9), at least in terms of its implications for Canada. To counter this concern, particularly on the part of Canadianists, my monograph deliberately develops a more inclusive and self-conscious methodological approach to the examination of English-language American and Canadian literary texts that explore the relationship between exceptionalism and refuge as portrayed on both sides of the Canada-US border.

In addition, many scholars of English Canadian literature and culture are deeply concerned that current approaches to Canada in border, transnational, and hemispheric (American) studies offer another opportunity to ignore or dismiss the particular in favor of broad generalizations that could undermine "the potential of the Canadian locale to interrogate the American" (Sugars 2010, 45). Winfried Siemerling and Sarah Phillips Casteel's 2010 collection, *Canada and Its Americas: Transnational Navigations*, offers the most thorough examination of the "hesitation … Canadianists" exhibit when engaging in "hemispheric discussions" (2010, 9). In their introduction, they contend that such a stance "may serve as an important corrective to some of the more troubling trends in the field of hemispheric American studies as it is currently taking shape, reminding us of the need to attend carefully to national and regional specificities even as we engage with transnational contexts"—that is, those who move across and between nation-state borders (2010, 9). Their book also includes essays that investigate the writings of Indigenous and Black authors on both sides of the Canada-US border. The former group, according to Siemerling and Casteel, may be read as using "the border between the United States and Canada to make the point that national boundaries are the consequence of white settlement and not primordial facts of thinking and belonging" (2010, 16), while the latter investigates the "problematic elision of race relations from foundational narratives and histories of Canadian literature" (2010, 19). These are two issues that I explore in this study, albeit from a different set of perspectives, by examining how American writers, both white and BIPOC, engage with Canada to probe and complicate presumptions of Canadian superiority.

For some Canadianists, focusing on American depictions of Canada may be perceived as diverting scarce resources and energy from a field still relatively young in its development. Cynthia Sugars' "Worlding the

(Postcolonial) Nation: Canada's Americas" expresses serious reservations about engaging with transnational and/or hemispheric studies in relation to Canadian literature. She argues that to "dismiss the viability of the nation form because it is essentially oppressive or homogenizing is to deny its very real effects and to risk disenabling the sites where the nation can be most usefully adapted for oppositional work in the present" (2010, 44). In particular, she recognizes "the potential for the Canadian locale to interrogate the American" (2010, 45). I would argue for the reverse to be true as well. In the second epigraph to this chapter, Sugars queries the cost of disengaging with border-crossing approaches because "[t]o opt out of the discussion of inter-American studies altogether may be to segregate Canadian literary study even further, to contribute to its hemispheric invisibility" (2010, 45). Indeed, this reality has been a long-standing source of irritation and even anger for Canadian literary scholars, whose field of study is often perceived of and treated as little more than an appendage of British and American literatures.[6]

Likewise, colleague and Canadianist Herb Wyile argues in an essay for *Canada and Its Americas* provocatively titled "Hemispheric Studies or Scholarly NAFTA?: The Case for Canadian Literary Studies" that the North American Free Trade Agreement, signed by Canada, the US, and Mexico and ratified in 1994 to facilitate preferential north-south trade agreements among the three nations, is a pivotal point. He fears that in "a comparative regime in which the literature of the United States dominates ... Canada, along with all the other 'Americas,' will be lost in the shuffle" (2010, 50). Such a perspective is not surprising given the emergence of "the New American Studies" over the past three decades (Rowe 1998, 13). This methodological shift in American literary and cultural studies pointedly acknowledges the US' "multiple histories of continental and overseas expansion, conquest, conflict, and resistance which have shaped the cultures of the United States and the cultures of those it has dominated within and beyond its geopolitical boundaries," including Canada (Kaplan 1993, 4). Despite the ostensibly self-conscious and intentional inclusive aims of such an approach, Rowe himself warns that "[i]n its claims to encompass the many cultures and political organizations in the Western Hemisphere, the new American Studies threatens its own kind of cultural imperialism" (1998, 15) and may lead to new-fangled forms of "the US ideology of manifest destiny" (Nischik 2016, 14).

As Canadian-based Americanist Bryce Traister explains, quoting Amy Kaplan, in "Risking Nationalism: NAFTA and the Limits of the New

American Studies," there is a danger in favoring models of pluralism that leave "national borders intact instead of interrogating their formation" (Kaplan 1993, 15; Traister 1997, 192) and that impact the hemisphere. To put it bluntly, navel-gazing from within (on either side of the Canada-US border) breeds insularity, even if it is undertaken ostensibly to cultivate diversity. This criticism has been repeatedly aimed at newer developments in American Studies, which tend to imperialize in the name of plurality and inclusivity, leading the idea of "America" to flood northward over the Canada-US border, or at least figuratively leak across the continent.

Given the relatively newfound recognition of English Canadian literature as a legitimate and separate field of study requiring its own scholarly expertise, Wyile expresses fears about the turn to transnational and hemispheric approaches to Canadian literature (and depictions of Canada by American authors) at the very moment when the field is finding its voice and when claiming its oppositional agency may result in its destabilization. But by refusing to consider what US perspectives on Canada might illuminate about the nation, Canadianists inadvertently ensure the thickening of the Canada-US border and the reification of narratives of US (and Canadian) exceptionalism, without considering how these have contributed to and been reconfigured by Canadians and Americans. Nonetheless, there are scholars who have vigorously engaged with and continue to probe Canada-US relations in the social sciences and humanities—for example, the "Borders in Globalization" project[7] and Harvey Amani Whitfield's groundbreaking historical study of slavery on the Eastern Seaboard, including the Maritime provinces, *North to Bondage* (2016). This holds true in literature and cultural studies, most prominently through a Leverhulme-funded project based in Britain called Culture and the Canada-U.S. Border (CCUSB), which lasted from 2012 to 2015.[8]

Many of the scholars who have continued to work on Canada-US comparative literary and cultural studies, including the principal investigators of the CCUSB, are located in Britain and Europe. Their own academic homes (usually in North American or American studies) foreground the necessity of border-crossing engagements and an understanding of the relationships between and among multiple national fields of study.[9] While the perceived threat—that Canada may get lost in the so-called transnational or hemispheric "shuffle" (Wyile 2010, 50)—warrants acknowledgment, I would argue that Canada and the field of English Canadian literary studies may benefit from more robust and thoughtful engagement with not only national, regional, and local contexts, but also transnational and hemispheric comparisons, particularly given Canada's history as a settler-invader nation with its own investment in narratives of (Canadian) exceptionality.

Rather than dismissing American depictions of Canada outright as cliché or stereotype, it would behoove scholars to consider why there is a long American tradition of writers who employ Canada literally and figuratively (frequently by moving characters across the Canada-US border) to explore American and Canadian concerns and why this fictional migration matters—both for Canadians and Americans. The US continues to cultivate and sustain US liberal fantasies of Canada, yet this perspective overlooks the reality that Canada and the US, as Adam Barker explains, "collectively form the northern bloc of settler colonialism" (2012, 329) and share in the creation and continued existence of a "'structure' of invasion" (2012, 329), most notably when it comes to Indigenous populations. Both Canada and the US have engaged in settler colonialism for hundreds of years, with the state wresting the land base of the nation from Indigenous peoples. As Elizabeth Carlson-Manathara argues, drawing on Tuck and Yang's pivotal essay, "Decolonization is not a metaphor," when "colonization [is] framed around settlement" (Carlson-Manathara 2021, 40), the result is the "total appropriation of Indigenous life and land" (Tuck and Yang 2012, 5). Moreover, in the case of settler colonialism, "the settler society becomes so deeply established that it is naturalized, normalized, unquestioned and unchallenged" (Battell Lowman and Barker 2015, 26). Certainly some of the works explored in this monograph probe and even undermine American and Canadian settler colonial perspectives, by exposing the structures that enable settler colonialism to dominate and flourish, albeit in distinctive ways, in both countries.

Of course, I am also mindful of the ease with which Canadians tend to view themselves as superior to Americans and to inscribe a national history that serves those desires. There is "significant resistance and reluctance to acknowledg[e] … Canada's colonial [past and] present," and the US has provided an excellent foil for evading responsibility for its own national history of racism (Battell Lowman and Barker 2015, 15). As Eva Mackey explains in *The House of Difference: Cultural Politics and National Identity in Canada*, "while one of Canada's defining and supposedly essential characteristics is tolerance to difference, one of the major socially acceptable forms of overt *in*tolerance has been that directed at the United States" (2002, 145).

Witness, for example, Black and Mi'kmaq author George Elliott Clarke's 2008 introduction to *The Refugee: Narratives of Fugitive Slaves in Canada* by American author Benjamin Drew (first published in 1865). In it, Clarke pointedly critiques Canadians for using these kinds of collections to "blame the practice of African slavery in North America [exclusively] on two-faced Americans" and, in turn, disavowing "our slave past and racist present" (2008, 10). For Clarke, there is danger in believing "our schooling that our settler ancestors, because they did not rebel against the British Crown, evolved a superior social order and liberty to that of the violence-prone ... United States": this assumption has led to widespread ignorance and denial of an ongoing history of Canadian racism, fueled by "a hint of anti-Americanism" (2008, 10). Even Drew's own construction of Canada as a "Paradise" in contrast to "the Great Republic" does a great disservice by creating a false binary between the two nations with respect to the treatment of Black enslaved people and BIPOC populations more broadly (10). Only by recognizing *The Refugee* as "a foundation of Canadian political philosophy ... and as a distinct set of *settler* narratives," Clarke contends, can readers "repulse imperial America's writ as an annexationist intellectual power" and engage fully with Canada's colonial legacy of slavery (2008, 11). Doing so, however, may raise fundamental questions about Canada's historical and contemporary self-positioning on the international stage, especially in relation to its neighbor to the south.

Debates about the meaning of the idea of Canadian exceptionality have continued throughout the past several decades. In 2017, the McGill Institute for the Study of Canada hosted a conference on "Canadian Exceptionalism: Are we good or are we lucky?" While the event focused on social sciences and public policy, the conference report noted that "[a] growing body of scholarly work, international commentary, and analysis ... [in the US, Canada, and beyond] has given purchase to the idea of Canadian exceptionalism" (Cooper 2017, 4, emphasis in original).[10] Support for this idea was prompted by increasing popularity of conservative values globally including the hardening of attitudes toward immigration and refugees, the growth of political parties and groups that favor a hard-right stance, and the thickening of borders (2017, 4). But such narratives are not new. In *The Homing Place* (2017), Rachel Bryant argues that Canadian exceptionalism, like American exceptionalism, has existed since Canada's time as a British colony by creating a "nobler idea of what a Western nation can or should be"—in Canada's case, through "a wilful separation from the United States" (2017, 77, 76). As Inderpal Grewal explains, the foundational idea of American exceptionalism is "a claim to anti-colonial origins that erases viewing the United States as empire" (2017, 8). Canadian exceptionalism employs a similar methodology, asserting a "set of beliefs through which Settler Canadians have continuously consolidated themselves against their perceived rivals (particularly the 'Americans')," by "articulating themselves onto a separate and higher moral plane" (Bryant 2017, 65). These claims to exceptionality are rooted in perceptions of national difference, creating a scaffolded relationship in which the exceptional nation is constructed as ethically superior. Hence, Chap. 2 of this monograph, titled "The Missionary Position: The American Roots of Northrop Frye's Peaceable Kingdom," extends Bryant's work by tracing the US origins of the "peaceable kingdom" through its use in nineteenth-century American folk art. It is a key phrase that Frye introduced in his 1965 "Conclusion" to his *Literary History of Canada* to differentiate Canada from the US, one that has been resurrected and deployed frequently in recent years in Canadian public discourse to sustain narratives of Canadian exceptionality (republished in Frye 1971).

Moreover, not everyone espouses American exceptionalism. This idea is epitomized in Dana Nelson's recent article, "We Have Never Been Anti-Exceptionalists," which argues that Americanists have "punctured the moralism of US exceptionalism only to set ourselves up in the same shop, constituting our moral superiority through our endless critical repudiation of American exceptionalism" (2019, e10). Nelson rightly suggests that such an approach leads to a self-fulfilling loop of logic rather than creating the opportunity for sustained and fundamental critique, because "we *need* US exceptionalism to keep the whole enterprise going" (2019, e10). Her astute observations should be heeded by Canadianists like myself, who may find themselves, over time, engaging in similar patterns of thought.

Finally, *Canada Through American Eyes* examines how and why Canada characterizes itself as a safe haven, as it explores the limits and contradictions of this self-positioning. Like the US, Canada has a long history of "welcoming the stranger" and, in turn, constituting "the nation" (qtd. in Roberts 2015, 14). But such claims to hospitality need to be scrutinized, particularly when framed by "myths of … benevolence" (qtd. in 2015, 14), as I do in the "Conclusion" to the book. Chapter 8 examines the illusion of national and racial inclusivity and compassion in three recent works of art, two Canadian and one American. I begin by comparing Michael Moore's 2003 documentary film, *Bowling for Columbine*, and the hit-Broadway Canadian-authored musical, *Come From Away*, both of which suggest that gun violence is exclusively an American problem. I then contrast these two works with *Nîpawistamâsowin: We Will Stand Up* (2019), Cree documentary filmmaker Tasha Hubbard's poignant investigation of historical and contemporary Canadian racism toward Indigenous peoples, particularly as manifested through gun violence.

Canada continues to present itself, however, as a more compassionate nation in comparison to its American neighbors, especially with respect to visibly marginalized populations. Yet, in *Policing Black Lives*, Maynard argues that this kind of strategic self-representation "invisibilizes Canada's role in supporting the root causes of Black (and brown) displacement," by naturalizing "race and racial hierarchies" (2017, 57) that have left these populations globally "shackled by poverty and debt" (2017, 60).[11] Maynard's work, when read in relation to Frye's representation of Canada as a "peaceable kingdom," offers a useful context for understanding the critiques of Canada explored in this book. Closely examining US literary and cultural depictions of Canada as a place of refuge for vulnerable populations enables thoughtful reflection about who benefits from the perpetuation of these specific national stereotypes, both north and south of the Canada-US border, and why they remain in circulation.

Carefully studying key nationalist narrative constructs is an uncomfortable yet necessary intervention that underpins *Canada Through American Eyes*. In particular, the novels—and occasionally paintings, films, and musicals—that are the subject of the book provide a deliberately varied set of case studies for examining how US texts, along with works of art produced on both sides of the Canada-US border, uncover moments in Canadian historical and literary studies that have been buried or occluded to protect Canada's self-representation as a "peaceable kingdom." Ford, Farmer, Duffy, Sunley, O'Nan, Whitehead, and Erdrich may initially portray Canada as a place of escape and refuge for individuals who find themselves marginalized or excluded from citizenship within the US because of their class, race, and/or sexuality. But my study additionally contends that these same texts also examine the ways in which the stories they tell expose Canada as a nation with its own hidden histories of racism, sexism, and classism.

The tendency to posit Canada as better than its southern neighbor is challenged and dispelled to various degrees by the authors under consideration, who refuse to perpetuate a singular virtuous vision of Canada. Moreover, by framing my examination of recent American-authored texts about Canada with Chaps. 2 and 8, I probe how ideas of American exceptionalism have been imported and refashioned to suit Canadian contexts and, subsequently, reinforced or challenged on both sides of the border, particularly as BIPOC writers question the legitimacy of Canadian claims to be a "kinder," gentler, and more inclusive nation than the US (Mackey 2002, 63). *Canada Through American Eyes* creates a richly layered comparative conversation that engages with both American and Canadian literary and cultural traditions to demonstrate the benefits of employing a perspective that shifts across the Canada-US border from both sides.

Richard Ford's novel, *Canada*, addressed in the preface to this book, is part of a long yet often overlooked history of Americans who have written about Canada from the American Revolution onward that warrants consideration here, precisely because it provides a useful framework for understanding the approaches and concerns of the contemporary authors examined in *Canada Through American Eyes*. Notably, most scholarship about how Americans envision Canada in literary terms has been produced by a handful of Canadian[12] and, occasionally, American academics. They typically focus on analyses of works by writers already deemed to be significant within American studies, among them Henry David Thoreau, Harriet Beecher Stowe, Henry Wadsworth Longfellow, Jack London, Wallace Stegner, Willa Cather, Marianne Moore, Elizabeth Bishop, Ishmael Reed, and Joyce Carol Oates. With few exceptions, the Canadian dimensions of their texts are typically treated as peripheral or secondary to the rest of their oeuvre and usually framed as part of a broader inquiry into their relevance to American literature. In other words, for Americans to write about Canada has historically been perceived as anomalous and unremarkable.

The few scholars who do examine American literary representations of Canada tend to focus primarily on the nineteenth century, a period when the US was struggling to develop its own cultural identity in part through literature and negotiating deep political, economic, and social divisions within the new nation. The most comprehensive of these is written by Canadian academic James Doyle, whose *North of America: Images of Canada in the United States, 1775–1900* (1983) provides a sweeping 11-chapter survey of American literary texts that portray Canada. The now-deceased Professor Emeritus of Canadian Literature at Wilfrid Laurier University begins *North of America* by arguing that "Canada has perennially figured as a vague, peripheral, and ambiguous concept" in the imaginative literature of the US because of "the comparative paucity and insignificance of the images of the northern country in the American literary tradition" (1983, 1, 2). For Doyle, the explanation is simple: "there are no American literary masterpieces dealing with Canada" and, even when canonical American writers "turn their attention briefly to Canada, the results are frequently disappointing in comparison to their best-known works" (1983, 2). Further, Doyle notes that, for American authors, many of whom never visited British North America or Canada, the lack of "obligation to empirical reality" is a catalyst for an exploration of the writer's own "national—or even personal—experience, rather than that of the country he is examining" (1983, 3). The abundance of American-authored texts about Canada may not represent "the country its own inhabitants know" (1983, 4) but are worth examining in their own right for what they reveal of both the US and Canada from an American perspective.

Doyle provides a detailed catalogue of American-authored texts about Canada from pre-Revolutionary captivity narratives, letters, journals, and diaries to a wide array of poems, travel and outdoor literature, guidebooks, nature writing, and various kinds of novels in the nineteenth century, highlighting the abundance and variety of works that, especially in the post-Civil War period, represent Canada as a site of fantasy and idealization, providing a locale for figurative and literal escape, albeit only temporarily. Typically, British North America and post-Confederation Canada are rendered as "more primitive and pure…, where man lives close to nature and the soil, [and] where intimations of peace and innocence are still possible" (1983, 47). The failures of the US' northern neighbor are usually attributed to the nation's tolerance of "French popery and Indian barbarism," which demonstrate an acquiescence to and perpetuation of Old World values and seemingly hinder a key colonial project, that of Indigenous genocide, though in reality, the subjugation and eradication of Indigenous populations was a central focus of post-Confederation Canadian governments (1983, 1).

Despite the Civil War, the US still emerges for most American writers as the more "complex, progressive civilization" (1983, 47). Further, even concrete examples of Canadian colonial nation-building, such as the completion of the Canadian Pacific Railroad, are perceived by US Americanists as "emphasiz[ing]… the geographical and sociological unity of the continent as whole" (1983, 7). Doyle's monograph may attest to the abundance of writing produced by US authors about Canada and the ways in which Canada's existence as a colony and a new nation gave writers a vehicle to explore "alternative possibilities" in increasingly concrete and realistic forms, especially in the last decades of the nineteenth century (1983, 6). But his book also demonstrates how narratives about Canada are always already relegated to the margins because they fail to live up to the "the imperatives of New World history" (1983, 47)—as determined by US writers, thinkers, and politicians who repeatedly position their nation at the physical and ideological center of the hemisphere.

Doyle's book is critical to this study, because his detailed catalogue of textual engagements by US authors with British North America and Canada demonstrates that, as the US' next-door neighbor, Canada has served a valuable and complex role in shaping American identity for several centuries, particularly at times of internal strife such as the American Civil War. However, as Doyle points out, the disconcerting or uncomfortable nature of comparisons between the two countries—and the ways in which Canada may expose the "intellectual elusiveness of such concepts as 'liberty' and 'progress,'" even when US writers "remain emotionally or rhetorically committed to the American assertion of such concepts"— makes it tempting for American authors and literary critics to avoid comparisons altogether (1983, 149). He concludes that rather than continuing to engage with Canada's distinctiveness, American writers of the twentieth century prefer to emphasize similarities "between the two countries" strategically (1983, 149).

This approach facilitates the projects of American imperialism and globalization, reflected in texts such as Jack London's *The Call of the Wild* (1903), Willa Cather's *Shadows on the Rock* (1931), and *Wolf-Willow* by Wallace Stegner (1962). While there are always exceptions to the rule (Ishmael Reed's satiric novel *Flight to Canada*, published in 1976, comes to mind with its sharply witty attacks on both American and Canadian treatments of BIPOC people),[13] Doyle's observations raise important questions about what has prompted a resurgence of interest in Canada by US authors in the first decades of the twenty-first century, following what might be called a relatively stagnant period in the closing decades of the twentieth century.[14] In other words, why Canada *now*?[15] And, more specifically, how have key canonical nineteenth-century texts produced by US writers about colonial and post-Confederation Canada been reimagined by contemporary American authors to address some of the political, social, and economic challenges faced by both the US and Canada?

In particular, Doyle devotes several chapters of his book to American renderings of the removal and displacement of Acadian and Indigenous peoples in elegiac terms, explicitly epitomized in Longfellow's canonical epic poem, *Evangeline* (1847), and to the ways in which pre- and post-Confederation Canada embody, however falsely, the promise of freedom from slavery for US authors, the most well-known being Harriet Beecher Stowe's *Uncle Tom's Cabin* (1853). Notably, the latter portrays Canada as a positive yet temporary place of respite for escaped enslaved Black Americans George and Eliza Shelby, who subsequently choose to travel to France, and then ultimately the Black African nation of Liberia, rather than returning to either the post-Civil War US or Canada. The same groups of people are at the center of Alyssa MacLean's 2010 doctoral dissertation, *Canadian Migrations: Reading Canada in Nineteenth-Century American Literature*, completed at the University of British Columbia in Canada. It recovers and examines "nineteenth-century representations of two major population movements across the Canada-US border": the 1755 Deportation of Francophone Catholic Acadians from eastern Canada to an array of American colonies and "the antebellum flight of free and enslaved African Americans north to Canada" (2010, 8). She contends that "[t]hese two instances of cross-border migration and state-sanctioned violence became flashpoints of literary conversation in the US in the mid-nineteenth century" at a time when America was working vigorously to "secure its external borders with other nation-states ... to define ideas of US citizenship and national identity, and to examine the relationship between race, nation, and empire as conceptual categories" (2010, 8).

In this study, I argue that, while circumstances may have changed, the legacy of these two forced movements and the depictions of Canada in US-authored literary texts about these specific historical events continue to play a central role in understanding contemporary relations between the two nations. Canada remains a critical tool for American writers to define, differentiate, and critique American representations of the US, especially when put into conversation with its northern neighbor. MacLean suggests that "[i]nvocations of Canada's similarities with the United States" have been historically "tied to much larger teleological arguments about the political, linguistic, and racial destiny of the New World" and fueled compelling arguments about "the 'purpose' of the United States as model for other nation-states" (2010, 20). Conversely, Canada has, from the American Revolution onward, proved to be a challenging neighbor for the US with its sustained resistance to annexation. So, while "[f]antasies of Canada as the Great White North often described a landscape that was historically blank and racially pure," MacLean persuasively argues in her doctoral dissertation that American depictions of Canada from 1826 to

1863 were used to challenge "the stability of US formulations of racial categories and definitions of citizenship" by offering "a political alternative within the hemisphere" (2010, 25, 26, 21). This is a role that Canada has continued to occupy in the American imaginary to varying degrees throughout the twentieth century and into the twenty-first.

For American authors, Canada has served as a crucial site of comparison and contrast. As MacLean explains, in the nineteenth century, Canada served "simultaneously as a symbol of the decline of European empires in North America, a site of linguistic otherness and racial miscegenation, a symbol of Anglo-Saxon supremacy and destiny in North America, and an alternative to established political structures in the US" (2010, 7–8). Canada's seemingly endless elasticity has enabled US Americanists to continue to advance critiques of their nation and to expose the US as a fictional construct in its own right without taking direct aim at their home country. The result is that Canada's fictional representations by Americans may be read, in some cases, as allegories of the American political debates of a particular era. Without dismissing the value of these narratives, one danger of reading depictions of Canada in this way is that incomplete or one-sided conversations about both countries abound, replicating clichés about Canada and/or the US that could instead form the basis of a sustained and reciprocal dialogue about relations between the two nations.

Using Peggy Phelan's theorization of strategic blindness and (in)visibility (1993), as employed by a broad array of variously marginalized groups, I argue that American-authored texts and cultural objects, such as paintings and films, provide new insights about what Americans and Canadians know (or may think they know) about each other. By attending to the ways in which Canada is represented or occluded in these works—some of which frequently reference Canada while others may merely gesture to Canada or the Canada-US border—I seek to reconfigure traditional approaches used to discuss (or ignore) Canada and the relation between Canada and the US, particularly by Americanists. That change in perspective includes employing a strategic mode of comparativism, modeled on Reingard Nischik (2016, 18–26), that moves beyond a single national framework "to consider regions, areas, and diasporan affiliations that exist apart from or in conflicted relation to the nation," while acknowledging "the complex ruptures that remain within but nonetheless constitute the national frame" (Levander and Levine 2008, 2). By looking primarily at novels that may fit uneasily into the study of "national literature," as well as reinvigorating works that may have been regarded as canonically nationalistic by resituating them in particular "comparative, transnational" frameworks, this approach puts into conversation "a wealth of new" and different texts and offers innovative perspectives on more established works (Adams 2009, 18, 19, 18).

To theorize US depictions of Canada that are central to this monograph, I also borrow and adapt Lee's concept of "ingenious citizenship," which he uses to describe examples of Americans who "contest their non-belonging" and, in doing so, expose "the unequal access to and realization of U.S. citizenship for … [those] unassimilatory subjects and the unseen systematic marginalization of non normative citizens in everyday liberal democratic life" (2016, 27, 2). Some of Lee's illustrations, such as suicide bombers, are extreme; yet much like Judith Butler's work on the prescriptive performance of gender normativity,[16] Lee's scholarship argues for the need to "break from habit" in reinforcing the "neoliberal script of citizenship" (dictated by the "symbolic and material structuring of whiteness") that is espoused and celebrated to varying degrees by the US and Canada (2016, 125, 46). Lee's focus on US cases is especially useful to explore select narratives in which those trying to live in America resist relegation to the margins by looking northward, and through this process (whether imaginative or literal), expose how Canada's self-presentation as a "peaceable kingdom" also regulates access to Canadian citizenship and limits sanctuary. I consider what "ingenious citizenship" can and does look like for those who cross the Canada-US border—or imagine doing so—and how this break from habit raises questions about what it means to find belonging.

In the chapters that follow, I trace the ways in which contemporary American depictions of Canada raise important questions about how we understand ourselves and our neighbors to the south. Chapter 2, titled "The Missionary Position: The American Roots of Northrop Frye's Peaceable Kingdom," explores the American foundations of Frye's familiar description of Canada as the "peaceable kingdom" by analyzing the folk art of Erastus Salisbury Field and Edward Hicks (who painted multiple versions of the "Peaceable Kingdom"). Frye's work illustrates the powerful influence of Canada's missionary position—both sexual and ideological—in shaping its relationship with the US to the present.

Chapters 3, 4, 5, 6, and 7 present case studies of novels that probe key aspects of Canada's representation as exceptional through the fictional rendering of key moments in Canada's historical and recent past. Chapter 3 examines Ben Farmer's *Evangeline* (2010), which rewrites Henry

Wadsworth Longfellow's epic poem *Evangeline: A Tale of Acadie* (1847). Farmer's character Evangeline offers a potential model of ingenious citizenship in the post-9/11 era, defying sexual and racial stereotypes of Acadians on both sides of the Canada-US border and highlighting the potentially genocidal aspects of the 1776 Deportation. Chapters 4 and 5 address untold stories of Canadian racism and sexism that have received little acknowledgment from Canadian governments or the wider Canadian public. The fourth chapter pairs Duffy's fictional portrayal of Avon Heist, a German-born Canadian citizen and local schoolteacher who is placed in an internment camp in Amherst in *The Cartographer of No Man's Land* (2013), with an analysis of exquisitely carved wooden objects produced by those who were imprisoned to argue for a model of ingenious citizenship that reconceives Canadian exceptionalism. In Chap. 5, I consider how *The Tricking of Freya* (2009) portrays the multi-generational impact and legacy of forced adoption on one Icelandic-Canadian family. Sanctioned by the Canadian government between 1940 and 1970, this practice resulted in the removal of roughly 300,000 children from their White unwed mothers, who were deemed unfit because of their marital status and/or mental health. I argue that Freya, in "becoming animal" and taking flight as she makes this discovery (Braidotti 2011, 84), is able to challenge notions of exceptionality on both sides of the border.

Chapters 6 and 7 explore a broad combination of concerns: the illusion of Canadian fiscal prudence; the revisioning of traditional discourses regarding Canada's favorable treatment of enslaved Black Americans who fled to Canada from the US; and the increasingly public critique of Canada's historical and contemporary colonization of Indigenous peoples through readings of three novels that look carefully at unexpected or non-traditional Canada-US border crossings, in some cases even rejecting the promise of northern salvation altogether. Stewart O'Nan's *The Odds* (2012) depicts a white middle-aged US couple's last-ditch efforts to save their marriage and financial future by taking a trip to gamble on roulette wheels in the honeymoon haven of Niagara Falls, Ontario. Their story, the focus of Chap. 6, reveals Canada's acquiescence to foreign investment and the ease with which Canadians and Americans attribute their financial woes to a racial other rather than probing the role domestic governments and corporations play in economic crises. Chapter 7 returns to the construction of Canada as a "peaceable kingdom" through Colson Whitehead's *The Underground Railroad* (2016) and Louise Erdrich's *Future Home of the Living God* (2017). Both novels explore how Canada functions as a receding mirage of the promise of a better life for a fugitive Black enslaved woman and an Indigenous female protagonist who finds herself living in a futuristic dystopian America; in their texts, Whitehead and Erdrich, respectively, trouble Canada's historical and contemporary virtuosity for BIPOC populations, suggesting that escaping to Canada may not provide the sanctuary presumed to exist north of the border.

Chapter 8 brings my inquiry full circle by comparing American Michael Moore's American documentary film *Bowling for Columbine* with the Canadian musical *Come From Away*, and contrasting these works with Cree filmmaker Tasha Hubbard's *Nîpawistamâsowin: We Will Stand Up*; the three texts present notably divergent perspectives on discourses of exceptionalism and refuge. As part of my conclusion, I reflect on the accessibility and portability of the novel form and suggest that given Canada's desire to see itself as a "peaceable kingdom," it may be more productive to consider how perception shapes representation and may preclude or facilitate new forms of ingenious citizenship.

NOTES

1. See Honderich and Gagdekar for coverage of the death of an Indian family who tried to cross an unregulated part of the Canada-US border in rural Manitoba in January 2022. The bodies of the adult couple and their two children were discovered on January 19. The family had frozen to death due to brutal winter conditions and a lack of appropriate winter gear. An American was subsequently charged with human smuggling. Their story echoes that of two Ghanian migrants who were "badly injured by frostbite" in 2017 while crossing the same geographical area. The men later had several fingers amputated due to the extreme damage done to their hands (2022).
2. See Andrews (2018a, 2021b), Maynard (2017), Roberts (2015), and Stewart (2014).
3. See Levander and Levine (2008), which references Canada throughout the edited collection titled *Hemispheric American Studies*.
4. See Braz (2011), Mayer (2014), Kerber (2017), and Umezurike (2021).
5. See Sadowski-Smith and Fox (2004, 6), Siemerling and Casteel (2010, 7–8), and Adams (2009, 14–20).
6. Sugars makes this point explicitly when she describes the categorization of English Canadian literature by the Modern Language Association (MLA). Founded in 1883 and based out of New York City, it is the largest and most well-known scholarly association of literary and language studies in

the world. She notes that within the MLA, the field of English Canadian literature historically is designated as one of the "literatures other than British and American" (qtd. in 2010, 42). At the MLA's annual convention, there is only one panel dedicated to Canadian literature (in addition to two panels on Margaret Atwood).
7. See https://biglobalization.org.
8. See https://www.kent.ac.uk/ccusb/events/archive.html.
9. See Siemerling (2005), Braz (2011), Nischik (2014, 2016), Harris (2016), Vernon (2019), MacLean (2010), Stewart (2014), Zacharias (2016), Chapman (2016), Roberts and Stirrup (2013), Roberts (2015, 2018), and Feghali (2019).
10. See, for instance, Marche (2016), Kingwell (2017), and Kendzior (2017) who connect the increasing popularity of treating Canada as exceptional in the wake of presidential election of Donald Trump in 2016.
11. See Dryden and Lenon (2015) for a similar set of arguments. They note that "the celebratory representations of Canada as a safe haven for African and African American refugees fleeing the institution of slavery in the United States ignores the realities of slavery and the treatment of the enslaved in Canada" (10). Much like the novels that I read in this monograph, Dryden and Lenon's collection pointedly "speaks back to … narratives of Canadian benevolence and exceptionalism while actively resisting the urge to look elsewhere," namely, to the US for examples of injustice and exploitation (11).
12. See, for example, Brown (1981, 1990), Blaise (1990), Lecker (1991), Thacker and Peterman (1999), Thacker and Hingham (2006), Thacker et al. (2010) for explorations of Canada-US border relations and Americans who write about Canada.
13. See Levecq (2002) for an examination of how Reed subverts the promise of Black salvation through the enslaved Black protagonist Quickskill's escape to Canada. Levecq argues that "stepping across the border" into Canada, at least in this novel, "signifies less a creative refashioning of identity and the nation than a reproduction, even an imposition, of the logic of that nation" (293). Likewise, Jerome Charyn's *New York Times* review of Reed's novel describes Quickskill's realization upon his arrival in Canada that the country is nothing more than a "carbuncle," meaning a pus-filled mound, "on top of the United States" (1976, 248).
14. There are always exceptions—among them, Joyce Carol Oates' novels and short stories, including *Wonderland* (1971) and *Crossing the Border: Fifteen Tales* (1976); Mary Morris' *The Waiting Game* (1989); *Affliction* by Russell Banks (1989); Jane Smiley's *A Thousand Acres* (1991); John Irving's *A Prayer for Owen Meaney* (1989); *The Parable of the Sower* (1993) and *The Parable of the Talents* (1998) by Octavia Butler; David Foster

Wallace's epic novel *Infinite* Jest (1996); and Howard Norman's *The Bird Artist* (1994) and *The Museum Guard* (1998).
15. There are many other novels that I could have explored in this monograph that were published post-9/11, each with its own fascinating and provocative depiction of Canada. They include Joyce Carol Oates' *The Falls* (2004); Philip Roth's *The Plot Against America* (2004); Ami McKay's *The Birth House* (2006); Jim Lynch's *Border Songs* (2009); *Last Night in a Twisted River* by John Irving (2009); Howard Norman's *The Haunting of L* (2002), *Devotion: A Novel* (2007), and *The Next Life Might Be Kinder* (2014), as well as *What Is Left the Daughter* (2010), which I have written about elsewhere; Robert Olen Butler's *Perfume River* (2016); *Red Clocks* by Leni Zumas (2018); *Africaville* by Jeffrey Colvin (2019); and Russell Banks' *Foregone* (2021).
16. See Lee 2016 for a useful summary of Butler's notion of gender performativity (162). See also J. Butler 1988 where she argues that "gender is in no way a stable identity ... [but is] instituted through a *stylized repetition of acts*" (519). Butler furthers this argument most famously in *Gender Trouble: Feminism and the Subversion of Identity* (1990) and then refines it in *Bodies that Matter: On the Discursive Limits of "Sex"* (1993) and *Undoing Gender* (2004).

REFERENCES

Adams, Rachel. 2009. *Continental Divides: Remapping the Cultures of North America*. Chicago: University of Chicago Press.

Andrews, Jennifer. 2018a. Escape to *Canada*: Richard Ford's Fugitive Novel. *Canadian Review of American Studies* 48 (1): 38–62.

———. 2018b. The Missionary Position: The American Roots of Northrop Frye's Peaceable Kingdom. *The Journal of Canadian Studies* 52 (2): 361–380.

———. 2021a. German Internment Camps in the Maritimes: Another Untold Story in P.S. Duffy's *The Cartographer of No Man's Land*. In *On the Other Side(s) of 150: Untold Stories and Critical Approaches to History, Literature, and Identity in Canada*, ed. Linda Morra and Sarah Henzi, 221–239. Waterloo: Wilfrid Laurier University Press.

———. 2021b. Reading *Evangeline* and *What is Left the Daughter*: Tracing American Projections of Grief onto Atlantic Canada. *Comparative American Studies*, November 30. https://www.tandfonline.com/doi/full/10.1080/14775700.2021.2008749.

Banks, Russell. 1989. *Affliction*. New York: Harper Perennial.

———. 2021. *Foregone*. Windsor, ON: Biblioasis.

Barker, Adam J. 2012. Already Occupied: Indigenous Peoples, Settler Colonialism and the Occupy Movements in North America. *Movement Studies* 11 (3/4): 327–334.
Blaise, Clark. 1990. *The Border as Fiction*. Orono, MN: Borderlands Project.
Braidotti, Rosi. 2011. *Nomadic Theory: The Portable Rosi Braidotti*. New York: Columbia University Press.
Braz, Albert. 2011. Reconstructing the Border: Jim Lynch and the Return of the Canada-US Boundary. *Comparative American Studies* 9 (3): 191–203.
Brown, Russell M. 1981. Crossing Borders. *Essays on Canadian Writing* 22: 154–168.
———. 1990. *Borderlines and Borderlands in English Canada: The Written Line*. Orono, MN: Borderlands Project.
Bryant, Rachel. 2017. *The Homing Place: Indigenous and Settler Literary Legacies of the Atlantic*. Waterloo: Wilfrid Laurier University Press.
Butler, Judith. 1988. Performative Acts and Gender Constitution: An Essay in Phenomenology and Feminist Theory. *Theatre Journal* 40 (4): 519–539.
Butler, Judith. 1990. *Gender Trouble: Feminism and the Subversion of Identity*. New York: Routledge.
Butler, Judith. 1993. *Bodies that Matter: On the Discursive Limits of "Sex"*. New York: Routledge.
Butler, Judith. 2004. *Undoing Gender*. New York: Routledge.
Butler, Octavia. 1993. *Parable of the Sower*. New York: Grand Central Publishing.
Butler, Octavia. 1998. *Parable of the Talents*. New York: Grand Central Publishing.
Butler, Robert Olen. 2016. *Perfume River: A Novel*. New York: Atlantic Monthly Press.
Carlson-Manathara, Elizabeth. 2021 "Settler Colonialism and Resistance." In *Living in Indigenous Sovereignty*, edited by Elizabeth Carlson-Manarthara, Gladys Rowe, 28–59. Halifax: Fernwood Publishing.
Chapman, Mary. 2016. *Becoming Sui Sin Far: Early Fiction, Journalism, and Travel Writing of Edith Maude Eaton*. Montreal & Kingston: McGill-Queen's University Press.
Charyn, Jerome. 1976. Flight to Canada. *The New York Times*, September 19: 248. https://www.nytimes.com/1976/09/19/archives/flight-to-canada-canada.html.
Clarke, George Elliott. 2008. Introduction to *The Refugee: Fugitive Slave Narratives in Canada*. By Benjamin Drew, 10–24. Toronto: Dundurn.
Colvin, Jeffrey. 2019. *Africaville: A Novel*. New York: Amistad.
Cooper, Celine. 2017. Report on *Canadian Exceptionalism: Are We Good or Are We Lucky? 2017 Annual Conference of the McGill Institute for the Study of Canada*. Montreal, February 9–10. mcgill.ca/misc/files/misc/misc_canadian_exceptionalism_2017_final_report_-04-18-2017.pdf.

Doyle, James. 1983. *North of America: Images of Canada in the Literature of the United States, 1775–1900*. Toronto: ECW Press.
Dryden, Omisoore H., and Suzanne Lenon. 2015. Introduction: Interventions, Iterations, and Interrogations That Disturb the (Homo) Nation. In *Disrupting Queer Inclusion: Canadian Homonationalisms and the Politics of Belonging*, ed. Omisoore Dryden and Suzanne Lenon, 3–18. Vancouver: University of British Columbia Press.
Duffy, P.S. 2013. *The Cartographer of No Man's Land*. New York: W.W. Norton.
Erdrich, Louise. 2017. *Future Home of the Living God*. New York: Harper.
Farmer, Ben. 2010. *Evangeline: A Novel*. New York: Overlook.
Feghali, Zalfa. 2019. *Crossing Borders and Queering Citizenship in Contemporary Canadian and American Writing*. Manchester: Manchester University Press.
Ford, Richard. 2012. *Canada: A Novel*. Toronto: HarperCollins.
Frye, Northrop. 1971. *The Bush Garden: Essays on the Canadian Imagination*. Toronto: House of Anansi Press.
Ghatak, Seemanti. 2020. How Will President Biden Affect Canadian Immigration? Only Time Will Tell. *New Canadian Media*, December 27. https://newcanadianmedia.ca/u-s-immigrants-to-canada-election-results/.
Grewal, Inderpal. 2017. *Saving the Security State: Exceptional Citizens in Twenty-First-Century America*. Durham: Duke University Press.
Harris, Jennifer. 2016. Black Canadian Contexts: The Case of Amelia E. Johnson. *African American Review* 49 (3): 241–259.
Honderich, Holly, and Roxy Gagdekar. 2022. The family That Froze to Death a World Away From Home. *BBC News*, February 11. https://www.bbc.com/news/world-us-canada-60290955.
Irving, John. 1989. *A Prayer for Owen Meaney*. New York: Harper.
———. 2009. *Last Night in Twisted River*. New York: Random House.
Kaplan, Amy. 1993. "Left Alone with America": The Absence of Empire in the Study of American Culture. In *Cultures of United States Imperialism*, ed. Amy Kaplan and Donald E. Pease. Durham: Duke University Press.
Kendzior, Sarah. 2017. When Trudeau met Trump: Canadian Exceptionalism, American Envy. *The Globe and Mail*, February 13. https://www.theglobeandmail.com/opinion/when-trudeau-met-trump-canadian-exceptionalism-american-envy/article34011537/.
Kerber, Jenny. 2017. Border Insecurity: Reading Transnational Environments in Jim Lynch's *Border Songs*. *Canadian Review of American Studies* 47 (1): 131–160.
Kingwell, Mark. 2017. No Exceptionalism Please, We're Canadian. *The Globe and Mail*, January 14. https://www.theglobeandmail.com/opinion/no-exceptionalism-please-were-canadian/article33619408/.
Lecker, Robert, ed. 1991. *Borderlands: Essays in Canadian-American Relations*. Toronto: ECW Press.

Lee, Charles T. 2016. *Ingenious Citizenship: Recrafting Democracy for Social Change*. Durham: Duke University Press.
Levander, Carolyn. 2013. *Where is American Literature?* Hoboken, NJ: Wiley-Blackwell.
Levander, Carolyn, and Robert S. Levine, eds. 2008. *Hemispheric American Studies*. New Brunswick, NJ: Rutgers University Press.
Levecq, Christine. 2002. Nation, Race, and Postmodern Gestures in Ishmael Reed's *Flight to Canada*. *Novel: A Forum on Fiction* 35 (2-3): 281–298.
Battell Lowman, Emma, and Adam J. Barker. 2015. *Settler: Identity and Colonialism in 21st Century Canada*. Halifax: Fernwood Publishing.
Lynch, Jim. 2009. *Border Songs*. Toronto: Random House Canada.
Mackey, Eva. 2002. *The House of Difference: Cultural Politics and National Identity in Canada*. Toronto: University of Toronto Press.
MacLean, Alyssa. 2010. *Canadian Migrations: Reading Canada in Nineteenth-Century American Literature*. PhD diss: University of British Columbia.
Marche, Stephen. 2016. Canadian Exceptionalism. *OpenCanada*, November 1. https://opencanada.org/canadian-exceptionalism/.
Mayer, Evelyn P. 2014. *Narrating North American Borderlands: Thomas King, Howard F. Mosher, and Jim Lynch*. Bern: Peter Lang.
Maynard, Robyn. 2017. *Policing Black Lives: State Violence in Canada from Slavery to the Present*. Halifax: Fernwood.
McKay, Ami. 2006. *The Birth House*. Toronto: Vintage Canada.
Moore, Michael. 2003. Bowling for Columbine. MGM Home Entertainment.
Morris, Mary. 1989. *The Waiting Room*. New York: Doubleday.
Nelson, Dana. 2019. We Have Never Been Anti-Exceptionalists. *American Literary History* 31 (2): e1–17.
Nischik, Reingard M., ed. 2014. *The Palgrave Handbook of Comparative North American Literature*. New York: Palgrave Macmillan.
———. 2016. *Comparative North American Studies: Transnational Approaches to American and Canadian Literature and Culture*. New York: Palgrave Macmillan.
Norman, Howard. 1994. *The Bird Artist*. New York: Picador.
———. 1998. *The Museum Guard*. New York: Alfred A. Knopf.
———. 2002. *The Haunting of L*. Toronto: Alfred A. Knopf Canada.
———. 2007. *Devotion: A Novel*. Boston: Houghton Mifflin.
———. 2010. *What is Left the Daughter*. Toronto: Vintage Canada.
———. 2014. *The Next Life Might Be Kinder*. Boston: Houghton Mifflin Harcourt.
O'Nan, Stewart. 2012. *The Odds: A Love Story*. New York: Viking.
Oates, Joyce Carol. 1971. *Wonderland*. New York: Modern Library.
———. 1976. *Crossing the Border: Fifteen Tales*. New York: Vanguard Press.
———. 2004. *The Falls: A Novel*. New York: Harper Perennial.

Phelan, Peggy. 1993. *Unmarked: The Politics of Performance*. New York: Routledge.
Reed, Ishmael. 1976. *Flight to Canada*. New York: Scribner.
Roberts, Gillian. 2015. *Discrepant Parallels: Cultural Implications of the Canada-US Border*. Montreal & Kingston: McGill-Queen's University Press.
———, ed. 2018. *Reading Between the Borderlines: Cultural Production and Consumption across the 49th Parallel*. Montreal & Kingston: McGill-Queen's University Press.
Roberts, Gillian, and David Stirrup, eds. 2013. *Parallel Encounters: Culture and the Canada-U.S. Border*. Waterloo: Wilfrid Laurier University Press.
Roth, Philip. 2004. *The Plot Against America: A Novel*. New York: Vintage International.
Rowe, John Carlos. 1998. Post-Nationalism, Globalism, and the New American Studies. *Cultural Critique* 40: 11–28.
Sadowski-Smith, Claudia, and Claire Fox. 2004. Theorizing the Hemisphere: Inter-Americas Work at the Intersection of American, Canadian, and Latin American Studies. *Comparative American Studies* 2 (1): 5–38.
Siemerling, Winfried. 2005. *The New North American Studies: Culture, Writing and the Politics of Re/cognition*. New York: Routledge.
Siemerling, Winfried, and Sarah Phillips Casteel, eds. 2010. *Canada and its Americas: Transnational Navigations*. Montreal/Kingston: McGill-Queen's University Press.
Smiley, Jane. 1991. *A Thousand Acres: A Novel*. New York: Anchor Books.
Stewart, Anthony. 2014. *Visitor: My Life in Canada*. Halifax: Fernwood.
Sugars, Cynthia. 2010. Worlding the (Postcolonial) Nation: Canada's Americas. In *Canada and its Americas: Transnational Navigations*, ed. Winfried Siemerling and Sarah Phillips Casteel, 31–47. Montreal & Kingston: McGill-Queen's University Press.
Sunley, Christina. 2009. *The Tricking of Freya: A Novel*. New York: St. Martin's Press.
Thacker, Robert, and Carol L. Hingham, eds. 2006. *One West, Two Myths: Essays on Comparison*. Calgary: University of Calgary Press.
Thacker, Robert, and Michael Peterman, eds. 1999. *Willa Cather's Canadian and Old World Connections: Volume 4, Cather Studies*. Lincoln: University of Nebraska Press.
Thacker, Robert, Françoise Pelleau-Papin, and John J. Murphy, eds. 2010. *Willa Cather: A Writer's Worlds: Volume 8, Cather Studies*. Lincoln: University of Nebraska Press.
Traister, Bryce. 1997. Risking Nationalism: NAFTA and the Limits of the New American Studies. *Canadian Review of American Studies* 27 (1): 191–204.
Tuck, Eve, and K. Wayne Yang. 2012. Decolonization Is Not a Metaphor. *Decolonization: Indigeneity, Education & Society* 1 (1): 1–40.

Umezurike, Uchechukwu Peter. 2021. The Euro (Centric) Border Man: Masculinities and the Nonhuman in Jim Lynch's *Border Songs*. In *Men, Masculinities, and Earth*, ed. Paul M. Pulé and Martin Hultman, 463–479. London: Palgrave Macmillan.

Vernon, Karina, ed. 2019. *The Black Prairie Archives: An Anthology*. Waterloo: Wilfrid Laurier University Press.

Wallace, David Foster. 1996. *Infinite Jest: A Novel*. New York: Back Bay Books.

Whitehead, Colson. 2016. *The Underground Railroad*. Doubleday.

Whitfield, Harvey Amani. 2016. *North to Bondage: Loyalist Slavery in the Maritimes*. Vancouver: University of British Columbia Press.

Wyile, Herb. 2010. Hemispheric Studies or Scholarly NAFTA?: The Case for Canadian Literary Studies. In *Canada and its Americas: Transnational Navigations*, ed. Winfried Siemerling and Sarah Phillips Casteel, 48–61. Montreal & Kingston: McGill-Queen's University Press.

Zacharias, Robert. 2016. The Transnational Return: Tracing the Spatial Politics of CanLit. *Studies in Canadian Literature* 41 (1): 102–124.

Zumas, Leni. 2018. *Red Clocks: A Novel*. New York: Little, Brown and Company.

CHAPTER 2

The Missionary Position: The American Roots of Northrop Frye's Peaceable Kingdom

[T]he rapid adaptation of the peaceable kingdom ideal suggests that Frye's search for imagery was over. For scholars, journalists, and politicians, the peaceable kingdom ideal is an historical certainty that provides a ready reference for touting Canadian nationalism, buttressing an argument, or even selling a product. (See 2018, 511)

The wolf also shall dwell with the lamb, and the leopard shall lie down with the kid; and the calf and the young lion and the fatling together; and a little child shall lead them.

And the cow and the bear shall feed; their young ones shall lie down together: and the lion shall eat straw like the ox.

And the sucking child shall play on the hole of the asp, and the weaned child shall put his hand on the cockatrice' den. (Isaiah 11:6–8, King James Version)

No government whose only acts are those of violence and cruelty ... and whose land is watered with the tears of widows and orphans, can long stand contiguous to a nation abounding in free institutions. O Canada, my own country, from which I am now exiled ... I love thee still .... I write that Canada may know her children will not silently submit to the most egregious outrages upon private property, and even life itself. ... how long will the people of Canada tamely submit? Will

> *they not soon rise in their strength, as one man, and burst asunder the chains that bind them to the earth and revolutionize and disenthrall Canada from the grasp of tyrants? (Lount, qtd. in Healey 2006, 166)*

Canada has long developed, reinforced, and promoted its own narratives of (literary and cultural) exceptionality, but often does so by using the US as a foil for its virtuosity. This chapter probes how Canada relies on and draws from specific American traditions to create the terminology and basis for a story of exceptionality that paradoxically depends on and is rooted in American culture. To do so, I explore the characterization of Canada as a "peaceable kingdom," a term used by Canadian scholar Northrop Frye in 1965 to articulate what makes Canada potentially distinctive.[1] In his famous "Conclusion" to his *Literary History of Canada*, Frye describes Canada as embodying a vision of "serenity" where man[2] can reconcile "with man and ... nature" (1995, 251). For Frye, this concept is epitomized by the notion of the "peaceable kingdom" celebrated in Isaiah 11: 6–9. Frye employs the term "peaceable kingdom" to reference Canada as a promised land in stark contrast to its American neighbor, yet as I will explore, US cultural materials provide the basis for this very portrayal. That Frye's term has endured in popularity well into the twenty-first century demonstrates that, as the first epigraph suggests, "[f]or scholars, journalists, and politicians, the peaceable kingdom ideal is an historical certainty that provides a ready reference for touting Canadian nationalism, buttressing an argument, or even selling a product" (See 2018, 511). This trafficking in cross-border exceptionality reveals the importance of looking to the US and its perceptions of Canada to better understand Canadian narratives of identity and history.

Frye's Missionary Zeal

Frye's literary criticism was shaped fundamentally by his knowledge of the Bible. He was deeply influenced by his religious roots; in particular, his maternal grandfather was a circuit-riding preacher.[3] Drawing on his religious background, including his ordination as a United Church minister, Frye blends "literary scholarship with Christian belief" in the "Conclusion" to create what Canadian literary critic Robert Lecker has described as a "pastoral version of English Canadian literary history" that attains coherence and a "transhistorical" mythological status through its ability to overcome, at least metaphorically, the challenges of Canada's size, sparse population, and close proximity to the US (1993, 284, 286). Like many of his works, Frye's "Conclusion" was characterized by "a missionary zeal" to "spread the word" (Dubois 2012, 66) by cultivating a pastoral myth that offered the promise of a return to a "prelapsarian" world, led by Frye himself as the "reader-hero" in a quest for the peaceable kingdom (Lecker 1993, 290, 284).

Although a literary critic and Biblical scholar, Frye also demonstrated a keen interest in and deep understanding of art history and the links between text and image. His first book, *Fearful Symmetry*, explored the work of English poet and visual artist William Blake and included various plates from Blake's work. Several of his most influential essays on Canadian art and culture are anthologized in *The Bush Garden*, including a study of painter David Milne and an introduction to the work of Group of Seven artist Lawren Harris.[4] While Frye references Canadian works of art in the "Conclusion," including the paintings of Tom Thomson and Emily Carr, his argument relies heavily on the power of American visual art. Frye cites "two famous primitive American paintings" to illustrate his key ideas in the "Conclusion" (1995, 249): Erastus Salisbury Field's "Historical Monument of the American Republic" and Hicks' "Peaceable Kingdom." He aligns Field with American technological dominance and uniformity as "a civilization conquering the landscape and imposing an alien and abstract pattern on it" (1995, 248). In contrast, Hicks' "The Peaceable Kingdom" is offered as a necessary antidote, epitomizing what could make Canada different from its American neighbor: the sustained search for a "vision of a serenity that is both human and natural" (1995, 251). For Frye, folk art, and especially the work of Hicks, offered an escape back to a kinder, gentler era that was no longer available to America and, by virtue of the US's pervasive impact on its northern neighbor, was gradually threatening Canada's sanctity.

Lecker, along with many other literary critics, has offered analyses of Frye's famous phrase, its role in concretizing the institution of "English Canadian literature," and the lasting impact it has had more broadly on Canadian culture and identity as a means of self-differentiation (1993, 283). However, my examination of Frye's essay differentiates itself from previous scholarly analyses of the "Conclusion" by Lecker and others[5] by closely examining the paintings produced by US artists that informed his understanding of the peaceable kingdom and their impact on his writing. Moreover, while Field's canvas provides an important point of comparison, Hicks' works are the primary focus of the chapter precisely because they offer unique insights about what the "peaceable kingdom" means for Frye in a Canadian context. In doing so, I explore the influence of American religions and their missionary traditions—specifically Quakers and Methodists (the latter of whom later joined the United Church)—on Frye's use of this phrase.[6]

This chapter considers how the historical flow of these religions across the Canada-US border, in combination with the influx of Loyalists northward and the subsequent commitment to missions that was part of "British rule in post-revolutionary colonial Canada," led to the lasting popularity of the concept of the "peaceable kingdom" (Christie and Gauvreau 2010, 112). In probing this complex intersection of influences, it becomes clear that Frye was indeed writing from what I am calling the missionary position in order to differentiate Canada from its southern neighbor, even as he was drawing on American traditions and ideas to do so. The missionary position commonly refers to a traditional heterosexual position, in which a man lies on top of a woman in a relationship of dominance, one that functions as an easy (all puns intended) metaphor for reading US-Canadian relations. But in this chapter, the missionary position can be understood as the position of the proselytizer, who spreads his or her beliefs in a deliberate effort to convert others to a particular cause—in the case of Frye, Canadian efforts to attain an ideal. As a missionary scholar, Frye makes a case for Canada as a place where Edenic peace and harmony, relatively untouched by technology, may potentially still be accessed.

Frye's coupling of the roles of scholar and missionary makes perfect sense given his personal and educational experiences in early twentieth-century Canada, a country shaped by both British and American traditions. Andrew Walls explains in *The Missionary Movement in Christian History* that "preaching and teaching" came to be regarded as "just different modes of evangelism," an option that appealed to Frye, who saw this phenomenon manifested in the teachers he encountered at Victoria College where he completed an Honors BA in Philosophy and English from 1929 to 1933 (1996, 203). Victoria College was the "first Methodist university" in Canada, stressing the idea of "an intellectualized Christianity," and produced a "cadre of clergyman-professors" to serve this mission (Christie and Gauvreau 2010, 73, 74). Raised as a Methodist whose first memories of the power of words were from "revival meetings," Frye understood his role as an academic to be a religious one; by teaching the Bible and Classical mythology, he would unpack the inheritance of twentieth-century Western society and make students into "active and responsible" citizens (Frye 2008, 33, 166).

Trained at Emanuel College to be a minister and ordained into the United Church in 1936, Frye held a "mission field" for a single summer in Saskatchewan before starting his Master's degree in English at Merton College and becoming a professor at Victoria College in 1939 (Frye 2008, 325). Yet when asked in a 1976 interview conducted by student reporter Philip Chester and published in the University of Toronto newspaper *The Varsity* if he saw himself as a missionary, Frye replied without hesitation, "Oh yes, yes," and described his teaching of literature at university as his "pastoral charge" (2008, 319, 325).

Canada's Conversion Narratives

Frye deserves enormous credit for creating and disseminating a powerful and persuasive set of what could be called conversion narratives that have secured Canada's status in the world as a country involved with and committed to social justice, liberty, and security. These ideas remain integral to the United Church mission and have been a critical part of Canada's self-positioning by scholars, critics, and journalists as an exceptional nation-state, both in the post-9/11 era and then with the advent of a Trump presidency. The concept of the "peaceable kingdom" is a critical part of the rhetorical toolbox used to differentiate Canada and to resist, at least linguistically, the infiltration of American culture and technology north of the Canada-US border.

Frye's essay may feel dated, especially given its gendered connotations; he published a far less influential revised version of the "Conclusion" in 1976.[7] Nonetheless, his idea that Canada has the potential to be a "peaceable kingdom" has remained popular over the past fifty-plus years and is frequently invoked to celebrate the country's (apparent) willingness to embrace diversity and reject violence, a tradition rooted in the idea that, unlike the US, where "revolution, civil war, ... lynchings, mobs, and the violence of the cities" marked the nation's birth, Canada was not born out of "a revolutionary celebration" (Torrance 1986, 100).[8] As Robert McGill argues, Lester B. Pearson's formation of a United Nations Emergency Force during the Suez Crisis of 1956 "inaugurated the notion of Canada as a peacekeeping country" (2017, 11). Pearson, who was also a Methodist and a graduate of Victoria College, would be awarded the Nobel Peace Prize in 1957 for this accomplishment.

It is worth noting here Sherene Razack's important efforts to challenge and dismantle Canada's subsequent self-positioning as a model of peacekeeping, both at home and abroad. In *Dark Threats and White Knights: The Somalia Affair, Peacekeeping, and the New Imperialism*, Razack assesses the ways in which taking up the role of peacekeeper has inspired "domestic unity" (2004, 33) among French and English Canadians and allowed Canada to cultivate and sustain "the myth of middle powermanship," turning vulnerability into an asset on the international stage (Donald Gordon, qtd. in Razack 2004, 33). Razack explains that by "claiming to possess the special qualities of the go-between—'a link between east and west, between haves and have-nots, and between whites and non-whites'" (33), Canadians are able "to tell a story of national goodness and to mark ourselves as distinct from Americans" (35), a stance that is reinforced by the perception that Canada has never "been a colonial power or engaged in aggressive occupations" (33). But as Razack reminds us, Canada has a long history of "internal colonialism" (33) that continues to be ignored and erased. By embracing its role as an external peacekeeper, Canada has been able to "grow up outside the shadow of both Great Britain and the United States" (34), while erasing its own legacy of settler colonialism. The contradictions inherent in this long-standing narrative of national identity are crucial to this chapter and this monograph more broadly.

The years prior to and following the publication of Frye's "Conclusion" were characterized by visible instability, racism, and violence in the US, with the Civil Rights Movement, the assassination of two Kennedys, the Red Power movement, and American military interventions abroad (most notably in Vietnam), which "spurred Canadians to see their own nation in a relatively positive light" (McGill 2017, 11). The term "peaceable kingdom" continues to hold its appeal as a shorthand that Canadians employ when comparing themselves with the US. For instance, the "Preface" to Judy Torrance's *Public Violence in Canada: 1867–1982* begins with the statement that "Canadians have long assumed that their society is relatively free of violence, particularly in comparison with that of the United States. They see themselves living in a 'peaceable kingdom' where problems are resolved without resort to violence" (1986, ix). While her work examines select examples of violence in Canada, Torrance insists throughout the book that Canada is still a remarkably safe nation whose "low level of toleration for violence" has been aided by the country's "legitimation of a strong interventionist government" (1986, 100, 102), one that prioritizes securing the state over American insistence on an individual's right to bear arms.

Likewise, note John Ibbitson's choice of words in a July 2016 *Globe and Mail* article when the federal government raised its Syrian refugee targets: "This peaceable kingdom [Canada] is an oasis of openness in a world of closing doors" (1). Ibbitson's use of Frye's famous phrase to describe Canada—"the peaceable kingdom"—in a national newspaper is repeated for effect at the end of his article in a cautionary manner, which asks that Canadians avoid falling prey to anger, intolerance, suspicion, and hatred. Ibbitson's invocation of "the peaceable kingdom" demonstrates its continued potency as a concept that embodies uniquely Canadian values and beliefs.[9] Yet, little attention has been paid to the primary source text for Frye's famous description of Canada—one of several canvases by nineteenth-century American folk artist Edward Hicks titled "The Peaceable Kingdom"—nor the context in which this image is presented and described by Frye. At a time in which Canada is facing an increasingly complex and contradictory relationship with its southern neighbor while holding onto its self-positioning as "nicer and less aggressive than the United States" (Razack 2004, 33), this phrase and its origins warrant a more careful examination.

NARRATING IMAGES

Despite the centrality of works of art to Frye's essay, there are no reproductions of any of the Canadian or American paintings Frye refers to in the "Conclusion" to his *Literary History of Canada*. Though the cost of publishing plates is not cheap (Donald Stephens remarks, in his 1965 review of *Literary History of Canada* in *Canadian Literature*, that the volume, at $18, is "far too expensive for a general reader" [1965, 13]), it is unlikely that the absence of these images was motivated by the fees involved in obtaining permissions or the expense of including reproductions. As general editor Carl Klinck was following the conventions of other national literary histories of the era published in Britain and the US, which typically contained no plates of any kind (reproductions of paintings or maps).[10] I would suggest that Frye's "deliberate shaping" of "Canadian literary history" and his effort to "construct Canada as the apotheosis of metaphor" makes the inclusion of visual productions unnecessary and even detrimental to the aims of his essay (Lecker 1993, 284, 285). But these paintings are an important part of the story behind the "Conclusion," offering their own Biblical allegories and religious metaphors in a distinctly American context, one that Frye employs comparatively through his readings of the canvases to illustrate Canada's potential. These artists complicate our understanding of "the peaceable kingdom" as a uniquely Canadian ideal.

Erastus Salisbury Field (1805–1900) was a deeply religious American folk artist who lived and worked primarily as a rural portraitist, producing "flat compositions" with "blunt directness," until, during a residency in New York City (1841–1848), he grew interested in "historical architecture and subjects" (Staiti 2011). Field was profoundly influenced by the Bible and thus used his paintings to create typological artistic works, employing Christian themes and Biblical scenes to depict America's past, present, and future. For Field, art was a tool for conversion, education, and faith-building. Field was a Congregationalist, a denomination that later became part of the United Church of Canada;[11] the Congregationalists were rooted in early American Puritanism and committed to missionary efforts both within the US and beyond.

Produced to celebrate the centennial of the Revolution, Field's massive canvas titled "Historical Monument of the American Republic" (1867–1888) depicts what Frye rightly describes as "an encyclopaedic portrayal of events in American history," offering a "prophetic vision of the skyscraper cities of the future, of the tremendous technological will to power of our time and the civilization it has built, ... [one that is] now gradually imposing a uniformity of culture and habits of life all over the globe" (1995, 249) (Fig. 2.1).[12] Field's canvas consists of ten massive marble towers atop a set of elegant Coliseum-like structures, each decorated with ornate reliefs. Some of the lower parts of the painting depict in a relentlessly graphic form "scenes of tragedy, chaos, invasion, oppression, and violence" (Staiti 1992, 33), including chained and lynched Black Americans and massacred Indigenous peoples. Field's painting likely appealed to Frye on aesthetic grounds with its complex layering of Biblical references and religious allegories—such as Lincoln being rendered as the Old Testament prophet Ezekiel who "imagined" the founding of "a new state when the Israelites were freed from bondage" (1992, 36). But for Frye, Field's painting also epitomizes the global reach of an American-defined homogeneity fundamentally rooted in technology. While Canadians, according to Frye, "seem well adjusted to the new world of technology and very efficient at handling it," he contends that within the "Canadian imagination there are deep reservations to this world as an end of life in itself" (1995, 250). The limitations imposed by a US-centered international perspective do not fully account for the ambivalence experienced by Canadians and expressed through the nation's literature and culture.

2 THE MISSIONARY POSITION: THE AMERICAN ROOTS OF NORTHROP… 35

For Frye, Hicks' paintings provided a useful contrast in his efforts to understand and portray Canada as distinct from and better than the US. Hicks (1780–1849) was a devout Quaker who used his sermons and his "easel pictures," which he gifted to friends and family, in the service of religion (Weekley 1999, 6). The canvases "were tangible reminders of the important beliefs and values Edward shared with the recipients … [and] [a]s such, their value transcended remuneration" (1999, 6). "The Peaceable Kingdom" became his most memorable series of paintings, which borrowed the idea from English artist Richard Westall, who illustrated Biblical stories, including those about the prophet Isaiah. In contrast with Westall, who was interested in "orthodox Christology and sacramental theology" (Sawyer 1996, 236), Hicks produced various versions of "The Peaceable Kingdom" to portray the shifting relations between and among the northeastern Quakers, a dynamic that grew

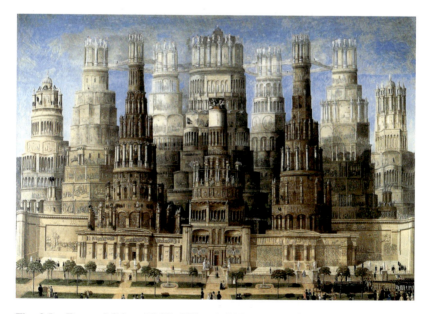

Fig. 2.1 Erastus Salisbury Field's "Historical Monument of the American Republic" (1867). (D'Armour Museum of Fine Art, Springfield, MA. Image available in the public domain: https://upload.wikimedia.org/wikipedia/commons/9/9d/Erastus_Salisbury_Field_-_Historical_Monument_of_the_American_Republic.jpg. Source: http://www.the-athenaeum.org)

increasingly complex in the late 1820s and early 1830s, the very period Frye cites in his "Conclusion."

In total, Hicks painted ten versions of "The Peaceable Kingdom," all of which could be dated to around 1830. Most of these canvases took a year or more to complete and are dated to reflect the entire period of their composition. Many of these versions found homes in public art galleries in the US, including at Smith College, Yale University, Swathmore College, and the Museum of Fine Arts, Houston. The variation among Hicks' canvases and Frye's decision to describe one specific version of "The Peaceable Kingdom" (although it is impossible to be entirely sure which canvas he was referencing) suggest that Frye was employing the art of both Field and Hicks strategically to demonstrate Canada's mythological potential at the very moment when it appeared to be most vulnerable to continentalism. Central to Hicks' "Peaceable Kingdom" and Frye's reading of a version of this painting are the prophecies of Isaiah, which employ a Biblical typology to create a symbolic system of animals as representative of key human traits and offer "insight about how aggressive animals must behave in order to achieve peace" (Weekley 1999, 53). For Hicks, Isaiah 11 offered a model for how states of concord could be achieved on earth and was a fitting analogy for the Quaker belief that "denial of self-will was the only means of establishing harmonious coexistence" (53). In other words, by following God's instructions as conveyed through "the Inward Light, the divine presence that guides and enlightens one's soul" without the necessity of "sacraments or regulate[d] forms of worship," one could achieve a state of peace (34). As the second epigraph outlines, by proposing unlikely pairings often of prey and predator—such as the wolf and the lamb and the leopard and the kid—within the animal kingdom, Isaiah's prophecy provided a powerful visual analogy for understanding how to reconcile differing groups. For Hicks and his Quaker community, this image of reconciliation and harmony would become increasingly useful in exploring what became a major religious division within the Quaker faith in the US and Canada.

THE QUAKER SCHISM

The schism was prompted by the claims of Orthodox Quakers (both English and American) whose affluence, urban lifestyles, and interest in the acquisition of material goods signaled a move away from quietism and the embracing of evangelical doctrines that "included 'the final outward authority of the Scriptures and the total depravity of human nature'" (Weekley 1999, 40). In contrast, there remained a group of rural Primitive Quakers, including Edward Hicks—and his famous uncle, Elias—who were eventually deemed heretical for rebelling against Quaker elders. The latter tightened "the limits of tolerance" in order to secure their power (40). The targeting of Elias Hicks and accusations of his "unsoundness as a Quaker minister" because of his emphasis on the Inward Light over scriptures and other "outward religious authorities" began in the early 1820s and reached its pinnacle at the 1827 Yearly Meeting in Philadelphia with the separation of the Orthodox and Hicksite groups (46, 42); the division led to lawsuits over property ownership of meetinghouses and graveyards in Pennsylvania, "acts of physical violence over the possession of official records" in New York and Ohio, and continued anger and frustration by Hicksites at the way in which English Quakers had influenced the outcome by bolstering the Orthodox cause (48).

Isaiah's prophecy served as an analogy for Hicks' beliefs in the face of growing scrutiny by Orthodox Quakers, and "The Peaceable Kingdom" canvases became a record of this shifting religious and political dynamic. The paintings enabled Hicks to pay homage to his uncle. Known for his self-described "hot-headed Americanism," Edward often avoided confrontational meetings but strongly defended his uncle, primarily through his art (Weekley 1999, 49). Because he regularly shifted the "compositions and principal elements" (54) of his multiple versions of "The Peaceable Kingdom," unlike his other works, they functioned as a catalogue of his efforts to articulate his feelings about a rapidly changing America.

Shifting Representations of Animals in the "Peaceable Kingdom" Series

Animals played a central role in the evolution of "The Peaceable Kingdom" canvases. The earliest known "Peaceable Kingdom" painting by Hicks has been dated to 1816–1818. It portrays a selection of representative "sweet and mild"-looking animals—a lion, a leopard, a wolf, a lamb, a young goat, and a calf—situated near one another in the bottom right corner of the canvas (Weekley 1999, 53). A single child rests his head gently on the mane of a lion, who in turn leans into the human body with an expression of tenderness and affection, reveling in the gentle caress. To the left is a lake, surrounded by green fields, trees, flowers, and a beautiful blue sky. The result is a bucolic scene that conveys the "harmony" and "unity" between and among animals and people (53).

As a Primitive Quaker, Hicks subscribed to older beliefs about the universe, including the idea of all living beings possessing certain dominant elements of the four humors, which shaped the personalities of people and animals, as well as the concept of the great chain of being, a hierarchical systematization of the world that equated "rulers or heads of state" with "lions, the kings of the beasts" (Weekley 1999, 55). Lions and the people they represented were prone to arrogance and pride, qualities that made them especially liable to making false judgments, having never denied their "self-will" (53)—a symbolic link that also may be read as a reference to the disappearance of the Hicks family fortune in the American Revolution.[13] So the choice of animals even in this early work demonstrates how Hicks' painting served as an allegory for his own life circumstance and the growing Quaker schism, which would ultimately target his uncle, Elias. For instance, in his famous Goose Creek sermon, recorded in 1837 and later published as part of his *Memoirs*, Hicks uses "a sanguine leopard" as a metaphor for Quakers engaged in sin, with the beast's sinuous beauty disguising its self-serving and cruel behavior (Weekley 1999, 60); likewise, he equates the spotted coat with the deceptive conduct of Quakers who were religious on their own terms, supporting "various sorts of reform" but only as it suited them (60). To convey his growing frustration with the Church divide, Hicks added more animals to his versions of "The Peaceable Kingdom" over time, including a bear who, in select canvases from 1828 onward, embodied the mercantile, or bearish, conduct of money lenders whose exorbitant interest rates he had struggled with firsthand, yet were embraced by the Orthodox Quaker churchgoers because of their wealth.

Changing Versions of the Peaceable Kingdom

By 1830, the date Frye uses to reference his description of "The Peaceable Kingdom," Hicks' paintings included several newer elements, among them on occasion an increasingly large vignette on the far left-hand side of William Penn and a group of Quaker men signing a treaty with members of the Leni-Lenape tribe inspired by Quaker artist Benjamin West's famous "The Treaty of Penn with the Indians" (1772).[14] This image of Penn, which was replicated in woodcuts and engravings, was an important inspiration for Hicks, who produced twelve canvases that depicted this scene between 1830 and 1847, including an 1830–1840 National Gallery easel that included the following statement in bold letters across the bottom: "Penns Treaty with the Indians, made 1681 without an oath, and never broken. The foundation of Religious and Civil Liberty, in the U.S. of America" (Weekley 1999, 162). For Hicks, this historical meeting represented a model of mutual consent and a powerful way to resolve conflicts in contrast to the schism. The wording Hicks used came from his own poetic adaptation of the Isaiah chapter, adding a final stanza to the heavenly scene that bridged the gap between the ideal of the "peaceable kingdom" and the Quaker enactment of the same values of self-denial and "transformation of ... brute nature by love into an ideal state" (Ford 1998, 41). Through its inclusion in the "Peaceable Kingdom," Hicks suggested that Quakers could fulfill this "prophecy" of harmony on earth, but only if they worked together, a possibility that grew increasingly remote directly before the artist's eyes (41).

Hicks' coupling of the Penn treaty signing, in its mythic glory, with the prophecy of Isaiah created a powerful mirroring effect between the foreground and the background of the painting; the animals were enacting, along with the cherubic child, the same kind of self-sacrificing behavior for the good of the community, and thus, offering hope to viewers that the kingdom of heaven could, in some form, exist on earth. But Hicks himself was confronted with a different reality.

As early as 1827, Hicks also began painting versions of "The Peaceable Kingdom" that displaced Penn's vaunted position and the promise of a historic peace with the Leni-Lenape in the upper left quadrant of the canvas with a more overt reference to the Quaker schism. This series of nine canvases, known as the "banner Kingdoms" (Weekley 1999, 116), celebrated the legacy of a group of Quakers whom Hicks championed, among them founding fathers George Fox, Robert Barclay, and William Penn with Elias Hicks, who died in 1830, at its center. Hicks continued to return to this visual metaphor to remind viewers of the legacy of the schism while celebrating his uncle's "ministry and exemplary life" (118). Although Frye does not reference this variant on "The Peaceable Kingdom," these alterations demonstrate Hicks' continued commitment to use his art in the service of religion—for the purposes of spiritual education.

Even as Hicks was painting banner versions of "The Peaceable Kingdom," he returned to canvases that included the Penn vignette in 1829, and it is most likely one of these paintings that formed the basis of Frye's interpretation, given the date of "around 1830" and the details that

Frye provides in the "Conclusion" to his *Literary History of Canada*: "Here, in the background, is a treaty between the Indians and the Quaker settlers under Penn. In the foreground is a group of animals, lions, tigers, bears, oxen, illustrating the prophecy of Isaiah about the recovery of innocence in nature" (1995, 251). Two of Hicks' canvases are dated 1829–1832 and closely resemble each other (Figs. 2.2 and 2.3). What is remarkable about these works is how Hicks employs the animals that appeared on the right side of the painting to embody the upheaval caused by his firsthand experience of religious factionalism. Art historian Carolyn Weekley, who curated a 1991 show of Hicks' "Peaceable Kingdom" works, argues that by the late 1820s, the "demeanor of the animals" began to change, growing "more alert and tense" (1999, 109). The number of beasts included in the paintings multiplied dramatically and covered a large part of the canvas, often with mates provided for specific animals to represent the strength and significance of family values. Children also proliferated in these works, increasing in number from one to three, often with their hands in the "*hole of an asp*" or on a "*cockatrice' den*," in accordance with the text of Isaiah 11:8 (Weekley 1999, 53). Most obviously, the leopard and lion were no longer languidly reclining, as had been the case with the latter in early versions positioned under the draped arm of a single child.

By the early 1830s, the lion is double the size of the adjacent child, who reaches out to stroke his mane but does not quite reach it, and the lion's enlarged yellow irises and black pupils stare straight at the viewer, impossible to avoid. Likewise, the leopard gazes directly from the canvas, with bulging pupils, ears erect, and the hairs around its eyes and mouth standing on end, alert to potential danger. In addition, a bear is situated in the lower right corner of the work, hoarding a cob of corn, while the cow beside it holds the stem of the tassel in its mouth. This juxtaposition highlights what Hicks calls in his Goose Creek sermon the treachery of the bear: it "appears more peaceable and contented than most of the carnivorous tribe, and will seldom … prey upon other animals, if they can find plenty of nuts, fruits, grains, or even roots" but its "sluggish" and "inert" appearance masterfully disguise a "worldly-minded man, wholly intent on the acquisition of wealth" (1851, 307). For Hicks, the desire for money had shaped the "decline of Quaker meetings in England, Ireland, and Scotland" and led to an unhealthy attachment to worldly goods, in direct contrast with the guiding beliefs of the Society of Friends and their emphasis on "true Christian charity" (Weekley 1999, 61, 62). The cow may

Fig. 2.2 Edward Hicks' "The Peaceable Kingdom" (1829–1832), oil on canvas. (Brooklyn Museum of Art, Brooklyn, NY. Image available in the public domain: https://www.brooklynmuseum.org/opencollection/objects/610)

graze with the bear, as the prophecy of Isaiah describes. But there is no guarantee that the bear will not eventually turn on and ultimately destroy its neighbor when profit is involved, just as the Orthodox Quakers have done, bolstered by their British supporters. Finally, the wolf, whose gaze up to this point has been angled away from the viewer, looks directly outward from Hicks' canvas, its ears dramatically pointed and its hair also standing on end. Like the leopard, the wolf's carnivorous appetites, solitary nature, and tendency to "devour innocent and helpless animals," according to Hicks, make it an ideal symbol of "hypocrisy and deception in the religious world" (1851, 276), especially when looming over a much more delicate lamb.

Fig. 2.3 "The Peaceable Kingdom" by Edward Hicks (1829–1832), oil on canvas. (Formerly owned by the Maier Museum of Art, Randolph-Macon Women's College, Lynchburg, VA, auctioned off by Christie's in New York after 2007 to pay the college's mounting debts, and was bought by a private collector

Cross-Border Schism

The Quaker schism, which Hicks documented with such energy in his paintings, was not confined to the US. The schism spread north of the US-British North America border; for instance, it reshaped the Yonge Street community Hicks first visited in 1819, although it is not clear if Hicks observed this schism during his time there. Originally from Pennsylvania, Philadelphia, and New York, Quakers migrated to Upper Canada in the late 1700s because of easy access to cheap farmland and the promise of religious freedom. Strong links to the US remained through ties to family members, friends, and marriage. Quakers were not the only American immigrants involved in the Yonge Street settlement. American Methodists were among those present and posed a special challenge to the

"Quaker hegemony" because they shared many of the same principles, including an emphasis on mission work and a belief in the inner presence of God (McIntyre 1994, 24). In his history of a sect of the Upper Canada Quakers known as the "Children of Peace," John McIntyre notes that despite the existence of a political border between British North America and the US, it is essential to recognize that groups like these need to be understood and studied as "part of the broader history of American religious communities" (xiv). As members of the New York branch of Quakers, the Yonge Street Quakers remained engaged in Church politics on both sides of the border. They learned about the schism through their representatives to the annual meeting, family and friends who came to see them, and visits from traveling ministers, including visiting English Friends who supported the Orthodox position and created further conflicts.

The use of paintings like those of Hicks to depict conflict and create strong messages of "belief and identity" was also evident north of the border with the "Children of Peace" sect who produced banners in the 1820s that depicted typological Christian images of women, children, and animals and included the word "peace" (McIntyre 1994, 30) to differentiate themselves. These banners anticipated Hicks' own banner versions of "The Peaceable Kingdom," created at the height of the schism. In *From Quaker to Upper Canadian: Faith and Community Among Yonge Street Friends, 1801–1850*, Robynne Healey describes some of the dramatic confrontations that resulted because of the schism in Upper Canada. They included a physical claiming of the meeting house by Orthodox Friends who outnumbered the Hicksites, the subsequent expulsions of Orthodox members by the Hicksites, and eventually increased activism as Quakers became more involved in the local community, calling for reformation on issues ranging from "[s]lavery" and "temperance" to "native education … [and] women's rights" (2006, 164).

Sadly, Quaker engagement with these broader concerns came at a price and revealed that the promise of a "peaceable kingdom" was no more accessible north of the US, a reality that has implications for Frye's representation of Hicks' work in the "Conclusion" to *Literary History of Canada*. Upper Canada resident Elizabeth Lount, for example, lost her husband, Samuel Lount, who was executed for treason because of his participation in the Rebellion of 1837. The Rebellion took aim at state support for the Church of England in the form of clergy reserves and the fining of Quakers who refused military service as part of their faith, payment of which violated their "peace testimony" (Healey 2006, 45). American Quakers who came northward found themselves being heavily taxed for their pacifist beliefs, but they did not want to wage war on family and friends south of the border. Yet, when war broke out between "the United States and Canada" in 1812, the cost of being exempt from military duty in Upper Canada went from 12 shillings—the tax in peace time—to five pounds. Those who did not pay faced confiscation of goods and could serve jail time (McIntyre 1994, 36). This was one of several issues that eventually prompted Quakers, among others, to rebel despite their commitment to pacifism.

In the aftermath of the Rebellion, Elizabeth, who had moved from the US to Upper Canada with her husband in search of prosperity, was refused access to her jailed husband. She was not allowed to say goodbye before his execution and could not claim his body afterward, indignities that led her to take her seven children and move back to the US. In response, she wrote an open letter to the judge who sentenced Samuel to hang. It was published in the *Pontiac Herald* newspaper in Michigan on June 12, 1838, and eventually circulated both south and north of the border, within the Quaker communities and beyond. As the third epigraph to this chapter illustrates, Lount's letter castigated the government for its behavior when compared with America, calling upon her "beloved" Canada to reform its ways (Healey 2006, 166). For Lount, the presumption of Quaker passivity and obedience to the tyranny of the current political rulers was unacceptable, motivating her to leave Upper Canada and call for a revolutionary action akin to the US Declaration of Independence to right what she observed to be fundamental wrongs in the colony government's conduct. Despite their commitment to pacifism, Lount's letter suggested that Quakers could no longer stand by and let themselves be exploited by the Canadian government, which was hardly a resounding endorsement of Canadian tolerance and peace, the same ideals readers of Frye have employed to champion Canada's uniqueness by referencing Frye's use of Hicks' circa 1830 canvas in his "Conclusion."

Returning to Frye's "Conclusion" to his *Literary History of Canada*

It is useful here, if only momentarily, to reflect on Frye's own ambivalence about Canadian literary excellence in the "Conclusion." Frye himself remains cautious about Canada's literary success to that point on the global stage, noting in the opening pages of the "Conclusion" that "[i]f evaluation is one's guiding principle, criticism of Canadian literature would become ... a debunking project" (1995, 215). He argues that "[i]t is much easier to see what literature is trying to do when we are studying a literature that has not quite done it" (216), comments that speak to the reality that Frye's ideals are based on the study of foreign, in this case canonical British (such as Shakespeare, Milton, Blake)—rather than Canadian—writers. This ambivalence is overlooked in popular analyses of Frye's symbolic relevance to Canada, like that of Ibbitson.

Nonetheless, when Frye invokes Hicks' "Peaceable Kingdom" as emblematic of Canada's potential, he is turning back the clock in his invocation of mythological contexts and American sources, displacing Field's large-scale representation of the industrialized US and pointed juxtaposition of the best and worst moments of his nation's history into a monumental Biblical allegory with what appears to be a far simpler message, one of potential harmony between and among humans and animals in the natural world. Through his missionary position, Frye's essay may be read as contributing to a cultural tradition that, as noted in this book's "Introduction," Bryant has rightly described as "Canadian exceptionalism" by taking up a position of simplicity framed by moral superiority (2017, 21). Not surprisingly, in Frye's case, that moral plane is Biblical and draws on his Methodist childhood, his training as a United Church minister, his Canadian and British university education, and American folk art.

Merging the missions of church and state, Frye can be read as suggesting that the founding myth of Canada's southern neighbor, that of a Biblical errand into the wilderness, is no longer the exclusive purview of the US but may be better suited to represent Canada's developing identity as a superior civilization built upon what Daniel Coleman has called "the Canadian Loyalist myth" of those like Frye's mythic ancestors who fled northward and resisted American capitalist greed (2008, 25). Frye discovered that his father's belief that his ancestors had left the US because of their loyalty to the British crown was untrue, explaining in an interview that "the Fryes fought on the other side in the revolutionary war and came across later, mainly because the land was cheaper" (Frye 2008, 1044). For Frye, his vision of the Hicks canvas "is a pictorial emblem of what [Frederick Phillip] Grove's narrator was trying to find under the surface of America," namely a "pastoral myth in its genuinely imaginative form" (Frye 1995, 251, 242). Moreover, it was free of the American literary clichés that he catalogues as lacking the authenticity that he perceives as inherent in the pairing of Penn with the Leni-Lenape juxtaposed with the animals of Isaiah's prophecy that "stare past us with a serenity that transcends consciousness" and enable a "reconciliation of man with man and of man with nature" (1995, 251).

What is telling about Frye's description in his "Conclusion" is his invocation of various images aligned with the US and Canada. Here, emblematic moments in American literature—among these, the seemingly pastoral aspects of Thoreau's Walden, Huckleberry Finn's raft, Emily Dickinson's garden, and Whitman's elegies—cannot measure up to "the haunting vision of a serenity ... in the Canadian tradition" (Frye 1995, 251). But in making this comparison, Frye creates an unresolvable paradox. He also insists that the search for a peaceable kingdom is, by definition, riddled with ghosts of the past—ghosts that include the Leni-Lenape tribe who were displaced and ruled by Penn,[15] suffered considerable losses during the Revolutionary War, and were eventually forcibly removed to Oklahoma, Wisconsin, and even Canada, where they were confined to reserves and sent to residential schools; the Quaker schism and persecution of his uncle that troubled Hicks so greatly that he dramatically altered the harmonious representation of Isaiah's prophecy; and the words of Elizabeth Lount whose husband was hung for his efforts to challenge the Upper Canadian government of the day, provoking her to retreat to the US to provide a more tolerant and accepting place in which to raise her now-fatherless family. To look beneath the surface of Frye's vision is to find the promise of a "peaceable kingdom" in crisis on both sides of the border. By examining the canvases of Field and Hicks, it becomes clear that the myth of the "peaceable kingdom" is just that—the idealization of a much more fractured and complex reality.

In the final pages of the "Conclusion," Frye describes the impact of an increasingly globalized world, one that poses a threat to the singularity of Canada. Here, the quest for the "peaceable kingdom" represents a search for stability, security, and plentitude. Writing from the missionary position, Frye weaves together former incarnations of his own faith to create a potential theological approach to Canada's identity in which the church and state function as one, putting forward a mythic vision of "the eternal frontier" as a model to be worked toward (1995, 252). Reflecting on American roots of Frye's "peaceable kingdom" and Frye's own ambivalence about Canada's potential to embody the "peaceable kingdom" offers tangible reminders that borders are porous and that those complex and contradictory origins need to be acknowledged as a critical part of Canada's self-construction.

NOTES

1. See Kilbourn's introduction to *Canada: A Guide to the Peaceable Kingdom* (1970) and Edwardson's argument that Frye's "peaceable kingdom" provided a useful and timely concept to differentiate Canada from its southern neighbor, one that remains relevant today (2008, 138). See's examination of "The Intellectual Construction of Canada's 'Peaceable Kingdom' Ideal" is also helpful in assessing its importance to Canadian historians and social scientists (2018, 524) as an idea that has been championed, but also revealed to be "problematic" (529).
2. Given the era, it is worth noting the sexism of the pronoun being employed.
3. See Bogdan 1986.
4. See, for example, Frye 1995, 201–214.
5. These include Lecker, David Bentley, and Philip Kokotailo. In Bentley's discussion of Hicks' painting, which he understands to be a singular work, he argues that Frye selected the canvas because it "represents the pastoral management of nature ... in the interests of achieving a level of social organization" (2009, 60). Bentley overlooks the significance of Frye's choice of an American painting and more precisely one by a Quaker whose missionary and pacifist beliefs align with the Canadian scholar's own Methodist roots. Kokotailo describes Hicks' American Quaker roots and notes the posthumous popularity of his folk art (1998, 5). He also acknowledges that Hicks created numerous versions of "The Peaceable Kingdom" but does not explore the individual canvases, the significance of the Quaker schism for Hicks' art, or the ways in which this schism traveled northward.

6. See the United Church website for a detailed history of the unions of churches that led to its creation; they include Methodist and Congregationalist Churches from Canada and the US.
7. See Frye 2003, 448–465.
8. See Torrance for an examination of Canada as a nation where violence is perceived of as both "illegitimate and illegal" (1986, 86). As a critical part of her argument, Torrance invokes the concept of "The Peaceable Kingdom" as painted by Edward Hicks in 1830, which motivated Frye to characterize Canada as a fundamentally law-abiding and tolerant society, and notes how it has been used to differentiate Canada from its southern neighbor. See also Anastakis for a playful and entertaining reconsideration of the "peaceable kingdom" in the new millennium; his *Death in the Peaceable Kingdom: Canadian History Since 1867 Through Murder, Execution, Assassination, and Suicide* employs a broad understanding of "death" to consider some of the more violent aspects of Canadian history (2015, xv).
9. See also retired diplomat Louis Delvoie's series of articles for *The Kingston Whig* in 2017 that repeatedly describe Canada as a "peaceable kingdom" (2017a, 2017b).
10. My thanks to Gwen Davies, Tony Tremblay, Carole Gerson, and Sandra Djwa for their speedy and thoughtful responses to my queries about the possibility of including plates. Davies offers the most persuasive explanation in a personal email communication, stating that "it was not a convention at the time to illustrate national literary histories." She notes that British and American literary histories from the same era suggest that "what was done in Canada in approximately the same time period is identical."
11. See http://www.united-church.ca/community-faith/welcome-united-church-canada/history-united-church-canada for information about the origins of the United Church of Canada, including a downloadable chart.
12. See Volume 9, p. 352, of the *Collected Works of Northrop Frye* (2002), which includes a reference by Frye to Field's masterpiece. It is not clear whether he saw the canvas in person or as reproduced in a catalogue. Thanks to Lisa Sherlock, Chief Librarian at Victoria College (the home of the Frye fonds), for her assistance in determining what versions of the paintings by Field and Hicks Frye was familiar with or made notes about over the course of his life. There are no comments about or references to the Hicks painting(s) in Frye's notebooks.
13. See Weekley 1999, 130.
14. See Newman's reassessment for Penn's legacy, as articulated by members of the more recent generations of the Delaware people who have come to perceive him as a "scoundrel" (2012, 131) and are eager to dismantle what

had been perceived as the beginning of a great and just relationship between Penn and the Leni-Lenape.
15. See Newman 2012, 103.

REFERENCES

Anastakis, Dimitry. 2015. *Death in the Peaceable Kingdom: Canadian History Since 1867 Through Murder, Execution, Assassination, and Suicide*. Toronto: University of Toronto Press.

Bentley, David. 2009. Jumping to Conclusions: Northrop Frye on Canadian Literature. In *Northrop Frye: New Directions from Old*, ed. David Rampton, 55–79. Ottawa: University of Ottawa Press.

Bogdan, Deanne. 1986. Moncton, Mentors, and Memories: An Interview with Northrop Frye. *Studies in Canadian Literature* 11 (2). https://journals-lib-unb.ca.proxy.hil.unb.ca/index.php/SCL/article/view/8052/9109.

Bryant, Rachel. 2017. *The Homing Place: Indigenous and Settler Literary Legacies of the Atlantic*. Waterloo: Wilfrid Laurier University Press.

Christie, Nancy, and Michael Gauvreau. 2010. *Christian Churches and Their Peoples, 1840–1965: A Social History of Religion in Canada*. Toronto: University of Toronto Press.

Coleman, Daniel. 2008. *White Civility: The Literary Project of English Canada*. Toronto: University of Toronto Press.

Delvoie, Louis. 2017a. Canada: The Peaceable Kingdom. *The Kingston Whig Standard*, January 27. https://www.thewhig.com/2017/01/27/canada-the-peaceable-kingdom.

———. 2017b. World Needs more Canada. *The Kingston Whig Standard*, June 29. https://www.thewhig.com/2017/06/29/world-needs-more-canada.

Dubois, Diane. 2012. *Northrop Frye in Context*. Newcastle upon Tyne: Cambridge Scholars Press.

Edwardson, Ryan. 2008. *Canadian Content: Culture and the Quest for Nationhood*. Toronto: University of Toronto Press.

Ford, Alice. 1998/1952. *Edward Hicks: Painter of the Peaceable Kingdom*. Philadelphia: University of Pennsylvania Press.

Frye, Northrop. 1995. *The Bush Garden: Essays on the Canadian Imagination*. Concord: House of Anansi Press.

———. 2002. *Collected Works of Northrop Frye: The "Third Book" Notebooks of Northrop Frye: 1964–1972: The Critical Comedy: Volume 9*. Ed. Michael Dolzani. Toronto: University of Toronto Press.

———. 2003. *Collected Works of Northrop Frye: Frye on Canada: Volume 12*. Ed. Jean O'Grady and David Staines. Toronto: University of Toronto Press.

———. 2008. *Collected Works of Northrop Frye: Interviews with Northrop Frye: Volume 24*. Ed. Jean O'Grady. Toronto: University of Toronto Press.

Healey, Robynne Rogers. 2006. *From Quaker to Upper Canadian: Faith and Community Among Yonge Street Friends, 1801–1850*. Montreal & Kingston: McGill-Queen's University Press.

Hicks, Edward. 1851. *Memoirs of the Life and Religious Labors of Edward Hicks, Late of Newtown, Bucks County, Pennsylvania. Written by Himself.* Philadelphia: Merrihew & Thompson.

"History of the United Church of Canada." *The United Church of Canada*. http://www.united-church.ca/community-faith/welcome-united-church-canada/history-united-church-canada.

Ibbitson, John. 2016. In a World of Closing Doors, Canada is Embracing Inclusion. *The Globe and Mail*, July 1. http://www.theglobeandmail.com/news/national/in-a-world-of-closing-doors-canada-is-embracing-inclusion/article30731700/.

Kilbourn, William, ed. 1970. *Canada: A Guide to the Peaceable Kingdom*. New York: St. Martin's.

Kokotailo, Philip. 1998. Creating *The Peaceable Kingdom*: Edward Hicks, Northrop Frye, and Joe Clark. In *Creating 'The Peaceable Kingdom,' and Other Essays on Canada*, ed. Victor Howard, 3–11. East Lansing: Michigan State University Press.

Lecker, Robert. 1993. 'A Quest for the Peaceable Kingdom': The Narrative in Northrop Frye's Conclusion to the Literary History of Canada. *PMLA* 108 (2): 283–293.

McGill, Robert. 2017. *War Is Here: The Vietnam War and Canadian Literature*. Montreal & Kingston: McGill-Queen's University Press.

McIntyre, W. John. 1994. *Children of Peace*. Montreal & Kingston: McGill-Queen's University Press.

Newman, Andrew. 2012. *On Records: Delaware Indians, Colonists, and the Media of History and Memory*. Lincoln: University of Nebraska Press.

Razack, Sherene. 2004. *Dark Threats & White Knights: The Somalia Affair, Peacekeeping, and the New Imperialism*. Toronto: University of Toronto Press.

Sawyer, John F.A. 1996. *The Fifth Gospel: Isaiah in the History of Christianity*. Cambridge: Cambridge University Press.

See, Scott. 2018. The Intellectual Construction of Canada's "Peaceable Kingdom" Ideal. *Journal of Canadian Studies* 52 (2): 510–537.

Staiti, Paul. 1992. Ideology and Rhetoric in Erastus Salisbury Field's "The Historical Monument of the American Republic." *Winterthur Portfolio* 27 (1): 29–43.

———. 2011. Erastus Salisbury Field, 1805–1900. *Traditional Fine Arts Organization Inc*. https://www.tfaoi.org/aa/3aa/3aa157.htm.

Stephens, Donald. 1965. The Literary History of Canada: Editorial Views. *Canadian Literature* 24: 10–14.

Torrance, Judy M. 1986. *Public Violence in Canada: 1867–1982*. Montreal & Kingston: McGill-Queen's University Press.
Walls, Andrew F. 1996. *The Missionary Movement in Christian History: Studies in the Faith of Transmission*. Maryknoll, NY: Orbis Books.
Weekley, Carolyn J. 1999. *The Kingdoms of Edward Hicks*. New York: Harry N. Abrams & Colonial Williamsburg Foundation.

CHAPTER 3

Evangeline's Revisioning: Reading Ben Farmer's Post-9/11 *Evangeline: A Novel*

Many Canadian anti-racist scholars have recently worked to re-educate themselves and broader Canadian society to the repressed elements of Canada's history of White British supremacy; so mainstream Canadians have been reminded about the extermination of the Aboriginal Beothuks in Newfoundland, the deportation of the French-speaking Acadians from Nova Scotia, the discrimination practised against Black Loyalists and their descendants from 1784 onwards, the head tax upon and eventual exclusion of Chinese immigrants after 1923, the internment of eastern Europeans during the First World War and of Japanese Canadians during the Second World War, the refusal of entry to Jews fleeing Nazi Europe, and the ongoing criminalization of Indigenous and Black Canadians. (Coleman 2006, 8–9)

[T]he conquest of Acadia was a foundational moment in the history of the Canadian state[.] (McKay and Bates 2010, 78)

It is the racialization of persons-on-the-move that is central to their ontologization as aliens by exalted citizens, who claim inalienable rights for themselves while helping to destroy those of Others. (Thobani 2007, 72)

As the previous chapter argues, Canada has been positioned in popular rhetoric as a nation that embraces diversity and rejects violence, offering the promise of Frye's peaceable kingdom characterized by harmony, safety, and security for all. But Ben Farmer's *Evangeline: A Novel* challenges this

© The Author(s), under exclusive license to Springer Nature Switzerland AG 2023
J. Andrews, *Canada Through American Eyes*,
https://doi.org/10.1007/978-3-031-22120-0_3

simplistic view by exploring a range of repressed elements of Canadian and American history, including the role played by both nations in the expulsion of Acadia in 1755. Published in 2010, American author Ben Farmer's *Evangeline: A Novel* rewrites the familiar story of an Acadian female heroine and her fiancé, separated on the eve of their marriage by the 1755 Deportation, to explore the challenges of faithfulness, the impact of betrayal (both sexual and psychological), and the violence of the Acadians' forcible removal from their community. Farmer creates a far more complex and contradictory portrait of this population's legacy and its contemporary relevance for both the Canadian and American nation-state than that of his predecessor, fellow American Henry Wadsworth Longfellow, who first published his epic poem *Evangeline* in 1847.[1]

Farmer's novel explores the ways in which nations choose to ignore or overlook elements of their creation in the service of creating a singular specific and dominant version of its past. Ernest Renan argues in his famous and still timely 1882 article "What is a Nation?" that "[f]orgetting ... is a crucial factor in the creation of a nation. ... historical inquiry brings to light deeds of violence which took place at the origin of all political formations, even of those whose consequences have been altogether beneficial. Unity is always effected by means of brutality" (1990, 11). Samuel and Elizabeth Lount, the Quaker pacifists described in Chap. 2, who refused to remain silent when exploited by a colonial Canadian government, offer a powerful and poignant reminder of the selective nature of narratives of nation-building and the (in)justices that are an integral yet too often overlooked part of the process of unification: who is deemed (un)worthy and thus, readily sacrificed to secure the nation.

This chapter probes the significance of Ben Farmer's *Evangeline: A Novel* for American and Canadian readers in a twenty-first-century context. Written a decade after 9/11—which put considerable strain on Canada-US relations—Farmer reimagines the famous story of Evangeline and her betrothed, Gabriel, to explore dominant versions of national exceptionality and the ways in which each country strategically includes and excludes specific populations to shore up that country's identity. Farmer, who was trained as both a historian and a creative writer, refuses to "quarantine" Canada's "uncivil past from the civil present" (Coleman 2006, 34) or to protect America from the hypocrisy of its own claims to exceptionality.

ACKNOWLEDGING TRAUMATIC HISTORIES

In the first epigraph heading this chapter, Coleman provides a lengthy list of historical events that have been buried or suppressed within dominant Canadian narratives of nationhood, precisely because they expose a Canadian legacy and ongoing tradition of violent exclusion and systemic racism rather than multicultural inclusion—including the Acadian Deportation of 1755. Coleman suggests that white civility is central to such Canadian narratives of exceptionality. As he explains, civility combines "the temporal notion of civilization as progress" fueling the colonial mission in a single evolutionary line, governed by the "moral-ethical concept of a (relatively) peaceful order" that claims to balance "individual liberty and collective equality" (2006, 10). The principles of "social order" that Coleman outlines are achieved through the provision of a "polite or liberal [colonial] education" combined with "good breeding" (2006, 10). They are notable because they rely on specific yet unacknowledged forms of exclusion, disguised as inclusivity by burying the existence of prior populations and their presence within Canada to this day. These "performance[s] of civility" (2006, 29) have been shaped by both the "'War on Terror' and the post-9/11 securitization of Western 'homelands'" (Wakeham 2013, 278) over the last two decades. This approach has led, paradoxically, to both the sustained use of states of exception to cultivate and sustain the suspension of legal rights and processes in the case of those who are perceived to be a threat and, conversely, encouragement of the strategic acknowledgment of certain traumatic histories. These histories typically are framed in an "elegiac discourse" that confirms the necessity of such losses "along the path of progress," including the presumption that "Natives" and Acadians were both examples of a "'vanishing race'" (Coleman 2006, 29).

As part of governmental management of these elegiac accounts of past wrongs, this period has also "been dubbed the 'age of apology' in response to the proliferation of gestures of contrition performed by nation-states" who are "grappling with … [their own] histories and presents of systemic violence" (Wakeham 2013, 279). Canadian literary scholar Pauline Wakeham proceeds to catalogue the Canadian government's "recent slate of apologies," including for the "internment and forced relocation of

Japanese Canadians during the Second World War, the Chinese head tax, and the [government-funded] residential schools system," which removed Indigenous children from their families and communities for over a century in order to assimilate them (279).[2] But, as she notes, "in the process of purportedly acknowledging these grievances, the federal government [also systematically] labours to depict them as exceptions to the imagined norm of Canadian civility" (279–280). In other words, these apologies paradoxically continue to reinforce the "national collective myth" of Canada as a "creation myth of the settlers' nation-state," one that excludes "[t]he stories" of those who are deemed not white or civilized enough (Episkenew 2009, 71).

Wakeham's observations are relevant to the Acadian Deportation. Since 9/11, the government of Canada has adopted a British Royal Proclamation, marking July 28 as the annual date of commemoration of the so-called Great Upheaval, but without offering an official apology or "recognition of legal or financial responsibility by the Crown in right of Canada and of the provinces" (Rosenberg 2003). The Canadian government also produced a commemorative stamp in 2005 to mark the 250th anniversary of the Deportation (having done so only once before in 1930 with the "Grand Pre" stamp, bearing the statue of Evangeline from the Grand-Pré site).[3] Finally, in 2019, nearly 30 years after the first "Heritage Minute" film was released, Heritage Canada produced a new Heritage Minute depicting the forcible removal of the Acadians from their homes.[4]

Despite these recent acknowledgments and commemorations of the Deportation in Canadian contexts, John Faragher notes in the final chapter of *A Great and Noble Scheme: The Tragic Story of the Expulsion* that the US government response has been even more muted. Within the US, the Royal Proclamation "attracted almost no attention" (2005, 479). The irony should not be lost that it was Warren Perrin, a lawyer and "Cajun descendant of Acadian exiles" in Louisiana, who began lobbying Queen Elizabeth II and the British government for an apology for the Acadian removal in 1990 (473). Faragher describes the enthusiastic response of the Société Nationale de l'Acadie (SNA) to the 2003 Proclamation, a group that represents contemporary Francophone Acadian communities in the four Atlantic Canadian provinces and that has affiliate members in Quebec, Maine, Louisiana, and France. As SNA spokesperson Euclide Chiasson explained, the proclamation ensured that the Deportation would be "not only Acadian history," but also a part of "Canadian history" (qtd. in Faragher 2005, 479). Faragher argues that the Deportation "was also American history," but readily refashioned by Longfellow who created "a tale of British perfidy" (479) with *Evangeline*. However, he observes that, "[o]nce New Englanders were implicated in the chain of responsibility the story was relegated to a dimly remembered chapter in the history of Canada, about which Americans are notoriously ignorant" (479). For Faragher, it is essential to recognize and understand that the Deportation was "an Acadian, French, British, Canadian *and* American story" (479) and that such historical events require American engagement with the "dark side of our past" (479–480). His observations provide a cautionary tale for both Americans and Canadians who may rely on nation-state borders to stage their distance from a shared brutal past or employ nation-state distinctions to bolster contemporary narratives of superiority.[5] Instead, the border-crossing conversations provoked by Farmer's novel—and the others in this book—encourage shifts in perspective and more nuanced thinking about what American writers may offer Canadian (and American) readers when exploring questions of national identity and belonging.

LONGFELLOW'S VERSION OF *EVANGELINE* AND ITS LEGACY

The story of *Evangeline* was first published as an epic poem by American writer Henry Wadsworth Longfellow in 1847. It is a narrative about tragic romantic love and thwarted opportunities, but also the resourcefulness and fearlessness of womanhood. For Longfellow, who "pretty much invented poetry as a public idiom in the United States and abroad," *Evangeline* was an opportunity to create a virtuous female heroine and a tale of unwavering loyalty that served the national cultural agenda of nineteenth-century America (Irmscher 2006, 3). In the poem, the pastoral existence of Evangeline and her Acadian community is destroyed when the British decide to forcibly remove the population, which stands in the way of new colonial endeavors. She and her beloved Gabriel are separated on the cusp of marriage. The real-life account of an unnamed Acadian woman's efforts over a lifetime to reunite with her betrothed whom she was set to marry on the day of the deportation was shared, at first, with Longfellow by his friend Nathaniel Hawthorne, both of whom recognized its literary potential; Longfellow, having initially encouraged Hawthorne to produce a prose narrative of the story, subsequently asked him to wait until he had attempted to write "a poem on the theme" (Griffiths 1982, 28). The resulting poem was a huge commercial and critical success with "at least 270 editions and some 130 translations" appearing in the first 100 years after its initial publication by Ticknor in Boston (28). Longfellow sold more than 28,000 copies of *Evangeline* in the US between 1847 and 1869, making him "the first American writer to make a living from poetry" (Charvat 1968, 155), and demonstrating the importance of this story to a new nation seeking to distinguish itself from its Old World (meaning European and British) roots.

Longfellow faced extraordinary challenges in writing *Evangeline* because of the paucity of "source materials" and the fact that he "had not travelled to Acadia" (Farmer, qtd. in Andrews 2018, 104). He had to rely heavily on secondary and tertiary sources, shaped by their own racial, linguistic, and religious biases and colonial aims. To understand the Deportation, Longfellow turned to Thomas Chandler Haliburton's *An Historical and Statistical Account of Nova Scotia* (1829). As a first-generation Nova Scotian with British and American Loyalist roots and trained as a lawyer, Haliburton used his two-volume study to catalogue "the boundaries, physical and natural characteristics, and human settlement" of the province, "county by county" (Taylor 1984, 55) championing a "heritage of struggle," which inevitably led to the Deportation (56). Despite its "detailed recounting of political ambitions, religious bigotries and the inter-play between national aims and colonial desires" (Griffiths 1982, 34), Haliburton's text ultimately regards the Acadians as an "unfortunate and deluded people" (Haliburton 1829, 196), whose removal was "the inevitable result of a process begun with a treaty signed more than 40 years previously" (Griffiths 1982, 34). For Haliburton, the Deportation itself may have been "totally irreconcilable with the idea … of justice" because it punished a "whole community … for the misconduct of a part," but expulsion, he concludes, was a necessary step for ensuring "the tranquility of the Colony" (1829, 196, 197). Whatever mercy was owed to the "misguided" Acadians, Haliburton insisted that Lieutenant-Governor Charles Lawrence behaved appropriately because to "temper justice" would have put the peaceful development of "British agricultural settlement" into peril (1829, 197; Taylor 1984, 65). Although Haliburton acknowledges the Deportation is fundamentally unjust, he is quick to defend the efforts of the empire to protect its colony, given the impossibility of determining, as he describes it, the Acadians' "future loyalty" (1829, 197).

Not surprisingly, Longfellow offers his own, distinctly Americanized perspective in his epic poem of whom justice serves and why. While the Deportation is characterized as tragic, Longfellow treats the outcome as inevitable given the mercilessness of the British. He reinforces this point through the voice of Basil, who embraces the need to exercise might and openly condemns "the tyrants of England" in the poem upon learning of the Deportation order (Longfellow 2004, 41). For Longfellow, Acadians exemplified the challenge of and failure to overcome powerful competing claims by the French and English on its land and culture. Seen as naïve, they were perceived as doomed to disappear—unlike America—and thus provided valuable lessons on what not to do.

For his portrait of the Acadian people, Longfellow also drew extensively on the work of "L'abbé Guillaume Thomas Raynal[,] ... a French historian and philosopher" who authored the "four-volume work *Histoire philosophique et politique des etablissements et du commerce des Européens dans les deux Indes*" (1770), which aimed to answer the questions "curious Europeans had about the rest of the world" by presenting readers with a vision of the Acadians as "simple, devout, charitable and apolitical" (LeBlanc 2003, 53–54; Griffiths 1982, 33). Raynal regarded the "expulsion ... [as] the tragic ruin of a Golden Age" (Griffiths 1982, 32), providing a deeply romanticized vision of a "people nobler than the contemporary European" (33) who were unfairly sacrificed in the service of empire building. By focusing primarily on Raynal's representation of the Acadian people and putting it in an epic poetic form, Longfellow enabled his American audience, if only temporarily, to "escape to a better, more European, more settled world, the 'Home of the Happy,' yet one tinged with that delicious nostalgia that came from knowing the transience of all such happiness" (McKay and Bates 2010, 73). Rendering Acadia as a "forest primeval" filled with "simple ... farmers" (Longfellow 2004, 9, 14) who appear to have an Edenic life also allowed Longfellow to sidestep an examination of the complex and often conflicted relationships between the English and the French colonial empires, between Acadian and Indigenous communities, and among the Acadians themselves.

Longfellow's poem was especially popular with nineteenth-century Americans eager to establish a distinctive cultural and literary tradition, while invoking some of the most appealing Old World European customs, and most importantly, justifying and solidifying a deep distrust of the British Empire. In Longfellow's text, the Acadian deportation is blamed squarely on the British and is the primary impediment to the long and happy marriage of the youthful and beautiful Evangeline to her husband, Gabriel. Evangeline's Catholic faith and unwillingness to sacrifice her virginity to any other man become symbolic of her saintly conduct and devotion to her betrothed in the decades that follow their separation from each other. Longfellow's verse stresses the glory of the suffering woman in a uniquely American fashion, attributing her transformation into a courageous and determined female to her search for a "Manifest Destiny" (Viau 1998, 54). This journey comes to offer a panorama of US history and geography from "agrarian colony to urban republic" covering the Western, Southern, and Eastern states over the course of the poem (Doyle 1983, 46). Her commitment to searching for her lost love ensures that the poem's elegiac tone continues even as the text tracks Evangeline's movement from "a static and idyllic Arcadia towards a constantly evolving, morally ambivalent, industrialized and urbanized society," and is reinforced by her eventual tragic reunion with Gabriel (46).

In Longfellow's version, after the Deportation, the still-faithful lovers find themselves relying on rapidly fading memories, as they travel vast distance across various regions of pre- and post-Revolutionary America. Late in the poem, Evangeline's journey is punctuated by her conversation with an "Indian woman" who is returning to her Shawnee tribe in the aftermath of her "Canadian husband['s] ... murder" (Longfellow 2004, 85). Borrowing from fellow writer Henry Schoolcraft's contemporaneous collection of Indigenous oral legends, Longfellow has the unnamed Indigenous woman share two stories that document a racialized woman's futile pursuit of love, setting up a clear parallel to be made between her and Evangeline. In one narrative, the "bridegroom" vanishes the morning after marriage and, in the other, the bride herself disappears into the forest, never to be found again. These stories reinforce Evangeline's belief that she too is "pursuing a phantom" (87)—and perhaps even becoming a ghost herself. The tragic narratives of this apparently childless widow pointedly offer a glimpse of Evangeline's future. Like her female Indigenous counterpart, she too is not destined to populate America. Evangeline may hold onto the belief that she will find Gabriel, but it is only at the very end of Longfellow's text that Evangeline and Gabriel physically reunite.

At the poem's conclusion, Evangeline, a Sister of Mercy working in Philadelphia who tends to those suffering from "pestilence," discovers Gabriel who is now an old man in an almshouse on his deathbed (Longfellow 2004, 97). Gabriel quickly dies in Evangeline's arms, having shared a single kiss, and relieves Evangeline of her "restless, unsatisfied longing" as she bows to God and thanks him for this moment of reconciliation (100). *Evangeline* ends on a poignant note with the lovers "sleeping. / Under the humble walls of the little Catholic churchyard, / In the heart of the city, they lie, unknown and unnoticed," but recognized as remarkable for having "completed their journey" (101). For Longfellow, Evangeline and Gabriel figure as constant reminders of a legacy of faithfulness and loyalty against all odds that, while deeply moving to readers, is readily displaced by the reality of the bustling American city with its New World dynamism. The now-reunited couple may be laid to rest in the midst of Philadelphia, but they represent a past that is no longer viable, nor suited to the vigorous growth of the US.

Most importantly, Evangeline and Gabriel do not procreate, enabling their story to remain one that secures the minority status of Acadians in America as they integrate and intermarry or, in the case of these lovers, die childless. Notably, those who arrive (like the deportees on Gabriel's ship) in Louisiana take advantage of the climate, plentiful and rich farmland, and the opportunity to build a homestead without fear of being driven away; they are rewarded with prosperity and security. For instance, Gabriel's father, Basil the blacksmith, tells Evangeline when she finally arrives, years later, that Louisiana has given him "a home, that is better perchance than the old one!" (Longfellow 2004, 78). He praises the region's milder weather and richer farmlands. Most importantly, Basil revels in the certainty that "No King George of England shall drive you away from your homesteads, / Burning your dwelling and barns, and stealing your farms and your cattle" (Longfellow 2004, 79). Basil also has taken a Louisiana Spaniard as his new bride, furthering his integration into the local community. With this gesture, Longfellow foregrounds the benefits of becoming American through marriage and procreation despite the circumstances of deportation, an approach that Acadian scholar Robert Viau explains affirms the notion that "les Acadiens de la Louisiane sont devenus des Américains" [the Acadians of Louisiana have become Americans] (1998, 57, my translation). While Evangeline and Gabriel are reunited in a divine version of Acadie through their deaths, the poem offers a much brighter future for men like Basil who embrace the entrepreneurial spirit of American self-reliance and assimilation and may ultimately, with their new wives and through subsequent generations, produce a line of US-born descendants.

In Longfellow's *Evangeline*, America becomes a beneficent nation and a champion of freedom from oppression, offering the promise of a future for those who integrate. This is despite the historical reality that pre-Independence American troops played a substantial role in the Acadian deportation and benefitted directly from the removal, as demonstrated by the migration of the New England Planters who relocated (at the invitation of the Lieutenant Governor of Nova Scotia) to the former Acadian lands shortly after the expulsion. In Longfellow's nostalgic conclusion, only a "few Acadian peasants, whose fathers from exile / Wandered back to their native land to die in its bosom," make it back to Acadie (2004, 102). Instead, the speaker notes that the area has been carefully repopulated with "another race, with other customs and language" (102), referring to the orchestrated migration of New England Loyalists into the region. Because Longfellow relied heavily on the writings of others to shape his poem, he was able to construct a vision of the Acadian homeland of Grand-Pré that functioned as a "veritable Paradise Lost (indeed Paradise Regained for the tourist, if not for the Acadians) whose 'tragedy' only lent an edifying melancholic tinge to its 'superlative [physical] beauty'" (McKay and Bates 2010, 103). The result is that *Evangeline* functioned for nineteenth-century American readers as a text upon which to safely project their "generalized emotions" and to share "broadly consensual sentiments" by reading a story that is relegated, at least chronologically, to an idealized yet ultimately tragic past (Irmscher 2006, 60; McKay and Bates 2010, 72). Longfellow's poem might depict the elements of "upheaval and destruction" experienced by nineteenth-century American readers just prior to the Civil War and on the cusp of the Industrial Revolution, but the narrative did not impinge directly on the present (72). The result was a poem that could provide catharsis for its American readers without burdening them with the complex emotions evoked by an immediate historical situation.

Marketing Acadie: Longfellow and *Evangeline*'s Canadian Legacy

Longfellow's poem provided the basis for long-standing and profitable tourist marketing campaigns within Canada—predominantly from the 1880s to the 1950s. These were underwritten by British companies, like the Dominion Atlantic Railway, that sold the "Land of Evangeline" (McKay and Bates 2010, 72) to affluent New England and Canadian travelers eager to escape urban industrialization and to experience the pastoral beauty of Longfellow's poem in person. This phenomenon can be read as consolidating the selective idea of "white civility" by quarantining Evangeline in a Canadian context as a character, relegated to the distant past, whose tragic story formed a solid yet malleable foundation for the creation of a single "Old World site" that carefully circumscribed the memorialization of the Acadian population (76). Geographically focused on the area of Grand-Pré, the location of the Deportation in Longfellow's poem—although it was only one of several places from which the Acadians were forcibly removed—the region itself offered a precursor to the "twentieth-century theme park" with its "nineteenth-century Land of Evangeline" (77).[6] The "formidable infrastructure" around Evangeline as a "brand" included substantial "advertising copy" and "postcards" (76–77), tools that enabled tourists to locate themselves in this Edenic past, if only temporarily.

Ian McKay and Robin Bates' *In the Province of History: The Making of the Public Past in Twentieth-Century Nova Scotia* features a chapter titled "This Is the Province Primeval: Evangeline and the Beginnings of Tourism/History" in which they argue that, as a result of Longfellow's poem, Nova Scotia became a "premodern, historic, picturesque zone," that "was organically related to the industrial capitalist revolution transforming London, Montreal and, especially in this case, Boston" (2010, 78). In an ironic twist, "frazzled Bostonians could decamp to Nova Scotia in quest of the very Acadians whose society their ancestors had so proudly demolished" (78). The creation of Evangeline Land served multiple purposes for both Americans and Canadians. The tourist site provided an otherworldly retreat to a kinder and gentler nation at a time of rapid industrialization in large urban centers. In addition, it promoted a vision of Canada—or at least rural Nova Scotia—as the embodiment of the peaceable kingdom, offering a pastoral and romantic alternative to the Acadian refusal to become British subjects.

Fittingly, images of Evangeline generated to accompany both the Longfellow text and the various promotional efforts to sell the tourist region known as the Land of Evangeline captured the female protagonist as a young and "comely" white woman who blended "purity and beauty" (McKay and Bates 2010, 84). Of course, "in this Arcadia," readers and tourists could savor Evangeline's good looks without guilt because "faith [and innocence] permeated life as a fail-safe against carnality" (85); it made it easy to participate and consume these images as one saw fit, without compromising her memory precisely because of her fictional origins. The commodification and sale of Evangeline's (un)touched (white) beauty, and her failure to age, provided yet another way for visitors and those who read the poem to participate in a sustained erasure of historical wrongs, by participating in and perpetuating the glorification of a character who does not impinge on the present moment.

Most notably, these tourist-driven representations of Evangeline and Grand-Pré as the iconic site of the Deportation relied heavily on the linkages between "necropolitics and geopolitics," which, as Grewal explains, refer to "the sovereign right to kill and the right to rescue" (2017, 9). Both are critical modes of nation-state power in the twenty-first century. Although Grewal uses this terminology to characterize the underpinnings of American exceptionalism, it is equally relevant for Canada, where the naturalization of white civility rests on a history of discrimination, "ethnic cleansing," and even genocide,[7] strategically invoked as necessary to "the path of progress" (Moss 2017, 92; Coleman 2006, 29). At the same time, and not a little ironically, Canada continues to celebrate its role as a peacekeeping nation, known for providing selective sanctuary to oppressed populations in the form of "rescue" while telling "a story of national goodness" (Razack 2004, 35) that frames the subduing of the nation's Indigenous (and other) populations as models of "peacekeeping" at its best (35).

In *Postcards from Acadie: Grand-Pré, Evangeline and the Acadian Identity*, Barbara LeBlanc catalogues the steps taken in the post-Confederation era by the Canadian government and private investors to consolidate Grand-Pré's significance as a cultural artifact ready for tourist consumption at home and abroad. The infrastructure was primarily aimed at facilitating timely travel to Grand-Pré, which included the creation of a railway line to Grand-Pré, opened in 1869 using locomotive engines. Ironically, several were named after Longfellow's famous couple, Evangeline and Gabriel, demonstrating the attractiveness of the poet's elegiac depiction of Acadians to tourists visiting the site. The resulting version of Canadian historiography granted sovereignty to the Canadian nation-state by ensuring that the Grand-Pré site remained a relatively empty space, devoid of concrete evidence of a tangible Acadian survival beyond the Deportation.

Moreover, efforts in the early twentieth-century to develop the immediate area of Grand-Pré, including unsealing a road with direct access to a replica memorial church that opened in 1922, were halted because local residents feared that this would prompt the return of Acadian residents as more than tourists and lead to the dispossession of English-speaking inhabitants: "While locals were not disturbed by tourists invading the land to revel in romance and nostalgia, they were definitely not interested in having Acadians [re]settle in the land of Evangeline" (LeBlanc 2003, 85). Evangeline also was championed by Quebecois and Acadian nationalists from the 1860s as an "unhappy victim of British imperialism" (McKay and Bates 2010, 89). But ultimately the liminality of Acadia as a homeland that "emerged before the abstract, fixed-and-firm boundaries of contemporary nation-states" made it easy to embrace her symbolic power nostalgically without being perceived of as threatening the sanctity of Canada (93). Rather "the dreamlike image of … Evangeline haunting the Grand-Pré landscape" (LeBlanc 2003, 85) provided an ideal vehicle for consolidating the Canadian nation-state and bolstering the region's appeal for American and Canadian tourists. The installation of a statue of Evangeline, funded by the Dominion Atlantic Railway and executed by two Quebec-based sculptors of Acadian descendent, in combination with "landscaping and a memorial church built with Acadian funds" offered what was deemed a "worthwhile … destination in the eyes of the visiting public" (84) because it reinforced the elegiac narrative cultivated in Longfellow's poem. LeBlanc notes that "not a single Acadian was present at the unveiling" of the statue, which was used by the railway company to celebrate the visit of British Empire Press Delegates (120).[8] In this case, "free publicity" was regarded as "an opportunity that could not be missed—with or without Acadians" (121)—reinforcing the lack of importance placed on contemporary Acadian engagement with the site and indeed suggesting that an Acadian lack of engagement was preferred.

The Acadian and Quebec populations undertook well-publicized pilgrimages to the area. These two groups had embraced their own translated reworkings of Longfellow's famous text to bolster the concerns of their individual communities—which condemned the brutality of the British forces, refused to champion American values, embraced the strength of the Catholic faith, and refuted racial slurs by granting the fictional Acadians "a flawless European pedigree" (McKay and Bates 2010, 95). Nonetheless, the site remained primarily a memorial. The Bicentenary celebrations marked the last event held at the park under private ownership, before the Dominion Atlantic Railway sold it to the Canadian government, no longer viewing it as a profitable enterprise with the shift from rail to auto tourism. The Bicentenary featured the unveiling of a bust of and plaque dedicated to Longfellow (made possible by "government financial assistance"), once again asserting the American poet's beneficial role in creating a saleable tourist narrative for the region and nation (Gagné 2013, 90). The park soon became part of a national project to designate, acquire, and preserve "Canadian historic sites," partly prompted by the findings of the 1951 Massey Commission Report, which encouraged the support of "institutions … [that] express national feeling" and "promote common understanding" (90) by inserting a "layer of official history into the national fabric" (Taylor 1990, 139). Just as Longfellow's poem had constructed a national imaginary for the US in the mid-nineteenth century, the figure of Evangeline and the Deportation would serve as carefully circumscribed markers of Canada's past within the framework of the Parks Canada system.

As Michael Gagné explains in "'Memorial Constructions': Representations of Identity in the Design of the Grand-Pré National Historic Site, 1907-Present," debates over the park's purpose and mandate continued throughout the latter part of the twentieth century. At the same time, "the federal, bilingual, and bicultural Canadian state" gradually moved toward a platform of official multiculturalism (McKay and Bates 2010, 124), while simultaneously aiming to "eliminate … narratives of British supremacy" that had shaped many Canadian historic sites founded in the nineteenth century (Gagné 2013, 93). The post-9/11 years featured the creation of a new interpretation center at the park entrance to reflect the material history of the Acadian people better. It also included a panel on the expulsion that "included the viewpoints of the Acadians and the Mi'kmaq, officials at Quebec and Paris, and Governor Charles Lawrence" (95). Nonetheless, the focal point of the park remained the sculpture of the eternally youthful and forever childless Evangeline, situated directly in front of the "Memorial Church" (96).

To this day, the site continues to prioritize the more saleable romantic ideals of "purity and rebirth," while marginalizing tangible feelings of the Acadian community of "pain and loss" (Rudin 2009, 272). Canada's shift toward a narrative of multiculturalism has, according to Wenona Giles and Jennifer Hyndman, muted "racism by unifying diversity under a banner of tolerance defined by the dominant settler society" (2004, 9). The recent integration of summer programming at Grand-Pré National Historic Site that includes weekly scheduled presentations of Mi'kmaq, Acadian, and Scottish traditions through a team of creative interpreters provides one way to temper efforts to activate retroactive justice or compensation for Acadians and still ensure a situation in which memorialization remains the dominant theme at the park.[9] Nonetheless, present-day Acadians throughout Atlantic Canada continue to probe the complexities of the figure of Evangeline and her legacies, with the Acadian Society of New Brunswick recently reviving the thorny question of "whether the British-led attempt to rid the region of Acadians between 1755 and 1763 was in fact a genocide" (MacDonald 2019). This query fundamentally undermines Canada's self-positioning as a country known for its "national goodness," both at home and abroad (Razack 2004, 35). Likewise, the story of Evangeline (based on a variety of source texts including the French translation of Longfellow's epic poem by Pamphile Lamay in 1865) is all too familiar to students in the Francophone school system in New Brunswick and elsewhere in Atlantic Canada; it continues to be leveraged to examine the historical injustices of the expulsion rather than merely functioning as a romantic vision of a lost past.[10]

Farmer's Revisioning of Evangeline

Farmer's *Evangeline: A Novel* (2010) can be read as fundamentally revisioning Longfellow's elegiac account of the doomed romance between Acadian sweethearts Evangeline and Gabriel and the legacy that is cultivated through the Grand-Pré National Historic Site. Farmer creates a version of Evangeline who, in contrast with Longfellow's character, is an assertive and "self-reliant" woman (Farmer, qtd. in Andrews 2018, 109). She may be guided by her faith, but she is also pragmatic and resilient. In an interview titled "Rewriting Longfellow's *Evangeline*," Farmer describes crossing out the poem's description of Evangeline as "Lowly and meek in spirit and patiently suffering all things," contending instead that the "journey that Evangeline makes … is not … [one] that a person could make if they were meek" (qtd. in Andrews 2018, 108), given the physical distances she travels and the challenges she encounters.

Farmer's depiction of the Acadian community is equally layered, reflecting the close relations between the Acadians and the Mi'kmaq as populations that were thought to have intermarried and produced offspring over multiple generations.[11] For example, he begins by describing Evangeline as having both Indigenous and Acadian ancestry, a decision that reflects the historical and contemporary complexities of determining relations between these two groups.[12] While there is much debate among both Indigenous and Acadian communities regarding the historical facts surrounding marriages and the offspring that may result from such unions,[13] Farmer employs the coming together of these two marginalized populations in a single resilient and self-sufficient female character to offer his own version of Evangeline. He goes so far as to draw connections between Evangeline's mother, Emmeline, and her daughter's darker complexion. Emmeline may have the benefit of having inherited, through her ancestors, an exquisitely "embroidered white lace wedding gown" (Farmer, qtd. in Andrews 2018, 116) from a childless French aristocrat to pass onto her daughter, but she is also part of a community in which the Acadians and Mi'kmaq have lived together for generations. In Farmer's novel, Evangeline is playfully nicknamed "my little squaw" as a child by her widowed father (Farmer 2010, 226), a reality that becomes far more visible post-Deportation when she compares her skin color with that of the "pastiness" of Marylanders (226). Indigenizing Evangeline foregrounds not only the close ties between the Mi'kmaq and the Acadians, but also highlights the contemporary challenges of determining one's identities in the case of two populations that continue to face systematic dispossession and erasure.

Even Evangeline's encounter with an Indigenous woman on her way to find Gabriel is reframed by Farmer to explore women's shared experience of caregiving for the sick, and to highlight the intergenerational and communal power of female nurturance, especially for those who have lost their fathers and mothers (as Evangeline has). In Farmer's novel, the Indigenous character speaks fluent French, which reflects her "mixed ancestry" (Farmer, qtd. in Andrews 2018, 115). The text foregrounds the close relationship between Indigenous, French, and Acadian communities in colonial Canada and the US, including the Shawnee who began trading with the French in the seventeenth century and later established a critical hub for "French and English fur traders" at Lower Shawnee Town on the Ohio River which existed from 1729 to 1753 (Clark 2007, 23).[14] Evangeline and her travel companions are initially welcomed to "Lower Shawnee Town," which is paradoxically situated near to a camp of "French-speaking white" male traders (Farmer 2010, 340, 339). Evangeline and her group pointedly contrast the more permanent feel of the "dozen wigwams and fire rings" built by the Shawnee with the transient and "sauvage" housing of the traders (340).

The Shawnee speaker who visits Evangeline's tent tells a story not of a vanishing bride or bridegroom but rather a "cautionary tale" of the "related but unexpected trauma" (Farmer, qtd. in Andrews 2018, 115) that can result from a woman's relentless search for her husband and how the loss of her grandmother has strengthened her and her mother's resolve to "help those who do not have their parents" continue their individual and collective journeys (Farmer 2010, 343). The speaker offers Evangeline "ground corn" and "tobacco," traditional staples of the Shawnee tribe, and wishes the Acadian woman and her companions "safe travels and a happy end" (343). Her inclusion reinforces models of female resilience, generosity, and fortitude that reach across racial lines.[15] Nor is it clear in

Farmer's text if the Shawnee woman has or will have a child. She garners sustained strength from her family and community, resisting stereotypes of nurturance and self-sacrifice dictated by a national agenda, by which the Acadian and Indigenous women in Longfellow's poem are characterized. The Shawnee female character's community is strongly rooted and resourceful, providing a clear example of survival and continuance, despite sustained efforts to eradicate Indigenous peoples on both sides of the Canada-US border from colonial times onward.

In addition, Farmer's novel takes a much more sophisticated historical approach to the Acadian Deportation by examining the central role played by volunteer soldiers from Massachusetts who carried out the British orders. In the novel, Evangeline herself narrowly escapes being raped by a Boston militia man during the Deportation. Having tried to visit Gabriel's ship still anchored in the harbor, Evangeline is turned away by a Bostonian militiaman whom she recognizes as "here to burn Grand Pre and pick its bones," much like the "birds and flies" who feast on the slaughtered animals that litter the path to the ships (Farmer 2010, 139, 138). The "dirty blue"-coated "colonial militia" (139, 138), despite being armed and part of a contracted group, provide most of the force used to execute the Deportation. However, they remain outside of the realm of British civil society with limited access to rights, if and only if they comply with the orders of Lt.-Col. John Winslow, the American military officer who helped execute the Deportation. Subjugated himself, the militia man whom Evangeline encounters exemplifies the desperation of those whom she meets later in her travels, men who have learned to dehumanize women and racial others in the service of their own sexual pleasure, and, in doing so, seize moments of power and control. He takes the opportunity to objectify her body, "staring at her as if he believed her muteness also blinded her to his lustful gaze," and mocks the absence of "real men" among the Acadian population because they are committed to neutrality (140).

Although the militiaman initially allows Evangeline to head back to the village, he soon follows her, chases her, and hits her, hoping to render her passive as he assaults her. In particular, the Boston militiaman, who reveals his name as Simon, expresses his anger at having been drawn into military service for groups of people who he does not believe are worthy of protection, telling Evangeline, "We weren't asked if we wanted to come here. They didn't even tell us what we'd be doing, fighting native bastards, guarding women and children and men without spunk" (Farmer 2010, 148). Feeling exploited and dehumanized, Simon perceives Evangeline as a vehicle through which to reassert his authority, if only temporarily.

Unwilling to remain on the open hillside, "littered with evidence of crimes already committed," Simon drags her into a refugee shelter, exposes his penis, and relishes the opportunity to try "a Catholic whore" (149, 150), using racialized, gendered, and religious slurs to justify his brutal attack on Evangeline's body. However, the knife that he initially carries soon becomes a weapon of reprisal, which Evangeline employs to stab the palm of his hand, and she escapes back to the village.

When Colonel Winslow learns of her assault within the camp at Grand-Pré, he takes justice into his own British hands, insisting that "Evangeline's attacker" be "dragged, naked and unconscious" to be tied to a whipping post located between "the soldiers' tents and the church" and that the spectacle be viewed by everyone: American militiamen, British "redcoats," and "nearly a hundred Acadians, the huddled refugees" (Farmer 2010, 152). This brutal punishment graphically reminds the militiamen that they are subject to the sovereign rule of the professionalized British soldiers. Farmer explains that "[t]he British are not empathetic, but they do follow the law. The law is the law" (qtd. in Andrews 2018, 112), although it is selectively invoked and reinforced. In "Necropolitics," Achille Mbembe notes that "colonies [like border zones] are the location *par excellence* where the controls and guarantees of judicial order can be suspended—the zone where the violence of the state of exception is deemed to operate in the service of 'civilization'" (2003, 24). Enforcement of the law—although it remains in constant flux—is deemed necessary by Winslow to maintain order.

Importantly, this section of Farmer's novel shows readers that "all the North American colonies were still administered by a common British colonial system of governance" (Coleman 2006, 189)—from which Canadian civility is derived. Canada may try retrospectively to deflect blame for the Deportation onto New England and to view white British civility in Canada as superior to American aggression, but these efforts ignore the shared values that shaped colonial behaviors on both sides of the Canada-US border. In other words, as the second epigraph of the chapter reminds us, "[t]he conquest of Acadia [can also be understood as] ... a foundational moment in the history of the Canadian state" (McKay and Bates 2010, 78). The Acadian Deportation has led to the construction of particular nation-state values and forms of justice that serve the colonizer, rather than those who are colonized or exiled, under the guise of enforcing civility.

In *Evangeline: A Novel*, Winslow even goes so far as to personally invite Evangeline "to attend the sentencing" (Farmer 2010, 152) and observe the imposition of justice on her attacker, despite her own extensive injuries. He provides her with a chair to sit and witness Simon receiving 50 lashes. Evangeline vomits in disgust at the relentless "wet smacking" (153). As the novel points out, the English in this version of the Deportation treat the American militiamen as "their vassals," wielding a might of their own, moderated by the same claims to beneficence that later characterize the "[w]hite British colonists of North America" by ostensibly protecting and championing vulnerable peoples (Coleman 2006, 47). Winslow's threat that "any other man who approaches any woman in this village" functions ambivalently: on the one hand, glorifying violence in the name of disciplining those who lack the ability to conduct themselves in a civil manner, while on the other hand also tempering the possibility of reproduction within the Acadian community (Farmer 2010, 153). Evangeline may serve as visible evidence of a legacy of Acadian and Indigenous cooperation and partnerships over generations. Nonetheless, the Deportation is designed to rid one part of the British empire of a population deemed to be an impediment to colonization.

As Farmer explains in the interview cited previously, *Evangeline: A Novel* "is concerned with justice and the fact that, really, justice is worthless in a lot of cases, and in this case, an English justice is worthless to the Acadian people" (qtd. in Andrews 2018, 112). Evangeline's "attempted rapist is punished," but the punishment does not alter the reality that she and her fellow exiles face as deportees (112). Critical race scholar Sunera Thobani explains, as evoked in the third epigraph, that, as "persons-on-the-move" because of their alien status, they are repeatedly targeted and exploited (2007, 72). Even Farmer's version of Gabriel is not exempt from his own encounters with differing versions of (in)justice, both before and after the Deportation. Basil's "berserker rush" toward the "British regulars" in the local Acadian church during the Deportation ends with Winslow's assertion that "[a]ny further attacks against a representative of the crown will be regarded as an act of war" and that punishment will be inflicted on both the primary instigators and any family members at Grand-Pré (Farmer 2010, 110, 111). Winslow places both Basil and Gabriel in British custody, explaining that "[s]ometimes the son pays for the father" (111). His decision to do so reinforces the Acadian priest Felician's assessment that the Colonel is guided by a desire to lighten his conscience matched by a fundamental commitment to exercise might over multiple generations of Acadians while retaining a veneer of civility.

Evangeline and Gabriel as Refugees

In *Evangeline: A Novel*, Farmer reworks Evangeline and Gabriel's story to explore how these Acadian exiles should be understood as "refugees" (Farmer 2010, 169) who have been denied basic rights in the name of securing the nation-state in both Acadia and the pre-Revolutionary US, a situation that may be seen to anticipate the curtailing of "civil liberties" and the erosion of civil rights for racialized populations (Faludi 2007, 294) during the post-9/11 "War on Terror." Unlike Longfellow, Farmer depicts the Deportation in graphic terms, devoting considerable time and attention in the novel to the process of removal and the "psychological weight" of the experience for the Acadians who were forcibly placed in "a refugee camp" in their homeland and then had to wait and watch their communities burn to the ground (Farmer, qtd. in Andrews 2018, 111). Farmer also tracks the ways in which the refugees, after they are sent to various parts of the US, continue to be exploited, marginalized, and denied the ability to exercise their rights, particularly with respect to movement.

In the same interview, Farmer notes that some of the ships carrying deportees were sent to communities outside of "Boston and New England," where the "militia men ... participated actively in the Deportation" (qtd. in Andrews 2018, 105). These towns received no warning or time to prepare, so in the case of places like Baltimore and Charleston, where Evangeline and Gabriel arrive, respectively, local officials "weren't told even how to treat the people when they came" (105). As a result, many Acadians found themselves in a situation of sustained statelessness, located between "prisoner and refugee status" for years and even decades (105). Some states required passports to circulate from "town to town" (105).[16] When select Acadians finally were given opportunities to leave American cities, they were put on boats and sent to other colonies, often in the Caribbean, a locale that had "as many similarities to Acadia as Winslow had to Evangeline" (Farmer 2010, 274).

Over the course of the novel, both Evangeline and Gabriel repeatedly witness how the use of social and political power dictates who lives and who dies. Gabriel observes the practice of necropolitics in the service of colonial warfare, most explicitly when he and his fellow refugees, shortly after being put ashore in Charleston, South Carolina, are recruited by the

French army as militiamen themselves, bribed with the promise of food and shelter. Fearful of an inevitable defeat by the approaching British soldiers, Gabriel and the other laborers help to empty a local French fort before burning it and discover that the French soldiers have their own plans for the "English" prisoners of war they have been housing (Farmer 2010, 219); the men are lined up and executed by direct gunfire, enacting a form of "military justice" that Basil and Gabriel refuse to witness (220). The bodies are then "dragged around toward the gate facing east, where the English army would approach," if the fort has not already burned to the ground (220). The visibility of these maimed English bodies is designed to send a clear message to the approaching British army—kill or be killed.

Evangeline encounters a similar scene when traveling on the Ohio River toward Louisiana with a group of Acadians. They come across a group of French soldiers who have been abandoned by their battalion after the end of the Seven Years War and have given up almost all aspects of white (European) civilized behavior. The men hold two Indigenous women hostage, hunt and kill more than they eat, and regard Evangeline and her fellow travelers as prey, with Evangeline ultimately shooting one of the men dead to fend them off. Once again, the exiled Acadians find themselves "on a different border" between and among competing empires, each with its own portable and malleable version of colonial justice grounded in what Mbembe characterizes as *"the right to wage war"* through the taking of life (2003, 23; emphasis in original). Farmer's novel demonstrates how the Acadian refugees employ similar strategies, despite their disgust, to survive as "persons-on-the-move" who are targeted because of their language, race, and lack of citizenship in colonial America (Thobani 2007, 72).

Farmer's novel also poignantly describes how those who traveled north in the hopes of returning to Acadia were "confronted by Scotsmen who plowed their fields and lived in earthen hovels erected over the fresh ruins" (2010, 274). The result was that "few now considered that Acadia could be home again" (274).[17] Evangeline and Gabriel, racialized and pathologized by virtue of their itinerant status, share a sense of alienation that is heightened by their physical separation. In the novel, both protagonists use travel as a political act to challenge the exclusionary dimensions of nation-state borders for those who are deemed unworthy of belonging. In doing so, Farmer raises fundamental questions about what justice looks like, and who has access to or is denied legislated forms of justice, both in the US, a country ostensibly built on life, liberty, and the pursuit of happiness, and in Canada, which claims to be a model of inclusion and equity through diversity.

SHIFTING DEPICTIONS OF GABRIEL

Gabriel's character offers the most dramatic alteration to the story of Evangeline in Farmer's novel. In Longfellow's text, Gabriel is portrayed simply as a "valiant youth" (2004, 22), who remains a loyal son to his father in the post-Deportation years in their new home of Louisiana. Little more is said about him until the poem's concluding scenes and the couple's death. By contrast, Farmer creates a far more complex and ambivalent portrait of Gabriel as someone who struggles intrepidly to hold onto his memories of Evangeline following deportation and over the decades to come.

In *Evangeline: A Novel*, Gabriel travels by ship with his now-disabled father, Basil, who sustained a head injury inflicted by a British soldier directly after the deportation order is read aloud. Basil, who confronted the soldier, was struck with a "wooden stock" (Farmer 2010, 110). Father and son are also placed on a boat that is sent farther south than the others—part of his penalty for being a perceived troublemaker. As a result, Gabriel and the other refugee men face squalid conditions throughout their voyage and upon arriving, eventually carving out lives on the outskirts of New Orleans, where the Acadians find a new community of exiles and runaways in the swamplands of Louisiana consisting of "Germans, … a few poor white creoles, … [and] former slaves" (240). In Farmer's novel, Gabriel even joins the local French militia, lured by the promise of "guns" and food in exchange for backbreaking labor (249). Eventually, Basil decides to settle down and constructs adjacent block homes in the swamplands, urging his son to hold onto the promise of a reunion with Evangeline.

Gabriel remains loyal to Evangeline for most of the narrative, despite being mocked by his fellow male deportees, who eventually realize that he has never been married—only engaged. Yet, he refuses to have sexual relations with another woman. Gabriel clings to the belief that he will "find" Evangeline (Farmer 2010, 245). He holds onto the knowledge that "he had a prospect, at least" (245), which provides him with some solace. Gabriel even refuses to move into his own home without her, carving a "solid cypress trunk" into a marital bed, along with a figure of Evangeline and the apple tree under which they were supposed to be married, in anticipation of their reunion (266).

Having remained faithful to his fiancé for a decade and watching friends marry and have their own families, Farmer's Gabriel finally yields to sexual temptation toward the end of the novel. He ultimately fathers a child with his best friend's wife, the daughter of a French captain in New Orleans. Shortly after, he returns to the home Basil has built for Gabriel and Evangeline, this time to destroy and burn the elaborately carved bed as a form of self-punishment for this infidelity. While Gabriel laments the potential state of his relationship to Evangeline if or when she arrives, Basil wryly responds that he "won't have a bed" to share with her (Farmer 2010, 267). Once the "impotent" best friend, serving in the French army in Louisiana, is killed in action, Gabriel marries his widow and claims as his own their male child, who is Gabriel's biological offspring. But he remains haunted by his betrayal of Evangeline, continually retreating to the swamp to avoid interacting with his new family (Farmer, qtd. in Andrews 2018, 117).

In a remarkable twist of fate, in the closing pages of the novel, Farmer's Evangeline finally tracks down Gabriel beside the murky swamp waters of the bayou. She first locates Basil, only to be informed that Gabriel has a wife and an infant child, but Evangeline remains committed to reuniting with her fiancé. After several days of journeying by boat to Gabriel's isolated location, Evangeline discovers him sick with a fever and possessing a swollen, gangrenous black tongue, that resembles the "tail of a ... snake" (Farmer 2010, 412), the same tongue that he used to promise he would be hers forever under the apple tree on the eve of their marriage decades before. Farmer's novel vividly depicts a Biblically inflected narrative of male betrayal, despite Evangeline's unwavering virtue and strength. Here, Farmer pointedly inverts the traditional Biblical scene in which Eve's inability to resist the snake's temptation—and eat the apple—leads to the fall of mankind.

Instead, in *Evangeline: A Novel*, Gabriel comes to embody the snake, who, despite "wait[ing]... as long as he could" (Farmer 2010, 406), finds himself in a loveless marriage to someone other than Evangeline. The betrothed couple has a short-lived reunion before Gabriel dies in her arms. Despite these significant alterations, in *Evangeline: A Novel*, Evangeline remains committed to Gabriel to the very end of the story. She has already come to terms with the reality that "Gabriel and I will never be young together" and has decided that "rather than giving my child as a servant to the Lord, I give myself" (Farmer 2010, 234). Hence, her search for Gabriel is one of necessity and provides resolution.

Farmer's novel depicts the precarity, violence, and injustice that Acadians and Indigenous peoples experienced in both pre-Confederation Canada and the pre-Revolutionary US. In *Evangeline: A Novel*, Farmer takes aim at Americans who may wish to distance themselves from the brutality of those who conducted the Deportation, a militia comprised primarily of 2000 volunteer soldiers from Massachusetts,[18] which was underwritten financially by "Boston merchants and bankers" (Griffiths 2005, 440)—and without whom there would have been no removal. His novel portrays the problematic and limited versions of justice that are advanced by the British, American, and French soldiers. His narrative also raises critical questions about Canadian complicity in perpetuating and profiting from the legacy of Longfellow's Evangeline to further Canada's role nationally and internationally as "a middle power" and thus perfectly positioned for the "role of peacekeeper and arbitrator on the world stage" (Coleman 2006, 27). *Evangeline: A Novel* can thus be read as refusing to accept Canadian claims to exceptionality and superiority that continue to place Acadian and Indigenous populations on the margins of Canadian civil society or erase them from existence altogether, except as a conveniently distant memory.

Ingenious Citizenship: Challenging Canadian and American Paradigms

The concluding pages of *Evangeline: A Novel* bring Evangeline and Gabriel together in an unexpected and decidedly messy fashion, which foregrounds the human foibles and strengths of each character. Evangeline is a woman who has survived an attempted rape, resisted captivity, and motivated others to travel across vast physical spaces to locate her fiancé. The version of Gabriel she finds is poisoned and dying, his black tongue serving, as Farmer explains, as evidence of his corruption and a visible phallic symbol of his sexual and psychological betrayal. Nor does the couple have much time together; he dies moments after she overcomes her initial horror at his physical state. But the journey to locate Gabriel indicates Evangeline's larger purpose, in this text at least: to prompt new imaginings of herself as a racialized female subject who refuses to be treated as a passive and vulnerable victim or as the pious and dutiful embodiment of a dying race.

As an Acadian and Indigenous woman who remains alive at the end of this American-authored revisioning of Longfellow's famous poem, Farmer's version of Evangeline defies efforts to be framed and contained by nation-state narratives that have relied on her death to perpetuate a mythic legacy on both sides of the Canada-US border. Refusing to serve as the literal bearer of nation, nor willing to adhere to the boundaries of the nation-state that have tried to limit her mobility, Evangeline resists reclamation as part of the humanitarian mission ascribed to Canadian immigration and refugee policies, particularly at the present moment. Instead, her story reveals the fragility of the conceptualization of the nation-state on both sides of the Canada-US border and the precarity of exceptionalist discourses by exposing their constructed nature. For Thobani, "[d]espite the most ardent claims of national mythology, the constitution of the [Canadian] nation as Euro-Canadian, that is, as white, was neither a natural nor a predestined inevitability" (2007, 22). Farmer's novel can be read as raising fundamental questions about the US desire to consign Acadians as a distinctive people to the distant past, before they were Americans, and a Canadian desire to overlook the brutality of the Deportation and its aftermath as an event that occurred prior to the creation of a nation-state, and for which blame is placed squarely on English and/or American colonial forces. Identifying Evangeline as both Acadian and Indigenous creates powerful parallels between the two distinct populations, emphasizing the similarities between their histories of containment, removal, and erasure. By modeling potential versions of what Lee calls "ingenious citizenship" through his novel (2016, 27), Farmer's Evangeline provides a provisional example of what social change might look like for multiply-racialized women who refuse to remain beholden to entrenched nation-state mythologies that have confined them to a falsified past or eradicated their existence altogether.

NOTES

1. See Moss for a detailed survey of historic and recent rewritings of Evangeline's narrative, including a 2011 book by Canadian-born American writer, Richard F. Mullins, titled *Evangeline: The Novel*. Mullins' story also "suggests a parallel between the dispossession of Native Americans and

that of the Acadians" (Moss 2017, 99). Moss does not mention Farmer's novel in her chapter.
2. See Authers (2021, 52–66) for another thoughtful discussion of the culture of redress in Canada.
3. See the Canada Post Corporation's post on its "Latest Stamps" from August 15, 2005, for more details about both the original stamp, released in 1930 on the 175th anniversary of the Acadian Deportation which "portrays the famous statue of Evangeline and the Acadian chapel at Grand-Pré National Historic Site." The 2005 stamp, designed by "graphic artist Pierre-Yves Pelletier," juxtaposes the original image with an "illustrated … Acadian flag in motion" with a "backdrop of waves, in a five per cent screen" representing "the sea voyage." As the blog's unnamed author argues, the inclusion of the Acadian flag with its gold star on the top left is critical because "[t]he star, Stella Maris, is the star of the sea and symbolizes the wanderings of the Acadians through the storms and dangers of life" ("Acadian Deportation 1755–2005" 2005).
4. See Starratt (2019) and Quon (2019) for media coverage of this new Heritage minute.
5. For further critical work on North American borders and how they were used to frame identities, see Hoy (2021).
6. See Deveau and Ross (1995, 63).
7. See Matthews and Basque for recent perspectives on the use of the term "genocide" to describe the systematic and violent targeting of racialized populations to consolidate a "hegemonic Western and white-coded Canadian national identity" (Matthews 2019, 2). Matthews contends that the "genocide finding" in the case of Indigenous peoples puts "truth to the lie of the picture of Canadian liberal tolerance" (4). In the case of the Acadian Deportation, Basque is one of many scholars who contends, for a variety of reasons, that "genocide" should not be used to describe "the Grand Dérangement. Acadie was not Armenia, and to compare Grand-Pré with Auschwitz and the killing fields of Cambodia is a complete and utter trivialization of the many genocidal horrors of contemporary history" (2011, 66). Nonetheless, the Société de l'Acadie de Nouveau-Brunswick formed a new committee in 2019 to look at "whether the expulsion of Acadians should be considered a genocide" (Bird 2019).
8. See also Moss (2017, 101).
9. See Mercer for recent coverage of the significance of Grand-Pré for Acadians, which describes the ways in which Acadians have continued to fight for recognition of their identity despite their decreasing numbers and systematic marginalization; Mercer argues that "their story is one of defiance and perseverance" (Mercer 2022).

10. See McKay and Bates (2010, 89–90) for a description of the Lemay translation, along with Bourque and Merkle (2008).
11. See Griffiths (2005, 35) for the significant role intermarriage played in the development of French and Mi'kmaq families in Acadia.
12. See Paul (2022, 86, 175) for descriptions of the close relationships between the Mi'kmaq and the Acadians from the arrival of the Acadians to after the Deportation.
13. See, for example, Laxer who claims that "[i]n Acadian communities, there were many families whose children were the product of unions between French and Mi'kmaq partners" (2007, 33). Likewise, Griffiths notes that "in terms of the genetic heritage of the Acadians, there is the question of marriage, according to Catholic rite, with the Mi'kmaq. As was mentioned in chapter 2, there is evidence that, during the 1730s and 1740s, members of the Lejeune, Thibodeau, and Martin families had Mi'kmaq spouses," and usually Mi'kmaq wives (2005, 172). In the case of Farmer, the invocation of this mixed-blood heritage, I am arguing, is gestured toward as part of his larger fictional revisioning of Longfellow's *Evangeline*, rather than grounded in irrefutable fact.
14. See Clark (2007, 75).
15. See Clark (2007, 40).
16. See Farmer (2010, 273).
17. See Faragher (2005, Chapters 14, 15, and 16 (392–498)), for detailed accounts of the dispersal of the Acadian population internationally from 1756 to 1785.
18. See Griffiths (2005, 440, 458, and 463).

References

"Acadian Deportation 1755-2005". 2005. *Canada Post Corporation*, August 15. https://www.canadapost.ca/web/en/blogs/collecting/details.page?article=2005/08/15/acadian_deportation_&cattype=collecting&cat=stamps.

Andrews, Jennifer. 2018. A Trio of Voices about American Literary Portraits of Canada with Authors Ben Farmer, Beth Powning, and P.S. Duffy. *Canadian Review of American Studies* 48 (supp. 1): 98–161.

Authers, Benjamin. 2021. Telling Harm: Time, Redress, and Canadian Literature. In *On the Other Side(s) of 150*, ed. Linda M. Morra and Sarah Henzi, 52–66. Waterloo: Wilfrid Laurier University Press.

Basque, Maurice. 2011. Atlantic Realities, Acadian Identities, Arcadian Dreams. In *Shaping an Agenda for Atlantic Canada*, ed. John G. Reid and Donald J. Savoie, 62–77. Halifax: Fernwood Press.

Bird, Lauren. 2019. Should Acadian Expulsion be Considered Genocide? New Committee Will Decide. *CBC*, June 17. https://www.cbc.ca/news/canada/new-brunswick/acadian-expulsion-genocide-1.5177808.

Bourque, Denis, and Denis Merkle. 2008. De Evangeline à l'américaine à Évangéline à l'acadienne: une transformation idéologique? In *Traduire depuis les marges: Translating from the Margins*, ed. Denise Merkle et al., 121–145. Québec: Nota bene.

Charvat, William. 1968. *The Profession of Authorship in America, 1800 to 1870*. New York: Columbia University Press.

Clark, Jerry E. 2007. *The Shawnee*. Lexington: University Press of Kentucky.

Coleman, Daniel. 2006. *White Civility: The Literary Project of English Canada*. Toronto: University of Toronto Press.

Deveau, Alophonse, and Sally Ross. 1995. *The Acadians of Nova Scotia: Past and Present*. Halifax: Nimbus.

Doyle, James. 1983. *North of America: Images of Canada in the Literature of the United States, 1775–1900*. Montreal: ECW Press.

Episkenew, Jo-Ann. 2009. *Taking Back Our Spirits: Indigenous Literature, Public Policy, and Healing*. Winnipeg: University of Manitoba Press.

Faludi, Susan. 2007. *The Terror Dream: Myth and Misogyny in an Insecure America*. New York: Henry Holt.

Faragher, John Mack. 2005. *A Great and Noble Scheme: The Tragic Story of the Expulsion of the French Acadians from the American Homeland*. New York: W.W. Norton.

Farmer, Ben. 2010. *Evangeline: A Novel*. New York: Overlook.

Gagné, Michael. 2013. 'Memorial Constructions': Representations of Identity in the Design of the Grand-Pré National Historic Site, 1907-Present. *Acadiensis* 42 (1): 67–99.

Giles, Wenona, and Jennifer Hyndman. 2004. Introduction. In *Sites of Violence: Gender and Conflict Zones*, ed. Wenona Giles and Jennifer Hyndman, 3–23. Berkeley: University of California Press.

Grewal, Inderpal. 2017. *Saving the Security State: Exceptional Citizens in Twenty-First-Century America*. Durham: Duke University Press.

Griffiths, N.E.S. 1982. Longfellow's *Evangeline*: The Birth and Acceptance of a Legend. *Acadiensis* 11 (2): 28–41.

———. 2005. *From Migrant to Acadian: A North American Border People 1604–1755*. Montreal & Kingston: McGill-Queen's University Press.

Haliburton, Thomas Chandler. 1829. *An Historical and Statistical Account of Nova Scotia*. Vol. 1. Halifax: Joseph Howe.

"Heritage Minutes: The Acadian Deportation". 2019. *Historica Canada*. https://www.historicacanada.ca/content/heritage-minutes/acadian-deportation#.

Hoy, Benjamin. 2021. *A Line of Blood and Dirt: Creating the Canada-United States Border Across Indigenous Lines*. Oxford: Oxford University Press.

Irmscher, Christopher. 2006. *Longfellow Redux*. Chicago: University of Illinois Press.
Laxer, James. 2007. *The Acadians: In Search of a Homeland*. Toronto: Anchor Canada.
LeBlanc, Barbara. 2003. *Postcards from Acadie: Grand-Pré, Evangeline and the Acadian Identity*. Kentville: Gaspereau Press.
Lee, Charles T. 2016. *Ingenious Citizenship: Recrafting Democracy for Social Change*. Durham: Duke University Press.
Longfellow, Henry W. 2004. *Evangeline: A Tale of Acadie*. Fredericton: Goose Lane.
MacDonald, Michael. 2019. Was the Acadian Expulsion a Genocide?: New Committee to Explore That Question. *CTV News*, June 18. https://atlantic.ctvnews.ca/was-the-acadian-expulsion-a-genocide-new-committee-to-explore-that-question-1.4471113.
Matthews, Heidi. 2019. What the Debate Around Indigenous Genocide Says about Canada. *Maclean's*, June 7. https://www.macleans.ca/opinion/what-the-debate-around-indigenous-genocide-says-about-canada/.
Mbembe, Achille. 2003. Necropolitics. *Public Culture* 51 (1): 11–40.
McKay, Ian, and Robin Bates. 2010. *In the Province of History: The Making of the Public Past in Twentieth-Century Nova Scotia*. Montreal & Kingston: McGill-Queen's University Press.
Mercer, Greg. 2022. At Grand Pré, Acadians Commune with Ancestors Driven from Their Land. *The Globe and Mail*, August 4. https://www.theglobeandmail.com/canada/article-acadian-days-grand-pre/.
Moss, Jane. 2017. Memorializing an Imagined Past: Evangeline and the Acadian Deportation. In *Landscapes and Landmarks of Canada: Real, Imagined, (Re)viewed*, ed. Maeve Conrick, Munroe Eagles, Jane Koustas, and Caitríona Ní Chasaide, 91–108. Waterloo: Wilfrid Laurier University Press.
Mullins, Richard. 2017. *Evangeline: The Novel*. Bloomington, IN: Trafford Publishing.
Paul, Daniel. 2022. *We Were Not the Savages: Collision between European and Native American Civilizations*. Halifax: Fernwood Publishing.
Razack, Sherene. 2004. *Dark Threats & White Knights: The Somalia Affair, Peacekeeping, and the New Imperialism*. Toronto: University of Toronto Press.
Quon, Alexander. 2019. New Heritage Minute Focuses on Dark History of the Acadian Expulsion. *Global News*, August 15. https://globalnews.ca/news/5766455/new-canadian-heritage-minute-acadian-expulsion/.
Renan, Ernest. 1990. "What Is a Nation?" Translated by Martin Thom. In *Nation and Narration*, ed. Homi K. Bhabha, 8–22. London: Routledge.
Rosenberg, Morris. 2003. Proclamation Designating July 28 of Every Year as 'A Day of Commemoration of the Great Upheaval,' Commencing on July 28, 2005. *Justice Laws Website, Government of Canada*, December 31. https://laws-lois.justice.gc.ca/eng/regulations/si-2003-188/page-1.html.

Rudin, Ronald. 2009. *Remembering and Forgetting in Acadie: A Historian's Journey Through Public Memory*. Toronto: University of Toronto Press.

Starratt, Kirk. 2019. Deportation Heritage Minute Shot in Annapolis Valley debuts on National Acadian Day. *The Chronicle Herald*, August 13. https://www.thechronicleherald.ca/news/provincial/update-deportation-heritage-minute-shot-in-annapolis-valley-debuts-on-national-acadian-day-340953/.

Taylor, C.J. 1990. *Negotiating the Past: The Making of Canada's National Historic Parks and Sites*. Montreal & Kingston: McGill-Queen's University Press.

Taylor, M. Brook. 1984. Thomas Chandler Haliburton as a Historian. *Acadiensis* 13 (2): 50–68.

Thobani, Sunera. 2007. *Exalted Subjects: Studies in the Making of Race and Nation in Canada*. Toronto: University of Toronto Press.

Viau, Robert. 1998. *Les Visages d'Évangeline: Du Poème au Mythe*. Beauport, PQ: MNH Publications.

Wakeham, Pauline. 2013. Rendition and Redress: Maher Arar, Apology, Exceptionality. In *Reconciling Canada: Critical Perspectives on the Culture of Redress*, ed. Jennifer Henderson and Pauline Wakeham, 278–295. Toronto: University of Toronto Press.

CHAPTER 4

German Internment Camps in the Maritimes: Another Untold Story in P.S. Duffy's *The Cartographer of No Man's Land*

A loyal Canadian these many years, a Canadian of German extraction, he was not allowed to enlist. Volunteered and was refused. Barred because of his name—a name that evokes the worst sort of bigotry. (Duffy 2013, 51)

The ... camp was located in an old and very dilapidated ... foundry that had been confiscated from its German owner. ... About eight hundred of us lived in these [cramped] conditions. ... Men hopelessly

---

Thanks to Nicole Richard and Ray Coulson, curators at the Cumberland County Museum and the Royal Nova Scotia Highlanders Regimental Museum, respectively, for their knowledge, time, and generosity.

Figure 4.1 is from the Cumberland County Museum Archives. The miniature spinning wheel is one example of the fine-woodworking skills used by the prisoners to produce miniature objects they could trade or gift. The photograph, presumably taken by a guard, was part of the internment camp's efforts to demonstrate that the prisoners were treated well during their time there. Author photos taken March 16, 2017.

Figures 4.2 and 4.3 are of the cello housed in the public exhibition about the regiment and the community at the Royal Nova Scotia Highlanders Regimental Museum. Author photos taken March 17, 2017.

© The Author(s), under exclusive license to Springer Nature Switzerland AG 2023
J. Andrews, *Canada Through American Eyes*,
https://doi.org/10.1007/978-3-031-22120-0_4

83

> *clogged the passages, elbowed their way through, lay down or got up, played cards or chess. Many of them practised crafts, some with extraordinary skill. … And yet, in spite of the heroic efforts of the prisoners to keep themselves physically and morally fit, five of them had gone insane. We had to eat and sleep in the same room with these madmen. (Trotsky 1930, 281)*

The year 2017 marked the 150th anniversary of Canadian Confederation; in the same year, the federal government also held major celebrations of the now century-old Canadian military successes of World War I at Vimy Ridge and Passchendaele. *The Cartographer of No Man's Land* portrays the less celebratory and more complex aspects of this war as it plays out on Canadian soil in Nova Scotia. The novel is authored by P.S. Duffy, an American who summered in Mahone Bay for 30 years and has Nova Scotian roots dating back 250 years. *The Cartographer of No Man's Land* (2013) explores how racism shapes the community's understanding of the war within their small fishing community, Snag Harbour, located on the south shore of Nova Scotia, near Lunenburg. As part of its multiple narrative strands, *The Cartographer of No Man's Land* tells the story of a German immigrant, Avon Heist, who teaches at the local school and befriends a young boy named Simon whose father and uncle are both in service overseas. The book addresses the complicated and confusing political ethics that unfolded in this community, portrayed through Heist's arrest and detainment at the Amherst Internment Camp and his continued correspondence with Simon throughout his imprisonment. Duffy rejects a resolutely positive portrayal of Canada and particularly the Maritime provinces, drawing attention instead to the flagrant racism and classism of the period directed at both Germans and select Canadians who were deemed undesirable.

In this chapter, I argue that Duffy's positionality as both insider and outsider to the Maritimes enables her to present a historical narrative about Canadian racism that, while compelling, has been overlooked or ignored by Atlantic Canadian critics because she resides south of the Canadian-American border. The story of Avon Heist's internment and its historical accuracy (which has been largely ignored in the Maritimes) demonstrates the ways in which Canadians, both regionally and nationally, remain ambivalent about acknowledging racism and classism north of the Canada-US border, particularly given that it has been easy to view Canada as more inclusive and tolerant than its neighbor to the south.[1] Duffy's novel also challenges what I have described as the ongoing "fantasy" of

Canadian exceptionalism,[2] which seems to flourish particularly in times of internal American conflict.

History of the Amherst Interment Camp

Amherst became the site of the largest internment camp in Canada during the First World War as a direct result of the lobbying efforts of a federal minister from the area and because of its proximity to Halifax. The real-life camp housed 853 prisoners and was located at the old Malleable Iron Foundry, which sat next to the railway tracks that were used to transport prisoners of war (P.O.W.s) to local work assignments. Those who were detained at the camp included "sailors from the *Kaiser Wilhelm der Grosse*, sunk in 1915, sailors from other ships, various untrustworthy, roughshod Canadians, and a large group of 'suspicious' aliens—many of German origin" (Duffy 2013, 321). The camp gained notoriety as the place where Leon Trotsky was held for a month in 1917, a historical detail that Duffy includes in her novel. In *The Cartographer of No Man's Land*, Heist aligns himself with the communist movement led by Trotsky to survive the brutality of camp life. The actual camp was closed in 1919. It was subsequently revitalized to serve two different purposes: initially, the camp provided barracks for the North Nova Scotia Highlanders Battalion (as of 1939), and then it later became the site of the annual winter fair until the buildings burned in 1958.

There has been relatively little attention paid to the internment camps themselves, and in particular, the Amherst one. The creation of the Canadian First World War Internment Recognition Fund, begun in 2008, has started to raise public awareness of these camps through its website and by funding over $2 million dollars in research, curriculum materials, and artistic projects about the camps.[3] The website includes a digital map of the camp locations across Canada, along with links to relevant newspaper articles published during each camp's existence. It also provides ready access to free curriculum materials about the camps aimed at educating students from Grade 5 to 12. The site offers a list of schools in Canada currently using the units in their classrooms—a group predominantly from Western and Central Canada. The Fund's mandate is national and much of the work focuses on the plight of Ukrainian-Canadians rather than the German-Canadians who populated Atlantic Canada; the former group primarily immigrated to the Prairie provinces and Ontario. As a result, the Maritime camps warrant more careful examination.

The Amherst area was originally a critical part of the seasonal migration of the Mi'kmaq who "encamped each year on the southern ridge above the marsh, establishing a principal village site ... near the meandering tidal creek" (Furlong 2001, vii). Over time, the land was claimed by Acadian settlers whose "unique system of dykes and aboiteaux" were ideal for managing the "tidal inundation of the salt marshes adjacent to the ... rivers of the Bay of Fundy" (vii). But the Acadian expulsion decimated the local communities, forcibly removing these long-established populations in a brutal fashion. In the aftermath, Amherst was reborn as a small village composed of under 200 residents, most of whom were Irish; four Acadians remained. Amherst continued to grow. It was incorporated as a town in 1889 and, by the turn of the century, was a thriving industrial hub. Amherst had gained considerable strength in the manufacturing sector and the local economy began to flourish, bolstered by a railroad line running from Quebec to Halifax that stopped in Amherst's downtown core.

Today, Amherst is a small town of under 10,000 people and evidence of the existence of the P.O.W. camp is scarce. Like many Maritime communities, outmigration is all too common, and the economy is struggling, a pattern that dates back close to a century. As Donald Savoie explains in *Visiting the Grandchildren: Economic Development in the Maritimes* (2006), the adoption of a "National Policy" in the post-Confederation period meant that manufacturing gradually shifted to vote-rich Central Canada, where urbanization far outpaced the Maritimes (33). The result was that between 1920 and 1926, manufacturing jobs in the region (including Amherst as a key hub) declined by 44 percent, and 150,000 Maritimers left the region. This pattern was exacerbated by the fact that the region was not the beneficiary of defense-related industries during the First World War (33).

The internment camp functions as the historical juncture for the shifting tide of Amherst's economic and political prosperity, a narrative that many would rather forget or refashion to suit their own purposes. For instance, a large plaque mounted on the side of the Casey Concrete headquarters, where the camp's footprint was located, acknowledges the significance of the site and describes the needless imprisonment of Europeans, including Germans and Ukrainians, in the Malleable Iron Works between April 1915 and September 1919. However, locating the plaque is not easy. Casey Concrete is situated on the edge of the Amherst industrial park, and the sprawling yards behind include an aptly named "boneyard," piles of concrete blocks, and a sign promising large fines if surveillance cameras catch one trespassing.

Other efforts to acknowledge the camp's existence vary. They include the 2001 installation of two granite headstones at the rear of a local cemetery recording the names of 11 of the 13 prisoners who died at the camp and performances of Cape Breton author Silver Donald Cameron's play about Trotsky's time at the camp. Called *The Prophet at Tantramar* (1988), the play premiered at Halifax's Neptune Theatre, was later turned into a CBC radio play and was subsequently revived in 2014 by an Amherst theater company as part of the town's 125th birthday celebration.

An increasingly prominent part of local recognition of the camp has involved the cataloguing of photographs and postcards of the camp's occupants, in conjunction with the recovery of the intricate wooden carvings, handmade musical instruments, and artwork made by prisoners at the camp that were marketed and sold or given as gifts to community members during the internment as souvenirs of the P.O.W. presence. As the curator of the Nova Scotia Highlanders Regimental Museum, Ray Coulson explained in an undated talk to the Amherst Rotary Club that these objects were "made and sold for money that … [prisoners] could use at the Canteen" in the camp or in exchange for tobacco (3). In addition, many black-and-white photographs were taken of the prisoners engaging in theatrical and sports events, performed for locals, or gathered at work sites where the P.O.W.s made a considerable contribution to the infrastructure of Amherst by clearing land at the local experimental farm, establishing the foundations of Dickey Park, and laboring for the railroad.

The postcards, printed locally, functioned as pieces of war propaganda, circulated by prisoners, Amherst residents, and travelers to the region as a record of the camp's existence that is benevolent, even arguably romanticizing camp conditions. This war propaganda bears a remarkable similarity to the marketing of the Acadian Deportation through tourism, as described in Chap. 3, demonstrating a pattern of Canadian exceptionality that relies on the cultivation of narratives of national inclusion rather than exclusion and racial discrimination.

There are two small museums in Amherst dedicated to preserving historical evidence of this camp: the Nova Scotia Highlanders Regimental Museum and the Cumberland County Museum. Fragile and complex wooden objects produced by prisoners have become a central part of the small displays created to inform visitors about life at the local internment camp. Often labeled "souvenir[s]" by their creators and consumers, the latter of whom were the residents of Amherst, these objects ranged from carved boxes, inkwell stands, and candle holders, to miniature models of boats, cannons, spinning wheels, the full-size card tables, trays, and even a full-sized working cello. Both museums use these objects to humanize and redeem the prisoners, by celebrating the intricacy and craftsmanship of these creations while downplaying the grim realities of life in the camp. The result is that these displays of these souvenirs continue to perpetuate what art historian Erin Morton calls "a fantastic sentimental alternative to troubling realities" (2016, 303) (Figs. 4.1, 4.2, and 4.3).

Much of the contemporary and retroactive coverage of the Amherst camp's history at these museums has been positive, stressing the habitability of conditions and the fact that prisoners were from 1916 onward able to work outside of the camp, bolstered by the efforts made to create a place that was physically and culturally stimulating. The archived photos of the camp are predominantly populated with images of the prisoners in costume, before or after the performance of a revue, or involved in sporting activities. The images include men jauntily attired in bright white pants and muscle tanks with barbells in plain view for a weightlifting competition; prisoners lined up in elegant formations wearing full fencing gear in the exercise compound; men playfully costumed in theater garb—whether a knight in shining armor, a cross-dressed cowgirl, or a bewigged ballerina—and even a full-sized orchestra composed of suit-wearing prisoners sitting beside a piano in the outdoor exercise compound.

But the description of the camp offered by Leon Trotsky in his autobiography, *My Life*, having himself spent a month detention in Amherst in 1917 (1930, 281), presents a decidedly different picture. The size of the camp totaled a quarter of a mile in length and was 100 feet wide. It housed not only the prisoners using communal bathrooms and kitchens, but also officers, guards, censors, and other staff, bringing the population within the camp to roughly 1100 men, surrounded by a high barbed wire fence. The second epigraph of this chapter comprises Trotsky's vivid observations of Amherst. As he outlines, the camp is horribly overcrowded and run-down, providing virtually no space for the prisoners to move around and leading to serious mental and physical health challenges among the men. Yet, some, he recalls, "practised crafts," creating works of art amid terrible living conditions, finding beauty in what they produce to remain sane (1930, 281).

Lubomyr Luciuk explains *In Fear of the Barbed Wire Fence: Canada's First National Internment Operations and the Ukrainian Canadians, 1914–1920* that life in these camps was typically harsh. Valuables were

Fig. 4.1 Miniature spinning wheel. Cumberland County Museum Archives in Amherst, Nova Scotia. (Photo courtesy of Jennifer Andrews, March 16, 2017)

confiscated as soon as internees arrived and often lost or stolen, never to be returned. The daily routine was strenuous and isolating as prisoners were "often denied access to newspapers … [and] their correspondence was censored. … They were forced not only to maintain the camps but also to work for the government and for private concerns, and their guards sometimes mistreated them" (2001, 20). In the case of Amherst, for example, following a 1915 riot that was attributed to "poor" discipline (Furlong 2001, 86), prisoners were dispatched on a daily basis to clear over 50 acres of land at a local experimental farm and charged with building a pool in an Amherst park, labor that was paid for in the postwar period at a reduced rate.

The immense "physical and mental toll" of imprisonment, including the limited activity in the crowded exercise yard, the endless "waiting,"

Fig. 4.2 Cello housed in the public exhibition about the regiment and community at the Nova Scotia Highlanders Regimental Museum in Amherst, Nova Scotia. (Photo courtesy of Jennifer Andrews, March 17, 2017)

and the constant confinement led to desperate attempts to escape at camps across Canada, including Amherst, despite the risk of being shot and killed (Luciuk 2001, 20, 21). Given the physical proximity to the US, which remained neutral for much of the war, Amherst prisoners were especially active in their efforts to escape by crossing the Canada-US border to evade Canadian authorities. This phenomenon directly confronts one of the most common tropes of Canadian identity—namely, the belief that Canada has provided and continues to provide a historic place of refuges for those escaping hardships and injustices faced by populations living in the US. Notably, the US served as a mediator for complaints made by the German government about the conditions of the camps, with the American consul traveling several times to Amherst to declare the state of the prison more than adequate. External Affairs provided professional photographs

Fig. 4.3 Cello head housed in the public exhibition about the regiment and community at the Nova Scotia Highlanders Regimental Museum in Amherst, Nova Scotia. (Photo courtesy of Jennifer Andrews, March 17, 2017)

of the men (the same ones collected and displayed by the Amherst museums) participating in camp recreation activities to demonstrate the quality of their treatment. However, in Appendix One of a 1921 federal government report filed regarding the internment camp operations, there is a list of ten prisoners who died or were wounded because of escape attempts. The file includes two names of Amherst detainees, Fritz Klaus and Kurt Becker, both of whom died as a result of gunshot wounds, the first in 1915 and the second in 1916. Four others from Amherst are named as being wounded yet eventually recovered.

Despite the existence of this material, the internment camps remain unfamiliar to most residents of Atlantic Canada and, more broadly, to Canadians. The displays that do exist are housed in local museums with very limited resources and little to no web presence, necessitating a trip to

Amherst to see the carved wooden objects and the photographs of the camp. The result is a hidden history of the region that challenges and complicates some of the foundational ideas of what differentiates Canada from the US.

COMPARING GERMAN IMMIGRATION IN CANADA AND THE US

Examining the history of German immigration to both the US and Canada provides an important framework for understanding why *The Cartographer of No Man's Land*—and the story it tells of the Amherst Internment Camp—has been marginalized. In *Building Nations from Diversity: Canadian and American Experiences Compared* (2014), Garth Stevenson points out that while "[w]hat happened in World War II is fairly well known, in its broad outlines if not in its details, and many who experienced it are still alive," yet "World War I, now almost a century past, has largely receded from memory or common knowledge" (2014, 123). He proceeds to argue that "[n]either Canada's claim to be a tolerant multicultural mosaic nor the proud American boast that theirs is a government ... of laws and not of men receives much support from a contemplation of these events" (123–124). In the case of the US, German immigration and its influence on American culture were significant from colonial times to the twentieth century; between 1820 and 1914, approximately "five and a half million immigrants," including "ethnic and linguistic minorities," came from Germany to the US, "more than any other country" (124). German immigration peaked in the 1880s, and then declined sharply, likely because of "increasing ... prosperity" at home (125). Nonetheless, prior to the First World War, public school language instruction in German was permitted in eight Midwestern US states, church services were delivered in German, and German-language newspapers and magazines were abundant, a situation that mirrors the prominence of Spanish in the US today.

The German "imprint on Canada" was less significant, although Germans played a critical role in "the settlement of Nova Scotia in the middle of the eighteenth century," the setting for Duffy's novel (Stevenson 2014, 126). There were small groups of Germans located across the country, ranging from Loyalists who moved to Upper Canada from Pennsylvania and neighboring states to Midwestern Americans who came northward in search of free land. Records of these groups were complicated by the fact that "the Canadian census, unlike the American, always enumerated people by ethnicity"—and being American was not considered a valid category (127). So "Germans" may have constituted "the fifth largest ethnic group (after the French, English, Irish, and Scottish)" in Canada but that included a wide array of populations, among them descendants of immigrants, German-speaking minorities from central and eastern Europe, and religious communities like "the Mennonites and Hutterites, which tended to isolate themselves from the rest of the population, … German or otherwise" (127). Because "Canada attracted very few immigrants from Germany in the nineteenth century" when compared to the US, the "process of assimilation for most German Canadians had been in progress for well over a century" by the time the First World War began (126). Despite the scattered nature of small groups of Germans across Canada, Stevenson highlights that there were "a few enclaves like Lunenberg (Nova Scotia) … where elements of their German heritage survived" (127) but that presence was far more muted in the Canadian education system, for example, than in its US counterpart.

The advent of the First World War brought about a dramatic shift in the status and treatment of Germans on both sides of the Canada-US border as a result of international law that allows the "interning [of] people who are citizens or subjects of a state against which war has been formally declared" (Stevenson 2014, 127). While "some German citizens residing in Canada returned home in 1914, often for the purpose of joining the German army," many others remained, hopeful that they would not be rounded up because they had been loyal to their adopted nation (127). The numbers of interned Germans in Canada totaled close to 8000 (including approximately 6000 "Austrians," many of whom were ethnic Ukrainians). In contrast, in the US, which joined the war effort in 1917, the number of German and German-Americans interned was roughly 6300, constituting a much smaller percentage of the German population, which totaled over two million people (127). The internment may have impacted a relatively small group of people, but it represented a much broader and more pervasive shift in public attitude in both countries—one of "hatred and hostility directed against every trace of German culture or heritage and against everyone who displayed evidence thereof, including persons who had been born in North America and had never seen Germany in their lives" (128).

The concept of the "melting pot" gained considerable traction when the US entered the First World War, putting immense pressure on the large German-American population to assimilate. Likewise, in Canada, "Germanophobia" was common (Stevenson 2014, 129), despite Canadian efforts to position their nation as more tolerant and inclusive of diversity. As Stevenson explains, the distinction between the US and Canada is often summarized as the contrast between the "melting pot" and the "mosaic" (3). The "melting pot," a term coined by Israel Zangwill, a Jewish immigrant to the US from the United Kingdom, was first used in his 1908 play. It called for Jews and Christians to "transcend their religious and cultural differences" (3). In contrast, Canadians embraced the notion of a cultural "mosaic" to describe the ostensible harmony among differing racial and ethnic populations within Canada from the 1920s to the post-Second World War period (3). Ideally, "immigrants in Canada ... [were] encouraged to retain their distinct characteristics and identities more or less indefinitely while immigrants in the United States face[d] pressure to conform to American cultural patterns and to lose their distinct characteristics as rapidly as possible" (4). Stevenson notes that the idea of the Canadian cultural mosaic was eventually displaced by a more inclusive synonym to reflect the federal government's public commitment first declared as an official doctrine in 1971, with the idea of "multiculturalism" (4). As Stevenson suggests, this contrast between Canada and the US has served as evidence of Canada's moral superiority over its nearest neighbor, creating a "cottage industry" in academia and the media focused on celebrating the nation's distinct brand of multiculturalism (4). However, it remains easy to overlook or dismiss historical narratives that counter this claim of virtuousness, among these the stories of interned people of German descent in rural Nova Scotia.

As Duffy's novel vividly demonstrates, historically, Canada has not been a beacon of inclusivity or necessarily accepting of the differences that shape its immigrant populations, despite its efforts to appear so. The story of Heist and Canada's treatment of Germans during World War I becomes a stark illustration of this reality. Persuasive British anti-German propaganda fueled public expressions of hatred and led to anti-German riots and vandalism against local German-owned businesses and families in Canada. Fear of Germans also led to the disavowal of the legacy of German immigration to Canada. Berlin, Ontario was renamed Kitchener after the "recently deceased British minister of war," who was featured on "recruiting posters throughout the empire"; the War Measures Act was invoked, which "disenfranchised ... [those] of 'enemy' origins" even if individuals had become British citizens in the 15 years prior; and a ban on "all

German-language publications" was instituted from 1918 to 1920 (Stevenson 2014, 129). *The Cartographer of No Man's Land* thus functions as a powerful reminder that Canada is no better than its southern neighbor when it comes to the treatment of immigrants.

Canadian Multiculturalism and the Story of Heist

In *The Cartographer of No Man's Land*, P.S. Duffy explores the conflicted nature of Canadian multiculturalism through the story of Mr. Heist, a "schoolmaster for the combined sixth, seventh, and eighth grades" in Snag Harbour, Nova Scotia, during World War I (2013, 50). When he first appears in the text, Heist has seized the end of the school day and his authority as a teacher to address a schoolyard fight in which German racial epithets have been used for "name-calling"—among them "*Kraut. Fritz. Hun.*" (51). In the second epigraph to this chapter, Heist claims to be presenting "A lesson in tolerance, if you will" (51) by presenting the example of Mr. Fritz:

> A loyal Canadian these many years, a Canadian of German extraction, he was not allowed to enlist. Volunteered and was *refused*. Barred because of his name—a name that evokes the worst sort of bigotry. (51)

Fritz, as Duffy explains in a recent interview, was an actual historical figure, whose tombstone was engraved with the ironic phrase "Fifteen years a citizen" because, despite his loyalty to Canada, he was not allowed to "join the Canadian army" (Andrews 2016, 3). What Heist proceeds to suggest to the students is that even citizenship cannot guarantee recognition or inclusion of German-Canadians, given shifts in political power. He reminds students that the Lunenburg area of Nova Scotia was populated in the eighteenth century by German Protestants "at the behest of the British. ... To make settlements against the [French] Catholics" (Duffy 2013, 51). The British merely displaced one population with another to secure British rule.

In the same interview, Duffy explains that the recruitment of Germans was prompted by the Governor General of the day who feared that British imports could not build a community, describing them as "drunk ... and ... slothful" (Andrews 2016, 4). As a result, the Governor General turned to Germany as a source for hardworking laborers who were regarded as more suitable to settle the new colony than the British. In a pointedly ironic twist, Duffy employs the character of Heist to mimic this same kind of racist attitude in his own classroom. Rather than taking aim at the Brits, Heist targets a specific segment of the German population: the Prussians. Heist argues that Germany, which he explains is composed of a variety of groups, is now being "held hostage by the few" (51). He pointedly contrasts the "rich heritage of [German] letters, music, science, and philosophy" with the "arrogant, unlettered" Prussians whom he describes as being "against freedom! ... Against culture!" and "Against parl-i-a-mentary government!" (53). Heist squarely blames Prussian leader Otto von Bismarck for subduing Germany, focusing only on military aspirations, and setting the stage for the outbreak of World War I, much to the horror of "the peace-loving peoples of Bavaria" and "[t]he rest of Germany" (54). For Heist, then, the Allies (including Canada) should be understood as a force of liberation, not only working to protect the freedoms of his students in Snag Harbour, but also bringing "freedom to the peoples of Germany" by crushing the legacy of the Prussian leader and his followers (54). The danger of Heist's claims to superiority is that the Germans, like the Acadians, are expendable at any time if they fail to represent British colonialist values.

Nonetheless, in *The Cartographer of No Man's Land*, Heist concludes his lecture to the students by insisting that the anti-German discourse that has been circulating on the school playground is exclusionary and unacceptable. He tells the students, "*Krrraut* and *Hun, Bosch* and *Frrritz*! I will not tolerate this intolerance" and calls on them to remember that, although local men possessing a "peaceable German heritage from all up and down this province, are this very minute fighting in the Canadian army," others such as "*Fritze*," "[a] man as Canadian as you," have been "Ostracized" and excluded from service (Duffy 2013, 54).

Duffy describes this moment in *The Cartographer of No Man's Land* as intentionally evocative of the paranoia of the era, a moment that may seem unbelievable to contemporary readers (including her own British editor), but which captures the genuine belief of the day that Germany could and would invade Britain if not stopped. The "florid language" drawn from original source material is coupled with Heist offering a "self-serving" and deeply ironic version of events (Duffy, qtd. in Andrews 2018, 149). Yet, for Duffy, the challenge of this scene in the novel is that the irony of Heist's stance "escapes almost every reader" (Andrews 2016, 4).

Given that, as Linda Hutcheon has argued, irony requires the recognition of its doubled edge by the discursive communities it addresses, in this instance, what emerges is a shared and sustained experience of ignorance on both sides of the Canada-US border. Duffy notes that, for American readers, the history of Nova Scotian settlement and Canada's contributions to the First World War are part of a broad lack of familiarity with the US' northern neighbor. Canadians, depending upon their location, may not know about the German colonization of Nova Scotia but likely have been exposed to Canada's successes in the First World War through school curriculum content, education programs, and the public memorialization that occurs on and around Remembrance Day. (Notably, four provinces, including Nova Scotia, do not recognize it as a statutory holiday.) However, most Canadians remain unaware of the existence of Canadian internment camps for Germans during that same war.

THE ROLE OF SIMON

In *The Cartographer of No Man's Land*, Duffy uses the character of Simon, a teen boy, to explore the challenges readers face when forced to engage with the undesirable aspects of Canadian history, particularly when one is both enmeshed in and physically removed from the actuality of war. Simon is too young to enlist, but his father, Angus, is serving overseas and his uncle, Ebbin, is missing in action. Over the course of the novel, Simon witnesses the increasing hostility shown toward his favorite teacher, once a respected leader in the community, simply because Heist is German.

On a daily basis, Simon is surrounded by propaganda such as war posters that are prominently displayed in the windows of local stores. In particular, Simon is obsessed with a military enlistment card he has mysteriously acquired. The card graphically depicts a "crouching ape in his German spike-tipped helmet" and pointed fangs. The ape threateningly clutches a "fainting maiden [with an exposed breast] in his brutish arm" (Duffy 2013, 65). The card includes an equally horrific backdrop with a "sinking navy ship, and beyond it, a town in flames." As Simon notes, the ape on the recruitment card carries "a spiked club with the word '*Kultur*' dripping in blood on it," evidence for Heist's claim that "[c]ulture and decency [are being] dragged into the mud by the Prussians" (Duffy 2013, 65). But, ironically, Simon hides his card in a book of poems written by Mr. Heist, concealing this brutal image within a work of cultural sophistication created by a German-Canadian man.

However, Simon accidentally drops the recruitment card during a local ladies' tea hosted by his mother to prepare comfort boxes for serving soldiers and to help the overseas war effort. The card prompts a strong reaction from the women. They are horrified by the bestial image of a German monster but are equally quick to condemn Heist, despite knowing him personally. Local British aristocrat Lady Bromley most vocally criticizes the teacher for "splitting hairs over who is and is not the enemy" (Duffy 2013, 66). She accuses him of "tricking our students" and labels him "[u]npatriotic" (67). Like Heist, who is "replicating the kind of rhetoric you see in [anti-German] recruitment cards," Lady Bromley employs her moral superiority as a community member with strong colonial roots and class status to counter his claims of innocence (Andrews 2016, 4). Here, propaganda triumphs over reason.

Simon is in the uncomfortable position of witnessing the turning of the tides against his teacher, who seems oblivious to the growing danger he faces by remaining in his hometown. Heist relishes the solitude of his cottage with a view of the bay, filled with books. Being a learned man, he naively believes that his status as a "loyal, upstanding member of the community … —fifteen years a citizen" and his role as a scholar and educator will keep him safe (Duffy 2013, 308), despite Simon's repeated warnings that his behavior is being read as suspicious by the community. However, his desire to watch local schooners and whales, his plans to build a lookout tower to better his view of the area's natural beauty, and his ritual of observing underwater life using a rowboat perversely lead to his firing, the search and seizure of Heist's belongings, and his eventual imprisonment.

An Alternative Voice of Reason and Resistance

Simon's grandfather, Duncan McGrath, who has become an adamant pacifist after losing his brother in the Boer War, counters the racist rhetoric of Lady Bromley by disbanding the tea and confronting Simon about his willingness to accept war propaganda as fact. He also models a version of resistance for Simon by standing up to local condemnation of Heist when the teacher's house is searched by the Royal Canadian Mounted Police (RCMP), when his belongings are seized, and when he is sent off to the Amherst internment camp: "It was Simon's grandfather, not Mr. Heist, who had to be physically moved from the door of Mr. Heist's cottage; … his grandfather who got roughly knocked to the ground when he tried to wrest the telescope from their hands" (Duffy 2013, 313–314). Heist, who is in a state of shock, remains seated quietly at his kitchen table.

And in a more visible symbolic gesture, on the Sunday after Heist's arrest, Duncan, who is a member of the local Protestant congregation, stands up and accuses the members of "turning on one of their own" before walking out with Simon by his side (Duffy 2013, 314). This gesture pointedly recalls Heist's lecture to his students about Britain's strategic use of Protestant German immigrants to counter the presence of French Catholics. Duncan, who is not German and thus far less vulnerable to imprisonment, is able to expose the disposability of Germans as a model minority in the case of Canada based on the state of contemporary international relations.

Heist's influence on Simon's life continues after his arrest and confinement at the Amherst camp. He asks Simon to care for his garden and borrow his books while he is being "detained," which as the young boy soon learns "turned out to be a nice way of saying 'held prisoner'" and "'camp,' a nice way of saying 'prison'" (Duffy 2013, 321). Heist is kept there, despite being neither "an alien," "an enemy combatant," nor an "enemy sympathizer" (321), and along with other prisoners finds himself "stacked up in bunks two deep and three high with hardly space to breathe," lines that closely echo the description of the camp by Leon Trotsky in his autobiography.

Unsurprisingly Mr. Heist's letters to Simon grow increasingly desperate, revealing that he is "miserable and heartbroken" at Amherst, losing hope on a daily basis (Duffy 2013, 344). Although he has been Simon's Greek tutor and initially encourages the boy to keep working on his translations, by November 1917, "there was no reference to the suffering of Agamemnon or Troy, only to the suffering of Mr. Heist in the wretched conditions in which he found himself. He said the search for a single thing of beauty was fading" (345). To cheer him up, Simon copies a meticulous sketch of the *Morpho didius* butterfly from a color plate in Mr. Heist's bound volume, *Lepidotera of North and South America*. The book is an insect catalogue of species, which he first learned about while visiting Heist at his cottage.

Morpho didius is a rare species, confined to South America, and named for its ability, as Heist explains, to undergo a "metamorphosis" (Duffy 2013, 182). With wings of iridescent blue on top and mottled brown on the bottom, this butterfly is a master of disguise and transformation. It ultimately shifts, according to Heist, from "caterpillar to chrysalis to ... butterfly, so light on its wing—that is pure beauty" (182). When Simon initially queries Heist about whether he collects butterfly species—or other specimens—the schoolteacher uses it as pedagogical opportunity to stress the value of observing the world and engaging with it rather than trying to control it. During the same conversation, Simon learns that Heist has "had three cousins killed in the war," losses that the boy later realizes must have occurred "on the other side of the line" (183, 185).

As Heist spends more time in the Amherst camp, Simon finds it increasingly challenging to bear witness to the complexities of his mentor's situation. Simon has been sending drawings to his teacher to keep his spirits up while witnessing Heist's growing desperation. Simon sees Heist unjustly suffering while the community views the teacher as a traitor. So, when Heist expresses interest in and respect for the ideas of Trotsky and his followers at the Amherst camp, Simon chooses the easiest interpretation (that of the prevailing culture) and treats Heist's decision to align himself with fellow prisoners as evidence of the teacher's duplicity. Simon's reaction mirrors the turning away of mainstream culture from complex narratives that ask a person to hold more than one perspective. Duffy's novel shares the story of Heist to complicate reductive and superficial narratives of Canadian national pride and inclusivity that ignore the intricacies of the Canadian nation-state and its own history of racism.

In his final letter to Simon, Heist describes how he has found allies among his fellow prisoners, "Dymetro and Johann, sturdy fellows who shared potato-peeling duty with him" and "rescued his spectacles when a fight broke out" (Duffy 2013, 360). Like the *Morpho didius* whose wing colors camouflage and thus protect the species, Dymetro and Johann "mercifully" take the aging schoolteacher "under their wing" and provide sanctuary from what he describes as the "louts and bullies that populated the camp" (360). Heist realizes that ensuring his survival necessitates aligning himself with his champions who become followers of Trotsky, who was imprisoned at Amherst for approximately a month in the spring of 1917 after being removed from a "Norwegian ship docked in Halifax enroute from New York to Europe" (Cumberland).

Seen as potentially contributing to further unrest in Russia that might derail the country's commitment to the Allies, Trotsky was separated from his family in Halifax and sent to Amherst, where he encountered a captive audience filled with men who had had little contact with the outside world and were eager to champion a cause. The result, as Silver Donald Cameron explains in his *Canadian Geographic* article, was that when Trotsky was interned in Amherst, he "bec[a]me a hero to the prisoners," providing an eloquent and persuasive vision of the value of revolution while also "vigorous in his complaints about the defects of the camp administration" (1988, 3). For Heist and his friends, Trotsky becomes a symbol of "change," giving the schoolteacher what he describes to Simon as "the courage to survive" (Duffy 2013, 360). Moreover, Heist informs his young protégé that Simon "probably didn't realize how critical this moment in history was," noting that "Few of your countrymen do" (360), a comment that devastates the boy, who views it as a betrayal of trust.

In anger, Simon tosses Heist's "books into the bay—his butterflies and Greeks. The key to his stupid cottage," taking the experience as a lesson that it is impossible to truly know or rely on other people (Duffy 2013, 361). He then heads out on the water with his teen friends in an unreliable boat and almost drowns, only to be rescued at the last minute by his father, Angus. Simon's reaction to Heist stands in stark contrast to that of Angus, whose story is woven throughout Duffy's novel as an example of someone who can comprehend the complexities and contradictions that shape both the reality of life on the frontlines of war and in rural Nova Scotia.

Early in the novel, Angus sets off to Europe in search of his brother-in-law, Ebbin, whose whereabouts are unknown. Despite having presumed that he would be far from the battlefield, Angus soon finds himself an active participant in the horrific brutality of trench warfare and realizes that his only goal is to "[s]tay alive" (Duffy 2013, 26). Over the course of his time in service, Angus also learns about what has happened to Ebbin. Ebbin has accidentally killed a fellow officer. Rather than face charges, Ebbin transforms himself into a hero and postpones the inevitability of death, if only temporarily, by acquiring the name and tags of another soldier. By the end of the story, Angus is seasoned by war and learns to appreciate the uncertainty of his brother-in-law's fate. So, while Simon responds to Heist's shift in alliances with anger and disappointment, Angus, who is newly returned from the frontlines of battle, takes a very different approach to the German internment camp prisoner. Angus has gained the experience over time to recognize and appreciate how individuals make decisions strategically and pragmatically to ensure their survival. For Angus, Heist's decision to befriend his fellow prisoners is a pragmatic decision, one he makes to secure his future.

THE LESSONS OF *THE CARTOGRAPHER OF NO MAN'S LAND*

For Duffy, Simon's impulsive reaction to Heist's perceived betrayal is juxtaposed with Angus' recognition that the German schoolteacher's behavior at the camp is motivated by self-preservation. The result is a novel that cultivates "ambiguity" (Andrews 2016, 6) in a deliberate attempt to raise questions about the moral and ethical complexities of the First World War, both overseas and at home in the Maritimes. By taking this approach, *The Cartographer of No Man's Land* rejects the often presumptively celebratory associations between Canadian national identity and the First World War, rhetoric that was echoed with the anniversary of the Canadian troops' triumph over German forces at Vimy Ridge, including free educational lesson plans posted on the Veterans Affairs site. Notably, a search of the site reveals a single photo of a Christmas Day celebration at an unnamed Canadian internment camp but provides no other records of this aspect of the First World War.

Instead, Duffy's novel prompts a closer look at one of the tourist souvenirs produced by those who were imprisoned. The Regimental Museum houses a hand-carved working wooden cello and bow, an object of remarkable beauty, produced by a prisoner at the camp. The skill and elegance of this piece bear consideration, because the cello head embodies a significant set of contradictions. Donated in 2007, the cello had been housed in an attic and mistaken for a fiddle, before being taken to be refinished by a professional cello restorer. It remains, as the framed explanation of the cello's origins outlines, "playable." In particular, the head of the cello is carved in a unique fashion, portraying what could be described as a caricature of a human face with wide lips, a strong, flat nose, and piercing eyes, while the scroll of the instrument forms two ears. The same museum description explains that "[t]he head of the cello was carved in the likeness of a sergeant the prisoners did not like." The carver of the head of the cello employs racist characteristics, typically associated with Black stereotypes, in order to mock a white sergeant whose treatment of the internment camp prisoners is regarded as especially egregious. The result is a layered ugliness with the cello head depicting a white person as Black to undercut their power and authority within the camp.

When placed in conversation with *The Cartographer of No Man's Land*, the cello head offers two powerful counter-narratives to the pervasive circulation of British war propaganda, which explicitly reduces the German population—including Mr. Heist—to the level of monstrous traitors, incapable of producing sophisticated cultural content. The cello, both head and body, attests to the fact that the interned German prisoners can and do create stylish and complex objects of beauty. But this musical instrument also subverts and challenges the racist tropes that pervade British war propaganda, by employing similar Black tropes to undermine white British and

Canadian authority over those being held at the camp. The prisoners reconfigure and demean the presumably white camp sergeant by creating what appears to be an object of high culture, yet the cello head holds its own mixed messages for those who recognize the invocation of Black stereotypes and critique of this figure of authority within the camp.

The use of racist tropes like those manifested in the cello head were a prominent part of late nineteenth-century advertising in most colonial nations. David Ciarlo explains in *Advertising Empire: Race and Visual Culture in Imperial Germany* that typically Black people were depicted as having "enormous red lips, oversized eyes and ears, and bumpy heads" (2011, 11). Advertising was employed to create and reinforce ideas of "nation- and race-building" (137), relying on the "popularity of the 'science' of race … [,] a broad fascination with an exotic 'Other,'" familiarity with the minstrel stereotype, and the "legacy of … slavery," to cultivate and sustain the most popular caricatured versions of Black people (2–3). Britain and the US employed racial imagery extensively to advertise products, with American print ads often depicting extreme versions of Black American racial stereotypes that in turn spurred German advertisers and graphic designers (many of whom became globally known) to use similar images.

The development of technology to create mass-market newspapers and magazines in Germany and the fact that "[b]y 1914 a coherent vision of racial difference was stereotypified and broadcast to virtually every person in Germany" (2011, 24) meant that "blackness" became the defining foil for the white German (315). According to Ciarlo, it was "nearly impossible to find images of blacks that do *not* deploy" the ingrained conventions of racialization (291). Of course, Germany, like the Maritimes, had its own Black populations, but these communities typically were ignored, enabling "highly visible constructions … [to obscure] social complexity in powerful ways" (19). As Harvey Amani Whitfield (2016) has documented, slavery existed in the Maritime colonies, and, despite the desire of Canadians to perpetuate a history of inclusivity, "anti-Blackness" remains a foundational part of Canada as a nation and "continues to hide in plain sight" 150 years after Confederation (Maynard 2017, 3). Similarly, Germany also drew extensively on the figure of the "African native" because of the Herero and Namaqua genocides in the early years of the twentieth century, which literalized the extermination of blackness in a colonial context (Ciarlo 2011, 276). Despite Canada's efforts to position itself as better than the Americans or Germans in its handling of racism, the cello provides evidence of intricate ways in which Black racist stereotypes are mobilized in Canada by those who find themselves persecuted, in this case by a white sergeant, for not being Canadian enough and therefore undesirable or threatening to Canadian security and harmony, especially in times of war.

By carving the caricatured face into a cello, an elaborate and complex handmade musical instrument with an illustrious role within the development of classical music, the prisoners ensured that this explicit inversion of racial stereotypes employing familiar stereotypes of Black people in Africa, Europe, and North America would be framed and contained by an adherence to high-culture norms. The cello head rendered the sergeant monstrously unrecognizable to everyone except the prisoners, who were presumed to lack "the ability to consciously manipulate notions of visuality" for their own purposes (Cobb 2015, 36), much like enslaved Black Americans who, as Jasmine Cobb argues in *Picturing Freedom: Remaking Black Visuality in the Early Nineteenth Century*, frequently employed "deliberate representational practices" to challenge their bondage while trying to avoid potentially deadly repercussions (76). Without equating the two populations or their situations, the cello is a powerful example of using one visual stereotype to counter another, creating a complex layering of meanings for the instrument's creator and his prison community. And, of course, high-culture norms kept the cello safely stored for decades in a local attic, despite its unusual head, ensuring its survival because it appeared to adhere to predominantly white community norms.

Like the cello that remains tucked in a corner of a small, chronically under funded regional museum, Duffy's narrative has been largely ignored by Maritime book reviewers and booksellers, despite being lauded throughout the US and the rest of Canada. The cello represents a very complicated, ugly, and confrontational depiction of a moment in time that Canadians would rather glorify than probe carefully. Similarly, *The Cartographer of No Man's Land* challenges some of the foundational beliefs that have defined Canada, and particularly Atlantic Canada, as different from and better than its neighbor to the south. As Herb Wyile points out in *Anne of Tim Hortons*, the "commonplace idea that Canada as a federation is a kind of mosaic," fueled by stereotypically bucolic images of "fishing sheds" in the "East Coast," has been fundamentally troubled by the uneven development of capital across Canada (2011, 7–8). Yet in order to survive economically, the region has trafficked in the rejection of "technological progress and mass consumption" (Wyile 2011, 148); the latter has created what Ian McKay famously described as "a Folk society, natural, and traditional" (2014, 32), including the production of "folk art," as part of a nostalgic vision of a "past of ethnic and cultural cohesion" free from "the burdens of sophistication" (Morton 2016, 19).

The Cartographer of No Man's Land problematizes such efforts by exposing the contradictory dimensions of nationalism during the First World War and Canada's discomfort in acknowledging publicly a complex history of racism that stains, especially in the case of the Maritimes, a folk culture that is essential to its economic survival. Duffy's text rejects the positioning of Canada as a site of refuge for populations that have been marginalized or perceived as a threat to national security by depicting the existence of the Amherst internment camp and exploring its impact on the local community. As camp records reveal, prisoners in fact looked southward to the US as a place of potential escape, reversing the perception of Canada as a safe haven from the American melting pot.

Duffy's novel also probes the difficult decisions that people make when confronted with fundamental threats to their humanity and asks readers to engage with these issues rather than ignoring them in the service of national unity or pride. Just as Angus recognizes Mr. Heist's shifting alliances while confined to the Amherst prison as a critical strategy of self-preservation, one that Simon struggles to understand, so too may Duffy's novel be read as cautionary tale for those who embrace Canadian exceptionalism, when it is all too easy to appear more inclusive and progressive. The cello and its carved head remind us that so-called aliens, those who were confined to the Amherst internment camp, serve as an important rejoinder and a significant voice for better understanding the Canadian legacy of World War I, particularly in Nova Scotia. Likewise, *The Cartographer of No Man's Land* offers a nuanced consideration of a chapter in Canadian history that has been primarily used to bolster Canada's identity as a distinct country. Instead, Duffy's book raises critical questions about how to understand the legacy of German immigration to the Maritimes and the ways in which this population has been both embraced and persecuted in the service of building a nation.

Notes

1. See also Kassandra Luciuk's graphic novel *Enemy Alien: A True Story of Life Behind Barbed Wire* for a compelling "Introduction," which describes her discovery of a memoir of a Ukrainian Canadian man interned at the Kapuskasing Internment Camp between 1914 and 1917. In it she notes that

"[i]nternment … was not a lone enterprise or isolated event; it was part and parcel of Canada's longstanding and unjust treatment toward populations it deemed 'undesirable others'" (2020, viii). Luciuk persuasively argues that "internment was not a regretful anomaly, but rather part of the regular functioning of nation building" (viii).

2. The opening sentence of Lauren Berlant's *The Anatomy of National Fantasy: Hawthorne, Utopia, and Everyday Life* states that "Nations provoke fantasy" (1991, 1). While Berlant focuses on the American dimensions of this argument, I argue in the "Preface" that this claim is readily imported to a Canadian context.

3. See http://www.internmentcanada.ca/index.cfm for information about this organization, which "exists to support projects that commemorate and recognize the experiences of all ethno-cultural communities affected by Canada's first national internment operations of 1914–1920." It is funded by a ten-million-dollar endowment, which was the result of a 2008 agreement between the federal government of Canada, the Ukrainian Canadian Civil Liberties Association, the Ukrainian Canadian Congress, and the Ukrainian Canadian Foundation of Taras Shevchenko.

References

Andrews, Jennifer. 2016. P.S. Duffy Interview Transcript: December 14, 2016. Interviewer's Copy. 1–11.

———. 2018. A Trio of Voices About American Literary Portraits of Canada with Authors Ben Farmer, Beth Powning, and P.S. Duffy. *Canadian Review of American Studies* 48 (Supp. 1): 98–161.

Berlant, Lauren. 1991. *The Anatomy of National Fantasy: Hawthorne, Utopia, and Everyday Life*. Chicago: University of Chicago Press.

Cameron, Silver Donald. 1988. Trotsky in Amherst. *Canadian Geographic*. https://www.silverdonaldcameron.ca/articles/trotsky-in-amherst-canadian-geographic-1988/

Ciarlo, David. 2011. *Advertising Empire: Race and Visual Culture in Imperial Germany*. Cambridge: Harvard University Press.

Cobb, Jasmine Nichole. 2015. *Picturing Freedom: Remaking Black Visuality in The Early Nineteenth Century*. New York: New York University Press.

Coulson, Ray. n.d. Transcript of a Public Lecture About the Amherst Internment Camp Given to the Amherst Rotary Club. 1–5.

Cumberland County Museum. n.d. The Amherst Prisoner of War Internment Camp, 1915–1919.

Duffy, P.S. 2013. *The Cartographer of No Man's Land: A Novel*. Toronto: Penguin.

Furlong, Pauline. 2001. *Historic Amherst*. Halifax: Nimbus.

Luciuk, Lobomyr. 2001. *In Fear of the Barbed Wire Fence: Canada's First National Internment Operations and the Ukrainian Canadians, 1914–1920.* Kingston: Kashtan.

Luciuk, Kassandra. 2020. *Enemy Alien: A True Story of Life Behind Barbed Wire.* Toronto: Between the Lines.

Maynard, Robyn. 2017. *Policing Black Lives: State Violence in Canada from Slavery to the Present.* Halifax: Fernwood.

McKay, Ian. 2014. *The Quest of the Folk: Antimodernism and Cultural Selection in Twentieth-Century Nova Scotia.* Montreal & Kingston: McGill-Queen's University Press.

Morton, Erin. 2016. *For Folk's Sake: Art and Economy in Twentieth-Century Nova Scotia.* Montreal & Kingston: McGill-Queen's University Press.

Savoie, Donald. 2006. *Visiting Grandchildren: Economic Development in the Maritimes.* Toronto: University of Toronto.

Stevenson, Garth. 2014. *Building Nations from Diversity: Canadian and American Experience Compared.* Montreal & Kingston: McGill-Queens University Press.

Trotsky, Leon. 1930. *My Life.* New York: Charles Scribner's Sons.

Whitfield, Harvey Amani. 2016. *North to Bondage: Loyalist Slavery in the Maritimes.* Vancouver: University of British Columbia Press.

Wyile, Herb. 2011. *Anne of Tim Hortons: Globalization and the Reshaping of Atlantic-Canadian Literature.* Waterloo: Wilfrid Laurier University Press.

CHAPTER 5

Becoming Bird(ie): Exposing Canadian Government Complicity with Forced Adoptions in Christina Sunley's *The Tricking of Freya*

> *Animals have long acted as boundary makers [and breakers] between fundamental categories. (Braidotti 2011, 84, my insertion)*
>
> *The movement of children (with or without their families) back and forth across the Canada-US border was hardly a new phenomenon in the mid-twentieth century. Large and small migrations across the 'world's longest undefended border' have been a feature of Canadian and American history for as long as the border has been defined. By the twentieth century, it was not uncommon for the same family to have branches in both countries, and occasionally children crossed from one country to the other to be formally or informally adopted by family or friends on the other side. (Balcom 2015, 6–7)*
>
> *Birdie nicknamed herself early on: she couldn't wrap her tongue around* Ingibjorg. *Birdie* stuck. *Because a bird can be so many things. A sadglad bird. A madmad bird. A mockingbird chattering at hummingbird speed. A snarky gull, a brooding raven. A finch smashing itself against windows. Or a woman who mistakes glass for air, words for wings. (Sunley 2009, 6)*

In *The Tricking of Freya*, American writer Christina Sunley examines how a toxic legacy of secrets involving a hidden story of mental illness and forced adoption shapes the narrative of an Icelandic family that first immigrated to Gimli, Manitoba, in the aftermath of the volcanic eruption of Mount Askja in 1875 and put down Canadian roots.[1] Sunley explores the

Icelandic and Canadian communities' efforts to maintain a veneer of respectability when it comes to the story of her twenty-first-century protagonist Freya Morris' origins. The novel also considers the power of healing when the truth is brought to light, offering up Freya's life as a potential metaphor for better understanding the complexities of Canada as a nation with its own increasingly secretive stories of misdeeds that threaten the country's comfortable narrative of a "peaceable kingdom."

Chapter 3 examines the representation of the Acadian Deportation in Longfellow's classic poem and Ben Farmer's recent novel, offering a comparative exploration of a relatively well-known event in Canadian history that has been rewritten to such an extent that there is national profiting from the romanticism associated with this tragedy. In contrast, the Amherst internment camp depicted in P.S. Duffy's *The Cartographer of No Man's Land*, discussed in Chap. 4 is much less familiar to most Canadians. The carved wooden objects that exist to document the intricate relationship of the prisoners to their captors along with staged photographs of the individuals being held at the camps, are, if shown publicly, relegated to displays at underfunded small museums, with little to no provincial or national circulation. Moreover, representations of the internment camp have been reframed and manipulated to suggest that the prisoners at Amherst were not treated particularly badly, despite facts that contradict this claim. Chapter 5 goes further by probing an American fictional depiction of a period in Canadian history that has been strategically hidden from public view: the trafficking of babies across the Canada-US border and the Canadian government's sustained involvement in and support of this practice. While all three of these historic events— the Acadian Deportation, the Amherst internment camp, and the trafficking of babies across the Canada-US border—represent the same colonialist values that shape this study in its entirety, each American-authored text about each historic event probes a specific moment in Canada's past to raise fundamental questions about Canada's self-positioning as a more virtuous and principled nation that its neighbor to the south.

The Tricking of Freya chronicles Freya's lifelong quest to uncover the truth about her family's origins, a journey that is made all the more complicated by the fact that hers is an immigration story that spans three countries: Canada, the US, and Iceland. Freya must overcome the reluctance of family, community, and country—all forces that seek to erase the narratives of immigrant women and children. Freya can feel the legacy of her past pulling at her and even threatening her life, though she does not learn the secret of her parentage until the end of the novel. By exploring this triangulated relationship of legal and illegal immigration, Sunley probes the complex and shifting links between Freya's Icelandic family lineage in Canada and Iceland and her life in New York City. Like P.S. Duffy's *The Cartographer of No Man's Land* discussed in the previous chapter, *The Tricking of Freya* tracks the gradual disclosure of familial and community secrets that span multiple countries and repeatedly cross the Atlantic Ocean in an effort to expose another series of untold stories about Canada's past, present, and future.

Babies and Borders

As Karen Balcom explains in *The Traffic in Babies: Cross-border Adoption and Baby-Selling Between the United States and Canada, 1930–1972*, which forms the second epigraph to this chapter, "[t]he movement of children (with or without their families) back and forth across the Canada-US border was hardly a new phenomenon in the mid-twentieth century. Large and small migrations across the 'world's longest undefended border' … have been a feature … for as long as the border has been defined" (2015, 7). Moreover, she notes that "it was not uncommon for the same family to have branches in both countries, and occasionally children crossed from one country to the other to be formally or informally adopted by family or friends on the other side" (7), the very situation that enables what Freya later learns was her own cross-border adoption.

Balcom's work focuses primarily on the relationships between and among child welfare professionals within Canada and the US and across the nations' shared border within the context of the for-profit adoption market. She describes how "[a]s babies crossed borders, they slipped between legal jurisdictions and arenas of governmental responsibility" (2015, 4). The result, she argues, was that "adopted children, adoptive parents, and birth mothers disappeared into the space between two (or more) sets of child welfare and immigration policies and law" (4).

In the concluding pages of *The Tricking of Freya*, Freya discovers a letter Birdie has written to her female cousin, Thorunn, whom she befriended while visiting Iceland. Confined to a Manitoba asylum since experiencing mania followed by deep depression while traveling in Iceland the previous summer, Birdie delivers a premature but healthy baby girl on February 18, 1965. She is given two choices by her mother, Sigga, and a nurse who befriends Sigga, Halldora Bjarnason: to surrender the infant in a "Blind Adoption" in which "*I would never see her again and she would never be able to learn who I am. Or, I can give her to* [her sister] *Anna to raise. Under the condition that she never knows who her real mother is!"* (Sunley 2009, 336). Fearful that she might be forever separated from her child, Birdie promises "to abide by this [secret] arrangement" (336). Despite clearly being coerced, she does not have the means to overturn the decision made by her *"mother[,] ... sister[,] ... doctors and the Canadian government"* (337). In contrast to the tradition of fostering and open adoptions in Iceland, Sigga immediately takes the infant across the Canada-US border to live with her "[b]arren" daughter, Anna, and her accountant husband in the US (12), a decision that has long lasting and tragic consequences, including Birdie's suicide on Freya's fourteenth birthday.

Birdie's baby is not sold for profit nor is Birdie completely cut off from her daughter, as evidenced by the extended trips Anna eventually takes to Gimli to visit her family, including her sister, with her adoptive daughter. However, by giving birth in an asylum in small-town Canada, Birdie is particularly vulnerable to familial exploitation along with provincial and federal legal systems that do not respect her parental rights precisely because she is unmarried and institutionalized due to mental illness. By placing Birdie's baby at a considerable physical distance from her birth mother, across a national border no less, Sigga and Anna hope to ensure that their secret will be safe. But they cannot account for the imaginative possibilities that Aunt Birdie offers to her unacknowledged daughter, Freya, promising her over the phone that when she visits Gimli, "I'll teach you how to fly" (Sunley 2009, 21). Bird flight becomes one way to challenge the concept of borders—whom they protect and whom they keep in and out. The metaphoric invocation of flight functions as a reminder to readers that nation-state borders are irrelevant to those bird species that migrate, including the millions of birds that travel yearly between Canada and the US, who have been protected by a joint Treaty since 1916, from being abducted, captured, killed, or sold, unlike Birdie's infant.[2] But Birdie remains locked out of the life of her child by a border, which is part of the impetus for her lifelong search for transcendence to animal.

In the first epigraph of this chapter, feminist philosopher Rosi Braidotti claims that "[a]nimals have long acted as boundary makers [and breakers] between fundamental categories" (2011, 84, my insertion). Sunley's Birdie is no exception. Using Braidotti's exploration of animals in *Nomadic Theory*, the roles of birds and other animals in traditional Old Norse mythology, and recent scholarship that examines the hidden legacy of forced adoptions in Canada, this chapter investigates how birds and their female human namesake in Christina Sunley's novel offer a way, by "becoming animal," to "destabiliz[e] the axis of naturalized difference" (81) that relegates unmarried pregnant women and the mentally ill to the margins of society and allows others to determine their future. Braidotti furthers this argument by positing "a qualitative shift" in the relationship between humans and animals that offers "an ethical appreciation of what bodies (human, animal, others) can do" (85). In a recent interview, Sunley explains that she sees birds as embodying "the magical possibilities of flight" (qtd. in J. Andrews 2020, 7) and connects "this interest in flying to creativity and … wanting to be part of some kind of extraordinary world" (7). These same qualities are central to Freya's and Birdie's characters as they refuse to play the preordained roles that they have been assigned as white, middle-class women of Icelandic descent, roles that favor propriety over the acknowledgment of their intimate biological and creative connection. *The Tricking of Freya* employs bird symbolism and bird metaphors—which will be discussed in more detail shortly—to explore the untold story of forced adoption in Canada, a practice that remains unfamiliar to most Canadians.

Unwed Mothers

As Valerie Andrews explains in her 2018 book (which started as a groundbreaking 2017 MA thesis), *White Unwed Mothers: The Adoption Mandate in Canada*, between 1940 and 1970, roughly 300,000 white unwed mothers in Canada were forced to surrender their newborn infants. In *White Unwed Mothers* Andrews documents how "young, white, respectable" women who produced children out of wedlock were viewed in Canada as "pathological subject[s] in need of a cure" (2018, 183). Andrews was motivated by her own experience as a 16-year-old white unwed mother who surrendered her son in a forced adoption in 1970. She reunited with her son as an adult, only to lose him to testicular cancer in 2008, prompting her to found a federal non-profit organization committed to advocating for the rights of adoptees and parents who were part of this phenomenon, and to begin researching the subject academically.[3] Andrews notes that "[u]nlike their [Black and Indigenous] counterparts, white middle-class unmarried mothers retained intrinsic social value by virtue of their whiteness" (22). Their reintegration into society was predicated on "adoption separation" (23). Ideally, once the infant was out of sight (and mind), the mothers could be rehabilitated "to the norms of legitimate marriage and normative white motherhood" (22–23). Australia,

New Zealand, the United Kingdom, and the US also introduced similar practices in the post-World War II era (21).

The coordinated provincial and national institutionalization of an adoption mandate in Canada marked a radical change from previous generations of babies born out of wedlock. Historically, "adoption was not widely used as a form of child transfer since the traits of the morally fallen were thought to be hereditary" (V. Andrews 2018, 23). While unwed mothers of babies in Canada in the nineteenth century had been cast as "fallen victims of seduction and abandonment" (61), these same women in the early twentieth century came to be perceived as "wilful actors and as a major cause of social ills" (61). In particular, a new discourse emerged after the release of a provincially commissioned report, *Upon the Care of the Feeble-Minded in Ontario, 1907*, which placed unmarried mothers in this category (V. Andrews 2018, 64). Pathologizing white women who gave birth out of wedlock, Andrews argues, reflected Anglo-Saxon Protestant anxieties regarding the lower fertility rates of white Anglophone Christians when compared to members of the French Catholic and "migrant communities" (64). By routinely sending "unmarried mothers ... to the psychiatric clinic" for assessment (65), government officials and healthcare providers ensured that these women's behaviors were stigmatized; the babies they delivered were also tainted. Medical eugenicists in Canada helped to limit the reproduction of so-called mental defectives (67) through the subsequent or simultaneous sterilization of unwed mothers.

These same women were also presumed to contribute to increased rates of sexually transmitted diseases in the inter-war period, making them into "sex delinquent[s]" in both Canada and the US, where they were routinely incarcerated or institutionalized (Kunzel 1993, 55). However, by the end of World War II, the medical, governmental, and public discourses surrounding the offspring of unmarried white women shifted dramatically as dominant beliefs in eugenics were displaced by "developmental theories" including the "clean slate" and the "clean break," respectively (V. Andrews 2018, 96–97), which viewed the newborn as untainted by its biological origins. Separating mothers from their babies at birth became common practice "to promote attachment to a surrogate as early in life as possible" (98). Priority was given to the needs of the adoptive parents in collaboration with the state and included the sealing of adoption records to protect the rights of the adoptive parents, a practice that continues to the present day in several provinces in Canada (among them Manitoba, where records disclosure still can be vetoed by either the birth parent or child individually).[4]

With the discharge of roughly 80,000 Canadian women who had either "served in the armed forces or worked in highly skilled jobs in the war industry" during the Second World War, there was "a renewed thrust of maternalism" (V. Andrews 2018, 153) in the postwar era. White middle-class females were urged to return home to fulfill more traditional roles in the private sphere. Cynthia Comacchio explains that in the US and Canada, this "postwar mother imperative" was "the central strategy of a politics of regeneration that would uplift both family and nation" (1999, 91). In the 1950s and 1960s, white married middle-class mothers on both sides of the Canada-US border were revered for their "ability to effect political change and nation building through their natural attributes as mothers" (V. Andrews 2018, 153). For those women who, despite possessing all the trappings of suburban affluence, were not able to produce biological children, adoption enabled them "to conform to the ideals of the nuclear family" (155), while also ensuring the redemption of the unmarried mother by releasing her from the burden of raising an illegitimate child. Birdie's story in *The Tricking of Freya* brings together various dimensions of this hidden history of Canada, as a white middle-class woman who, already pathologized because of her bipolar disorder and institutionalized by her family, becomes an ideal and forcibly compliant surrogate for her sister, Anna.

The Shame Is Ours

July 3, 2018, marked the release of a Canadian Senate Report titled *The Shame is Ours* calling on the federal government of Canada to issue a formal apology to all the women who were pressured into these kinds of agreements. Until this time, there had been no official acknowledgment of this chapter in Canada's history, despite allegations of abuse and coercion from over 500 mothers, adoptees, and fathers. The report was authored by members of the Senate Standing Committee on Social Affairs, Science, and Technology. It was based on research and substantive testimony delivered over three days in March 2018 by organizations, churches, government officials, scholarly experts from Canada and Australia (where an official federal government apology was delivered in 2013),[5] parents, and adoptees. The report provides "a detailed picture of this shameful period" in Canada "when human rights may have been violated" and laws potentially broken as a result of federal funding initiatives in the form of "social assistance grants and programs" intended to "address the needs of children, pregnant women and mothers" (Eggleton et al. 2018, 1–2).[6] While "adoption policies and practices are the responsibility of the provinces and territories" in Canada, the report specifically points to the ways in which the federal government facilitated forced adoptions, especially in the case of those that crossed "national borders because of its authority over immigration and citizenship matters" (2). In *The Tricking of* Freya, Birdie's story is complicated by her confinement to two different asylums while pregnant in Iceland and Canada, which echoes the early twentieth-century desire in Canada to treat unwed mothers as abnormal.

The story of Birdie's hidden pregnancy—the familial and institutional pressures and threats exerted on Birdie, when combined with the "clean break" process used to separate mother and child—follows the conventional patterns of forced adoption by ignoring the mother's wishes in favor of societal norms and values (V. Andrews 2018, 97). Birdie may be part of a highly literate second-generation Icelandic immigrant family, but her white middle-class lifestyle, level of education, fertility, and unmarried status also make her a perfect biological vessel (despite her bipolar disorder) to fulfill the destiny assigned to her sister. Indeed, Birdie's surrender of Freya is framed by Icelandic family friend and asylum nurse, Halldora Bjarnason, "as the greatest gift one sister can give to another" (Sunley 2009, 337), a sentiment that underlines for Birdie the perverse cruelty of this forced adoption and anticipates a legacy of pain for mother and child.[7]

Valerie Andrews' work on forced adoption in Canada also highlights a key scientific and consumer development: "the introduction of baby formula" (2018, 22). While absent from the Senate report, it played a fundamental role in facilitating forced adoptions that required newborns to be transported over considerable distances to their adoptive families, without ready access to breast milk. An article by Stevens et al., "A History of Infant Feeding," published in *The Journal of Perinatal Education*, describes the challenges of creating infant formula throughout the late nineteenth and early twentieth century, which led to the regulation of its composition and product advertising in the decades that followed: "By the 1940s and 1950s, physicians and consumers [in the US and Canada] regarded the use of formula as a well known, popular, and safe substitute for breastmilk" (2009, 36). In *The Tricking of Freya*, Freya pointedly recalls a photograph of herself as an infant in the arms of her grandmother Sigga, "expertly tilting the bottle to my lips" while "[m]y mother stands to the side, peering over at me[,]" looking "tentative [and] …

perplexed[,]" an image that hints at the use of formula rather than mother's breast milk precisely because Anna had not produced a baby, nor presumably attempted to induce lactation (Sunley 2009, 13).[8] Andrews notes that with the decline of breast-feeding, "bottle feeding became the norm," so while it did not cause the "adoption mandate," this innovation "served the mandate well" by ensuring that the separation of mother and child could be undertaken without compromising—at least visibly—infant health (V. Andrews 2018, 111).

When trying to make sense of her own past at the beginning of the novel, Freya argues, based on family photographs, that her parents were not "unhappy with their childless life," one that they appear to have accepted and even embraced (Sunley 2009, 12). Anna and her husband initially purchased a home in "the baby-booming subdivision where they'd planned to raise a family, ... [before moving] to an older neighborhood inhabited mostly by retirees. Not a tricycle in sight" (12). Freya speculates that while her parents, and especially her mother, had been ostracized for their status as "fruitless" and "sterile," they led "orderly lives" until Freya's arrival, which created a "startling splash into the calm waters of my parents' middle age" (12). Repeating her relative's constructed narrative of her birth, Freya describes her grandmother, Sigga, taking "the train down from Canada, arriving shortly before my birth, [and] remaining three months after" (12). As mentioned, Freya notes Sigga's competence in cradling and feeding her, in contrast with Anna, clues that coupled with the bottle, suggest a very different story.

Yet, as Freya explains, "I don't claim to remember Sigga from this postnatal visit, and it would be seven years until I would see her again, seven years before I would meet my Aunt Birdie" (Sunley 2009, 13). Moreover, though Freya recognizes the disconnect between her own boundless energy and love of adventure as a young child and her mother's uncertainty regarding how to manage Freya, the ability to understand and make sense of this relationship can only happen by learning the truth of her origins. Sunley's novel provides a deeply compelling fictional account of this until recently unacknowledged chapter in Canadian history, using her narrative to explore—from the intimate first-person perspective of the grown adoptive child and through the letters of the birth mother—the lasting physical and psychological impacts of this separation of mother and daughter for both generations.

Becoming Animal

To understand the consequences of forced adoption and its pivotal role in creating what Lee in *Ingenious Citizenship* calls "normative citizens" (27) who comply with and replicate familiar and acceptable life narratives, Sunley employs birds, literally and metaphorically, to explore how so-called abject subjects attempt to and occasionally succeed in disrupting and appropriating these standardized scripts. By performing acts of "ingenious citizenship," these "abject subjects" work to "improvise more humane and inhabitable spaces for themselves" (Lee 2016, 27). Birds have a long and illustrious history in Old Norse mythology[9] but take on equal complex meanings for the New Icelanders in Canada. In particular, *The Tricking of Freya* specifically considers how the migration of the "Goolies" (supposedly from an Icelandic term meaning "blond" or "gold") to Canada, a nickname given to Icelanders by Anglo-Canadians when they first arrived in Canada, cultivates and perpetuates the marginalization of citizens like Birdie who value their Icelandic heritage but do not conform to post-World War II Canadian (and US) values which favored traditional heterosexual unions with wives functioning exclusively as homemakers for and caregivers of the next generation (Sunley 2009, 26).

In "Animals and Other Anomalies," Braidotti observes that relationships between humans and animals have been "framed" by the "dominant human and structurally masculine habit of taking for granted free access to and consumption of the bodies of others, animals included" (2011, 81). This mode of relations is inherently "violent" (81). For Braidotti, Jacques Derrida best captures the significance of this "human power over animals" with the word "carnophallogocentrism" (82), a term that Matthew Calarco glosses as "Derrida's term for the dominant model of the subject as speaking, virile, and carnivorous" (2003, 7). Through this neologism, Derrida exposes the problematic positioning of the white, Western, masculine speaking subject at the top of the hierarchy that underlies the "sacrificial structure" of Western philosophical, religious, and political discourses, a hierarchy that creates space "for ... [the] noncriminal putting to death" of animal-others (Derrida 1995, 279). In his efforts to unpack the significance of carnophallogocentrism, Ken Stone explains that "[t]he most obvious examples of a 'noncriminal putting to death' ... involve animals, whom we allow ourselves to kill without penalty for food, clothing, experimentation, and numerous other reasons," precisely because "we seldom grant ... [animals] the status of subject" (2017, 262). But Stone argues, in ways that resonate with Braidotti's analysis of the contradictions that are integral to "this human power over animals" (Braidotti 2011, 82), that "the 'noncriminal putting to death'" is not exclusively performed on "non-human animals" (Stone 2017, 262). Stone notes that "we frequently sacrifice ... humans as well, not only through literal and legal killing (one thinks of warfare, drones, the death penalty, and stand-your-ground laws in the United States) but also, Derrida notes, through our symbolic consumption and appropriation of others" (262). Certain categories of humans are equated with animals—and viewed as equally consumable.

In a well-known interview with Jean-Luc Nancy called "'Eating Well,' or the Calculation of the Subject," Derrida argues that it is "very difficult" and even "impossible to delimit" the distinctions between literal and symbolic sacrifice (1995, 278). Krishanu Maiti connects the blurring of moral and ethical boundaries to the ways in which "various minority groups ... have been denied the basic traits of subjectivity" (2013, 98). Like animals, certain humans "are excluded from the status of being full subjects," among them women, children, and those who are part of the subaltern (98). While Sunley's novel arguably depicts relatively economically privileged female characters from birth to death, descendants of Icelandic immigrants who may not fit the abject status of "people who are located in lowly, marginalized, and impoverished material conditions defined and produced by liberal societies" (Lee 2016, 14), *The Tricking of Freya* explores how Birdie and Freya negotiate the erasure of their bond as mother and daughter by aligning themselves with and refiguring themselves as animal-others. Regardless of their relative affluence, they do so at great personal cost.

For Braidotti, "becoming-animal" is one way of challenging a "mode of relation" that is "structurally violent and saturated accordingly with projections, identifications, and fantasies" (2011, 81) that include both "[d]esire and fear" for both "the animal outside but also the animal within" (82). In *The Tricking of Freya*, the animal within takes the form of women who struggle with mental illness—vividly described by Freya as the "madmad bird" legacy of her birth mother, who is forced to surrender her child to the care of her sister and eventually takes her own life (Sunley 2009, 6). Braidotti explains that while the young white male has traditionally been deemed the "rational animal," or the virile human who consumes animals, those (like Birdie) who don't fit this model are cast as deviant and monstrous (2011, 82).

Throughout *The Tricking of Freya*, the process and product of "becoming-animal" (Braidotti 2011, 84), in the form of metaphorical and occasionally literal birds, provide a way for the narrator of Sunley's text to create an "ethical code that can reconnect humans and animals" and, conversely, challenge "methodological" and ideological forms of nationalism that divide territories by relying on hierarchical structures of "speciesism" that favor certain humans over (animal-)others (85). Using the characters of Birdie and Freya, Sunley asks readers to re-examine the "moral and cognitive bestiary that uses animals as referents for values, norms, and morals" (84), to query deeply engrained clichés about women and mental illness, to probe the legacies of colonization and forced adoption, and, likewise, to think differently about dominant national stereotypes, which all too often envision Canada as more progressive and inclusive when compared with the US.

In contrast with her married sister, Anna, who "can sing and play the piano, embroider and knit ... But [is] no poet," Birdie traces her direct lineage to the "greatest Viking poet, Egil Skallagrimsson"; her father's uncle, "the famous farmer-poet Pall"; and her own father, Olafur, whose letters back to his homeland after he immigrated to Canada motivate Birdie to travel to Iceland to recover them (Sunley 2009, 2). Birdie aspires to continue this tradition (despite being female). Her goal, however, is partly thwarted by her pregnancy and the forced adoption of her daughter and later by the jealousy of an authoritative male relative and preeminent scholar of traditional Icelandic literature, Ulfur, who recognizes her brilliance but fears the innovativeness of her writing.

When she finally shows her free verse epic poem, "*Word Meadow*," to Ulfur during a secret trip to Iceland with 13-year-old Freya, he describes it as "*Arnaleir*" or "eagle muck" (Sunley 2009, 161). Ulfur's word choice is especially hurtful to Birdie. Eagles are symbols of male "strength and power" in Old Norse mythology and commonly associated with Odin, the father of the gods, who "according to the Eddic poems ... transformed himself into an eagle" (Gräslund 2006, 128). Notably, one of the mythological poems of the *Poetic Edda* (dating back to the thirteenth century) contains a description of the elaborate doors into Odin's hall: "a wolf hangs in front of the ... doors / and an eagle hovers above" (Gräslund 129). Given that Ulfur's name means "wolf in Icelandic," as Freya explains in Sunley's novel (2009, 163), Birdie comes to view him as a predator in his human and animal forms—one who is known to attack and consume more vulnerable creatures and their offspring. By equating Birdie's experimental poetry with bird excrement, he makes clear that she may wish to take flight metaphorically through verse but that she will never become the famed poet she aspires to be, thanks to Ulfur's seemingly unrelenting preservation of the male-dominated Old-World Icelandic literary canon. As Ulfur's son, Saemundur, explains to Freya, his father is uncomfortable with contemporary Icelandic writing, especially by the descendants of immigrants, but unable to recognize his own biases. Ulfur thus routinely "reads modern work, [and] then condemns it" (Sunley 2009, 151), ensuring that it remains unpublished, as part of his own ambivalence about acknowledging the contributions of those who left Iceland. Ulfur's dismissiveness of Birdie's epic poem contributes to her descent into mania, which ends with Birdie's suicide back in Canada.

References to people taking on animal forms and characteristics—especially those of birds—are littered throughout *The Tricking of Freya*, pointedly blurring the boundaries between and among species. From the opening pages of the novel, the young Freya, who begins summer visits to Gimli, Manitoba, in her eighth year of life, accompanied by her adoptive mother, Anna, looks forward to visiting her Aunt Ingibjorg because she promises during a weekly telephone call to "Our People in Canada" to fulfill Freya's desire to "learn to fly" (Sunley 2009, 19, 21). The aptly nicknamed Aunt Birdie, of course, insists that she can deliver on this wish, telling Freya when she queries Birdie's knowledge, "Why do you think they call me Birdie?" (21). As the third epigraph for this chapter reveals, Birdie has renamed herself in an effort to move beyond the confines of her world because "a bird can be so many things" (6). Yet, in doing so, she risks hitting the proverbial glass ceiling that confines Icelandic-Canadian women in mid-twentieth-century Canada to their roles as wives and mothers by mistaking her poetic talent as a viable form of liberation that will bring her recognition at home and abroad: "glass for air, words for wings" (6). Not surprisingly, Anna has delayed bringing her daughter to Gimli repeatedly based on the premise that she is "afraid to fly" (20), but also because of her fear as to what Birdie might do when they finally visit.

In the meantime, having moved to Connecticut to marry an American who dies suddenly of a heart attack before Freya turns two, Anna finds herself a widow with a small child, stuck in the "bland Connecticut suburb" of Windsor (Sunley 2009, 14), where she does not fit in because she lacks skills to integrate into this affluent US bedroom community. She doesn't excel at tennis or bridge, the main preoccupations of her white, female neighbors who form her immediate cohort. As Freya explains, Anna "radiate[s] … foreignness" (14). She refuses to own a television, creating a sheltering yet isolated cocoon around herself and her daughter. The living room mantel, with its myriad of framed photos of Gimli relatives and her late husband, becomes a literal "shrine," reflecting Anna's desire to replicate and hold dear the values of her New Iceland community. Freya sees her mother as frightened by "[m]odern America" (14). Anna especially fears images of the "Vietnam War, with its body bags and massacres" (14), yet is unwilling to move back to Canada, a seeming contradiction given that Canada refused to support the US involvement in the war.[10] In fact, Canada became a favored site of refuge for dodgers and deserters of the Vietnam War. But remaining in the US provides Anna with an escape hatch from a different kind of war—what she perceives as the seductive and destructive nature of her sister, Birdie, whose unpredictable moods are a reminder of the animal within both Birdie and, potentially, her adopted daughter Freya, both of whom embrace their affinity with animals and ability to take on animal (especially bird-like) characteristics.

Animal Transformations

Shortly after arriving on their first trip to Gimli, Freya pretends to be a dog, sticking her head out of a car window much to Anna's chagrin, a playful transformation that Birdie embraces, leading the young girl to believe that ultimately, she can become a bird and take flight. Birdie deliberately compares Freya to an "egret" (Sunley 2009, 1), a white plumaged vagrant that was nearly wiped out in the US because it was hunted for decorative feathers to be used by milliners during the nineteenth century. Leslie Kemp Poole explains that "[t]he feminine desire for hats adorned with long plumes and bright bird wings, heads, and bodies arose in the post-Civil War decades [in the US, Canada, Britain, and Europe] and, by the 1880s had accounted for the deaths of hundreds of thousands of birds" (2007, 300). Poole notes that the most coveted feathers were "'aigrettes,' the showy plumage that appeared on egrets during mating and nesting season" (300). Due to extensive conservation efforts from the 1880s into the next century, the egret population recovered and subsequently became the symbol of the National Audubon Society.[11] Yet Birdie's choice of bird species also can be read as a pointed critique of Anna's decision to live in the US, where, she tells Birdie, "they don't teach Icelandic in … elementary schools" (Sunley 2009, 34). By enabling Freya's assimilation and distancing her from her Icelandic heritage and language, Birdie sees her sister as failing to live up to her side of the arrangement, pitting Birdie against the "respectable Anna the American" (337).

Conversely, Birdie recognizes the ways in which bird names can be used, like the pathologizing of her illness, to relegate people to otherness, as is the case with the stereotyped description of the Icelanders in Winnipeg, whose nickname, "Goolie," was said to recall an Icelandic word for the color "gold" (referencing the immigrant population's startling light-blond hair) (Sunley 2009, 26). Freya equates "Goolie" with a "ghost" when she first arrives in Manitoba for a visit before being corrected. It is a slippage that articulates her uncertain relationship with her own identity as well as the racism faced by Icelanders in the New World (26), a racism that she experiences throughout her childhood and university years in the US because of her startling blondness. But the term "Goolie" also invokes the clichéd and primarily negative associations with gulls as a species, birds known for their carnivorous appetite, predatory behavior, and effective scavenging and mobbing techniques (26). Like egrets, gulls often rely on kleptoparasitism, or the stealing of other animals' food, to feed themselves.[12] Ironically, Birdie's own family does precisely this when they facilitate the internal transfer of Freya to Anna against Birdie's wishes.

As Birdie points out, the secrecy of this process is in direct contradiction to that of the story her Icelandic cousin, Thorunn, tells her of siblings who were "*given away to families in the district who couldn't have children of their own*" but that this was done in a completely open manner: "*they always knew who their parents were. ... There was ... no government cover-up*" (Sunley 2009, 337). What Freya learns, long after Birdie commits suicide, is that the family has "*gotten the court to declare*" her "*unfit to raise a child*" (337), legitimating the stealing of Freya to feed, literally and figuratively, social expectations of appropriate behavior for white middle-class women on both sides of the Canada-US border. Anna reinforces this view in the post-adoption years by repeatedly describing Birdie's various nameless boyfriends as "Fly-by-nights" (338), extending the metaphoric dimensions of Birdie's animal-otherness to critique her sister's refusal to marry and settle down. This legal and moral marginalization of Birdie accords with the shift in the "postwar adoption mandate [in Canada]" to make the "prospective adoptive parents" (V. Andrews 2018, 23–24), in this case Birdie's sister Anna and her husband, the primary focus of attention rather than attending to the health and wellness of mother and child.

Birdie's efforts to hold onto her baby are thwarted by a "collusion" among her mother, her sister, the doctors at the asylum, the federal and provincial governments, and the court system, which prevent her from keeping the child, relegating her to the status of "a sadglad bird. ... A mockingbird chattering at hummingbird speed. ... A finch smashing itself against windows" (Sunley 2009, 337, 6). Birdie may have named herself as a child, but her bird-like qualities, paradoxically, are used to demonstrate her inability in adulthood to care for her newborn daughter, as her transformations through various stages of bipolar disorder cross boundaries between and among bird species and behaviors in ways that contest the hierarchical relationship between person and animal.

The "clean break … practice of removing babies from unmarried mothers immediately at birth so as to prevent bonding" has devastating consequences in Sunley's narrative for mother and daughter (V. Andrews 2018, 97–98). By prioritizing the attachment to the surrogate, as was common in hospitals across Canada from 1940 to 1970, and removing babies from their legal mothers prior to the "signing of a legal consent" (107), women like Birdie are violently and unethically coerced into surrendering their parental rights. Birdie is left with empty arms, "weeping" breasts, and continued confinement in the Asylum, ostensibly to "guard against postpartum depression" (Sunley 2009, 337). But as she rightly argues, the removal of her child puts her at much higher risk of relapse than anything else: "It is having your child kidnapped by your closest relatives in collusion with agents of the government! How could such an act not crush one's very soul???" (337). The family's insistence on Birdie's need to sacrifice her baby to fulfill a familial obligation, shaped by "the drive to achieve heteronormative gender roles and nuclear families in the immediate postwar decades" (V. Andrews 2018, 100), comes at a great cost for multiple generations of women whose bodies and minds look to escape the strictures of a white Western North American society that tethers them to the ground by "becoming-animal" (Braidotti 2011, 81).

What Is in a Name?

Birdie's only source of comfort in the forced adoption process is that she has had the opportunity to name her baby girl Freya, after an Icelandic goddess. Through this act of defiance, Birdie ensures that her Icelandic heritage is passed on to her daughter, a decision that undermines Anna's desire to facilitate her adopted daughter's assimilation into a North American (and ultimately US) society. As Birdie explains to the child years later while sitting on a beach in Gimli, realizing that Freya still knows very little about the significance of her name, Freya was "the goddess of love ... of birth ... [and] also the goddess of magic" but most importantly she is both "a seer extraordinaire" and "a shape-shifter" who "could turn herself into a bird and travel great distances, into other worlds, wearing a cloak of falcon feathers" (Sunley 2009, 54).

But Birdie brings another dimension to this imaginative exercise by giving Freya the knowledge to connect with her Icelandic roots, as well as a path to "becoming-animal" (Braidotti 2011, 81), in direct contrast with her adoptive mother, Anna, who shortens her name to "Frey," having forgotten that "Frey" is one of several names for "Freyr," a "male ... fertility god" (Sunley 2009, 42). As Birdie pointedly explains to her sister, "when you call her Frey instead of Freya, you're calling that darling child *a giant phallus!*" (42), revealing the absurdity of Anna's efforts to assimilate into white Anglophone North American culture. In contrast, Birdie highlights the Icelandic fertility goddess' strength and independence, telling her daughter: "some giant or other was always trying to carry her off, but Freyja called the shots when it came to men" (54). She also notes the strategies used by men within traditional Icelandic narratives to denigrate Freyja's achievements, including accusing her of "sleeping with various elves and gods" (54). Birdie even recalls the efforts of a male poet leading Iceland's conversion to Christianity who describes "Freyja as a wild pig in heat, a she-goat bitch roaming the countryside" (54).

While Freya may not fully understand the significance of Birdie's summary of her namesake's origins, Birdie educates her daughter as to how the act of animal-othering is used in Freyja's case to denigrate her power within Icelandic mythology and to send a clear message about acceptable female behavior within the Christian Church hierarchy and, over time, in the Canadian world of the New Icelanders. Braidotti notes that "[t]he wild and passionate animal in us may be cheered as the trace of a primordial evolutionary trajectory ... but it also calls for containment and control," disciplinary practices that take aim at the "disposable bodies of 'others'" (2011, 82). By naming Freya as Birdie does, but also explaining through the story of her namesake how alternative "modes of embodiment" and "categorical otherness" are marginalized by the dominant society, Birdie provides Freya with the tools (unbeknownst to the child) to imagine alternate ways of being in the world, yet also outlines some of the hurdles she will face in doing so (82).

Shortly after that conversation, Freya dreams of her aunt coming to her, "arriv[ing] ... at dawn outside my window trailing a cloak of feathers" and gathering the young girl up in her arms to take flight over the lake and "into the lightening sky, the feathers of her cloak soothing the burned surface of my skin" (Sunley 2009, 56). Birdie may not fulfill the conventional role Anna does—of the safe, dependable mother-figure. But Birdie does provide strategies for negotiating the complexities of her identity as an Icelandic Canadian-born American woman who needs to take flight to discover who she is—by traveling to Iceland and New Iceland. Freya will use this same approach to help her to reconceive her origins and goals once she uncovers the family secret.

In contrast, Freya's grandmother and Birdie's mother, Sigga, represents the Icelandic community's efforts to be part of the Canadian mainstream. Sigga goes so far as to tell her young granddaughter that "Nobody believes in Freyja anymore. That was a long, long time ago. Now people only believe in one God. Or none at all" (Sunley 2009, 58). Sigga's comments echo the assimilationist rhetoric and behavior that Birdie mocks, the desire to "fit in" in Canada that leads, in Birdie's words, "all good Goolies" to go to church on "Sundays" (26). Nonetheless, Freya refuses to accept her grandmother's dismissal of her namesake goddess' powers, even uttering "I believe in Freyja" under her breath in the hope that she will "fly again" (58). Freya demonstrates a persistence, curiosity, and imagination that eventually enable her to uncover the truth of her birth and forced adoption.

Over the course of *The Tricking of Freya*, Freya specifically struggles with the fact that she feels and behaves differently from her adoptive mother, Anna. Her need to be active, to spin and move, "to climb" trees and gaze down on her surroundings is countered by her mother's ever cautious nature and constant surveillance of her (Sunley 2009, 13). It is only when she encounters Birdie that she finds someone who understands what she means when she says, "My wings itch" (37). Nevertheless, like Birdie, Freya falls prey to the strictures of her Icelandic family in Gimli when, during a welcoming tea party, filled with "grown-up talk" (41), she accidentally frightens Birdie, prompting her aunt to spill coffee on her elegant floral dress. To cheer Birdie up, Freya performs—for the first time in her life—a cartwheel in Sigga's crowded room, bringing a beloved heirloom china cabinet stocked with teacups down on herself. While the young girl is unhurt, Anna panics and faints, hitting her head on the edge of a telephone table, which puts her in a coma.

Freya blames herself for the accident and Anna's subsequent inability to fully function. For a time, Freya stops imagining flight, explaining "I was the girl who put her mother in a coma: I no longer deserved to fly" (Sunley 2009, 46–47). The only solace Freya finds is through Birdie's sharing of Icelandic stories and her efforts to teach Freya the Icelandic language in the aftermath of the accident. The narratives fuel the young girl's desire to take flight once again and build a special bond between the birth mother and her secret daughter. Learning Icelandic, while incredibly challenging for Freya, is bolstered by Birdie's promise to take her to Iceland. As the summer passes, Freya begins to think of Birdie "as a kind of *volva* [or female prophet] …, an enchantress folding me into her wings with words, soaring us far from the scene of my cartwheel crime" (67). Moreover, when Anna is finally released from hospital, she has no memory of what has happened, creating another layer of deception among family members and feelings of guilt for Freya that continue even after her adoptive mother's death.

The Hidden Costs of Forced Adoption

Central to the recent Canadian Senate report is the realization that forced adoptions have had serious and lasting consequences for adoptees and mothers alike. The outcome for the mothers has been overwhelmingly poor, a fact that Sunley's novel confirms. Many mothers have struggled with depression, "anxiety disorders, pathological grief, post-traumatic stress disorder, and other mental health issues preventing them from trusting others and developing healthy relationships" (Eggleton et al. 2018, 10). Close to a third of the women who underwent forced adoption never gave birth to another child; they felt "too traumatized or … ashamed and unworthy to go through pregnancy again" (11). Even though Birdie has limited access to Freya during her childhood, she is unable to share the truth of their relationship or recover what has been lost as a result of the forced adoption. Birdie's manic voyage to Askja, a gesture intended to show Freya her namesake's power and ward off the threat of the imagined wolf, Ulfur, perversely ensures the end of their contact as Freya learns that Birdie has taken Freya out of Canada without the required permission of her mother, prompting extensive searches for the young girl throughout Manitoba before she is discovered in Iceland. In an ironic reversal of Freya's journey from Canada to the US, Birdie is accused of "kidnapping" (264) the child she had forcibly surrendered. Freya returns to Winnipeg and then Connecticut, with her mother vowing never to return to Gimli. No charges are laid but Anna refuses to let Freya "mention Birdie's name again" (190), an act of repression that fails miserably, with Freya continuing to contemplate Birdie's fate once grounded south of the Canada-US border.

The Tricking of Freya demonstrates the substantial and cumulative harm that occurs because of Freya's forced surrender to Sigga and then Anna. For Birdie, the end of Freya's summer visits to New Iceland results in immense trauma, often rendered through bird imagery, with what Anna describes as "*Birdie's god-awful scenes*" (Sunley 2009, 91), a description that doubly marginalizes her sister's behavior as sacrilegious and absurdly selfish rather than recognizing Birdie's pain. At the end of each summer, Birdie begins to fall into a deep depression, punctured by rage and silence that even leads to threats of suicide, conduct that both Sigga and Anna dismiss as selfish and narcissistic. When Anna tries to orchestrate an early departure from a Gimli trip, Birdie comes "flying down the driveway screaming, 'Plotters! Schemers! *Traitors!*'" (92) in gull-like fashion, embodying the "sadglad bird" (333) whose bipolar disorder is worsened by the secret knowledge of Freya's parentage and limited presence in her life.

As mentioned, Birdie eventually takes the 13-year-old Freya on an unapproved trip to Iceland, during her summer vacation in Gimli. This final flight to reclaim her daughter is made possible by the distraction of an annual traditional summer Icelandic festival, known as "*Islendingadagurinn*," in Gimli (Sunley 2009, 94). The festival includes the crowning of "an upstanding matron" or "*Fjallkona*" to reign as queen of that year's festivities (93). Sigga is a past recipient; the pictures on Anna's mantel include one of "Amma Sigga in her *Fjallkona* costume" (15). When Freya asks whether Birdie might be chosen, Birdie explains to Freya that she is a "crazy spinster" who has no hope of getting selected, despite Birdie's commitment to keeping the Icelandic culture and language alive (95). Nor is Anna a suitable candidate to be crowned the "upstanding matron of Canadian Icelandichood" because she is an "American housewife" and thus not a Canadian "pillar of the community" (94, 95), an observation that reinforces the potency of the border that separates Birdie from Freya.

The secret trip to Iceland enables Birdie to deliver on her promise to take Freya "flying!" (Sunley 2009, 102), despite Anna's insistence that such a journey would be far too expensive. While Birdie typically embraces the social dimensions of the Icelandic festival, which prompts a "yearly infusion of visitors" (95)—Icelandic immigrants from all over Canada and the US as well as Icelandic tourists who gather together to celebrate their shared heritage and traditions—she seizes the distraction of the large gathering to take Freya to the Winnipeg airport and, ultimately, Iceland. Freya, despite her reservations, is a naively willing participant, longing to escape the "limbo" of "life with Mama in Connecticut" that is shaped by regret and self-punishment for the harm she believes she has inflicted on Anna (100).

Initially the trip overseas appears to be Birdie's effort to introduce Freya to Iceland. Yet Freya also finds liberation from acting as her adoptive mother's caregiver as she encounters, firsthand, a country where animals—most often sheep—graze freely all over the island, disregarding property lines, roads, or other barriers erected by humans. Freya even begins a teenage romance with Ulfur's son, Saemundur, who despite his initial dismissiveness of the "American princess" becomes a confidante and tour-guide for the duration of the trip (Sunley 2009, 124).

However, Ulfur's devastating critique of Birdie's epic poem derails the journey and triggers a manic episode for Birdie. She flees Ulfur's home with Freya in tow, steals a jeep, and commences a treacherous drive around the island, during which they face adverse weather conditions. Freya is terrified, having recognized that Birdie is in a manic state and speeding through dangerous terrain covered in a veil of fog. Freya is especially devastated when Birdie hits a sheep, and rather than stopping, simply drives around the bleeding carcass, refusing to check on or care for the wounded animal. She is horrified to see how carelessly Birdie dismisses the value of these animals and the emotions of her own daughter. Through this scene, Sunley dramatizes the tension between "becoming-animal" (Braidotti 2011, 81) and Birdie's own willingness to sacrifice those who stand in her way. Birdie may extol the value of sheep's wool for keeping Icelanders warm. But she also recognizes their passive abundance, mockingly telling Freya as a child, "We owe our lives to those sheep! Bless the sheep!" (Sunley 2009, 219).

Birdie's dismissiveness of certain land-bound animals as lacking the ability to escape the clutches of predators becomes especially significant later in the novel when Freya learns more about her adoption. Freya gains deeper insight into how she is more like a land-bound sheep than she ever realized when she connects the story told by Sigga with her own birth. Sigga tells Freya about a dream in which an eagle takes a lamb, prompting the ewes to stop producing milk, a tragedy that is only resolved when the recovered skin of the dead lamb is sewn over a live lamb to restart milk production. For Freya, the dream narrative serves as a riddle that explains her adoption: "the real trick: the bird's lamb=Birdie's lamb=Birdie's child" (Sunley 2009, 236).

Birdie's blind and careening flight around Iceland ends at the remote Askja volcano, a site that for Birdie represents her connection to her ancestor's gift of prophecy and her own calling. Birdie and Freya are recovered by an Icelandic search-and-rescue team.[13] Birdie's erratic behavior and endangerment of Freya are all part of a manic episode that risks Freya's life and nearly leads to Birdie's death.

Though Birdie is first hospitalized in Iceland after she and Freya are discovered at the volcano, she is soon sent back to Canada and confined once again to the Selkirk Asylum, the same place where she was forced to surrender her newborn. Two days after Birdie's release to Sigga's care, she is found dead—apparently of an overdose. Years later Freya learns that Birdie hanged herself from a rope tied into the ceiling by pushing her desk, with its books and typewriter, "all the way over to the [open] window" of her bedroom and stepping off, a final attempt to take flight into the natural world despite the efforts of Ulfur, Halldora, and her own family (Sunley 2009, 271). Halldora, for example, dismisses Birdie's behavior as irrational and selfish: "The suicidal mind is always hard at work…. They see a window and think *leap*" (268). Freya, however, recognizes Birdie's hanging as both an act of self-punishment, "a sentence Birdie had handed down upon herself" (268), and a last desperate effort to make herself airborne, demonstrating a connection with her mother that reaches far beyond Halldora's cruel observation that "[e]veryone has their crosses to bear, … but we don't all up and kill ourselves now, do we?" (268–269). Halldora relegates Birdie to the status of animal-other because of her mental health challenges. Even in death, Birdie is being judged—as she is so acutely aware—for her unwillingness to conform to established social conventions among the New Icelanders in Gimli, Manitoba. Birdie experiences a cyclical pattern of illness that is generated by the policies and responses to vulnerable populations, like unwed mothers, who get in the way of colonialist values.

Exposing Secrets and Accessing the Power to Heal

In the years after she returns from Iceland and loses Birdie, Freya comes to embody a differently kind of "Goolie" or "gull," living as "shell" or ghost of her former self (Sunley 2009, 26, 193). She engages in self-destructive behaviors, defies Anna, and is haunted by dreams of her trip abroad (193). Even while attending college nearly a decade later, Freya is unable to find her place, despite her efforts to learn about "the immigrant Icelanders" in her "history classes" (192). She realizes that in the context of American immigration, Icelanders constitute a mere "droplet lost among the million-size waves of immigrants who flooded North America's shores" (192). Moreover, she recognizes that the Icelanders who did come "assimilated more quickly than most" (192), just as she has at college, relying on ironically accurate stereotypes—such as the "*Norse goddess*"—to explain her "wispy white-blond hair" and "near-albino looks" to those who query her origins (193).

When Anna dies during Freya's junior year, she plunges into a deep depression, finding solace by apprenticing at the underground darkroom of a photo lab in New York City. Comparing this period in her life to a hibernating bear instead of a bird, Freya speculates that "[w]hen I was good and ready I'd emerge from my lair, hungry for world again" (Sunley 2009, 196–197), a "shape-shifting" that begins when she finally travels to Gimli for Sigga's centenary celebration (228) and hears rumors about Birdie's secret child. For Freya, the possible existence of a relative who is her contemporary offers the promise of family for this only child.

Freya's return to Gimli—which includes assisting her "uncle Stefan," Birdie's former suitor, in packing up Sigga's home (Sunley 2009, 24)—awakens her desire to know more about her unacknowledged cousin, prompting her to set off on a series of journeys that eventually culminate in a return trip to Iceland during which she once again becomes animal. Having confirmed the existence of a baby ostensibly given up, according to Halldora, in a "blind adoption" and protected by sealed government records in Canada (270), Freya leaves her job and apartment in New York, taking on the role of detective to discover the truth. But instead of looking for lost letters in Iceland, Freya searches for Birdie's child's father.

Once in the capital of Reykjavik, she begins a dramatic self-described "transformation" (Sunley 2009, 315) that echoes her childhood feelings of liberation during her first trip to Iceland with Birdie. Freya relishes the "vivid[ness]" of her surroundings (288) in Iceland, explaining that "[l]ife seemed expansive, full of possibilities" (314). Freed from her work obligations and subterranean life in "grimy crowded Manhattan," she enjoys the natural beauty of the "island of endless light" (314). Freya even works up the courage to confront her host, Ulfur, now an aging man, about his relationship with Birdie and learns of his regret in dismissing Birdie's poetic genius. He may not be the father of Birdie's child but is deeply saddened by his inability to recognize Birdie as "mentally ill" during her manic phase (295). Unexpectedly, it is Ulfur, wolf turned sheep, who creates a list of a dozen possible suitors, leading Freya to reinvigorate her efforts to discover more details about this secret child.

Like Birdie, Freya is deeply affected by the Icelandic environment, especially the endless brightness of the island in the summer months, which dramatically interrupts her sleep patterns. During her visit, she reunites with her teenage crush Saemundur, the so-called black sheep of the family who runs his own wilderness tour company into the interior of Iceland (Sunley 2009, 290). Freya also finally learns the truth about her birthmother from Thorunn, the recipient of Birdie's desperate letter in the aftermath of Freya's birth and forced adoption. Just as Birdie takes flight through mania over the course of her travels 17 years earlier, so too does Freya find herself developing "*hypomania*" (314), triggered by Iceland's endless light. Though initially devastated by Thorunn's revelation about Birdie, a discovery that plunges Freya into her own deep depression—during which she is "curled into a comma" (333)—Ulfur and Saemundur recognize her mental illness and can get Freya the medical care she needs to stay alive and finish her story.

At the conclusion of *The Tricking of Freya*, Freya still fears becoming a "sadglad bird," and "ending up like ... Birdie my mother" (Sunley 2009, 333). But the revelation of her forced adoption enables her to recognize her family history. She learns how to properly treat her own bout of mania and to find a routine that grounds her, without plunging her into "[n]othingness" (332). In contrast with Birdie, Freya is able, with the help of a female physician, to moderate her exposure to light and prevent "*circadian rhythm disruption*" (333; emphasis in original). Through this care, Freya avoids hospitalization altogether. Once recovered, Freya recognizes the "conspiracy" of her forced adoption. Uncertain of where to go after her breakdown (333), she returns briefly to Gimli, once again crossing the ocean and, in doing so, unexpectedly resolving the final piece of the puzzle: the identity of her father. Changed by her time in Iceland, Freya starts to perceive those around her differently, including Stefan, Birdie's jilted yet ever-loyal friend and suitor who works as the local high-school English and history teacher during the school year and pursues his passion project in the summers—an inclusive New Iceland family genealogy. He stores and catalogues the objects of deceased New Icelanders with the goal of starting a local museum to honor the accomplishments of this immigrant community.

At first glance such a project may seem to romanticize Icelandic experiences in Manitoba. However, Stefan's description of himself as a "collector. ... A scavenger" prompts Freya to recognize how he uses his "gull"-like tendencies to better understand the complexities of the past and to become the parent she has longed for (Sunley 2009, 255). James Gorman notes that "gulls" are known for their devotion to their children, and their ability to survive in a "harsh and unforgiving world" (2019), characteristics that have led to Halldora, Sigga, and Anna's kleptoparasitic behavior and Freya's forced adoption. Stefan, however, reveals a different side of "gulls," namely their willingness to co-parent, which is a distinguishing trait of the species.[14] In fact, his translation of Birdie's desperate letter to Thorunn from the asylum after the forced adoption of Freya is the catalyst for Freya's discovery of her father's identity. Not only does Stefan promptly provide a carefully typed and complete translation of the document to Freya, but he also helps Freya to fill in the missing parts of the story, drawing on his private memories to conclude that he is Freya's father (the result of a single night of passion). As part of his new role, Stefan becomes Freya's researcher in Canada as she translates Ulfur's letters, conducting "background research" about the New Iceland settlement to ensure that Freya can construct her own transatlantic family story (Sunley 2009, 340).

Having reconnected with Saemundur and ready to learn more about her ancestral country, in the concluding pages of the novel, Freya describes her decision to reside in Iceland for the immediate future. She recognizes that it is a place where she can take flight, while still caring for her health. Iceland's landscape is punctured by the collision of two tectonic plates—the North American and the Eurasian—creating cracks that are visible to humans. Her residence in Iceland can be read as embodying her efforts to accept the cracks in her own "egg," the "ovoid" that Birdie has insisted, during one of Freya's childhood visits to Gimli, is "[r]eady to hatch" (Sunley 2009, 90). She enrolls "at the University of Iceland, majoring in Icelandic literature with a minor in history" (331), and "put[s her] ... faith in words" (341), following in Birdie's footsteps. Living in a country where "[m]arriage has lost its popularity" (332) and literature, regardless of the writer's gender, is valued, Freya finds support from Saemundur (in contrast to Birdie's dismissal by Ulfur), who reads and recognizes the significance of her notebooks, to publish the story of her tricking. While she will "always be something of an outsider" (341), and still is identified by older Icelanders as "a *Vestur-Islendingur*, Western Icelander, the name given to those who went west to Canada and America" (341), she also thinks of herself "as an American" (341). In doing so, Freya honors her two mothers—adoptive and birth—without being confined to the strictures of Gimli, the Icelandic colony named after the best location in the palace of Heaven, or the reach of the Canadian government.

Once well settled in Iceland, Freya starts having prophetic dreams about earthquakes and the cracking open of planets, yet soon comes to realize that her dreams are of "an[other] egg hatching" (Sunley 2009, 341). Freya negotiates her own feelings of ambivalence over having a child with Saemundur, recognizing that the pregnancy and postpartum period could worsen her depression or result in offspring that may "bear these same mood-sick genes" as Freya and Birdie (341). For Freya, "[w]hat matters is not our fate but what we make of it," viewing her fate as a "seed that unfurls itself over the course of our lives" (341). In stark contrast with Birdie's secret pregnancy and Freya's forced adoption as a newborn, Freya faces no major social stigmas as an unmarried woman in getting pregnant. Saemundur is eager to have a child with Freya.

But Sunley refuses to provide a definitive answer or conventional happy ending to *The Tricking of Freya*. Freya herself rejects her namesake's prophetic role, allowing herself to shape her own future beyond the strictures of marriage and motherhood that led to her own adoption: "Saemundur could leave me if I won't have a child. Or I could leave him. Fly back to New York. Don't ask me. I'm no *volva*, I've got no gift of prophecy" (Sunley 2009, 342). Instead, Freya uses her bird-self to challenge the ways in which Canada has concealed the stories of mothers and children of forced adoption and to imagine a life in which the creation of a child, though it may be terrifying for an unmarried woman who struggles with mental illness, will not prompt nation-state interference.

The Tricking of Freya offers an intimate look at how the process of "becoming-animal" can be read as subverting—albeit in a limited fashion—the strictures of the Canadian and American nation-state and, particularly, the hidden history of forced adoption in Canada. Birdie commits suicide after losing access to her child yet again, a desperate act of self-assertion that is one of the few available to her as a mentally ill, unmarried woman living in Canada in the 1960s and 1970s. Freya, however, begins to take flight—metaphorically at least—over the course of the novel, unraveling the truth of her immediate family tree and reuniting with her father and extended relatives through a transatlantic migration that ends not in Canada or the US but in her ancestral homeland.

Andrews observes that "[i]t is impossible to know the exact number of Canadian infants of unmarried mothers that were sent to the United

States … [between 1940 to 1970]. Many of these now adult adoptees seek their lost Canadian roots and citizenship. Others may still have no idea they were born in Canada" (2018, 175). Through Freya's story, Sunley challenges the ways in which Canadian exceptionality—including the inclusivity attributed to the Canadian cultural mosaic in contrast to Freya's observations about the lack of acknowledgment of New Icelanders in US college history classes—has led to the suppression of key historical moments that do not support a celebratory vision of the US' northern neighbor. Much like Dell Parsons of Richard Ford's *Canada*, whose high-school students cannot imagine why he would want to be anything other than a Canadian citizen, *The Tricking of Freya* maps Freya's nomadic alterna(rr)ative, a story that refuses to reify Canada's exceptional status. Instead, Sunley exposes the limits of a "moral and cognitive bestiary" that relegates animals to the role of moral symbols without acknowledging the possibility that such nomadic connections between and among those who become-animal provide a space for Freya and other women to claim the power to shape their own lives and resist being confined by the borders that divide nation-states (Braidotti 2011, 84). Freya is undoubtedly relatively privileged, as a university-educated white woman with some financial resources and extensive family support who ultimately makes her home in the highly progressive political country of Iceland. It is worth noting that despite being from an immigrant family and burdened by a genetic legacy of mental illness, her Nordic heritage and appearance of "whiteness" allow her to occupy a position "of normalcy" within Canada and the US (Coleman 2006, 7). Nonetheless, her story provides another pivotal example of how recent American authors continue to disrupt the dominant Canadian national narratives through innovative and provocative examinations of key moments in Canada's hidden histories.

Notes

1. See Sunley (2009, 17–18) for the story of the volcanic eruption that Anna shares with Freya as a child to explain their ancestors' immigration to Canada and subsequent settlement in Gimli, a town named after the "most beautiful room in the palace [in heaven], where the very best people went after they died" (18).
2. See Pope (2016) for an introduction to the animated map created by the Cornell Ornithology Lab "showing the migratory movements of 118 bird species over the course of a year" across the Western Hemisphere. See

Greenspan (2015) for a brief history of the Migratory Bird Treaty Act, an act first signed in 1916 by the US and Britain (on behalf of Canada) to protect migratory birds, "'mak[ing] it a crime to 'pursue, hunt, take, capture, kill,' or 'sell' a migratory bird or any of its parts, including nests, eggs, and feathers."
3. See Andrews (2018, 17–20).
4. See Andrews (2018), who notes that "Although the current trend in adoption practice is openness, as of this writing, adoption records continue to be sealed in Prince Edward Island, and Nova Scotia, and only semi-open subject to a veto in British Columbia, Alberta, Manitoba, Saskatchewan, Ontario, Newfoundland, and New Brunswick. In Quebec, only adoptees have a right to information if not vetoed, not mothers, as in other provinces" (108).
5. See Eggleton et al. (2018, 13–14), for a section of the Senate committee's report titled "The Australian Experience," which details the steps taken in Australia to prepare for and deliver a formal federal apology to those impacted by the forced adoption policy in that nation. The report notes that "Australia's Commonwealth Government also invested in counselling and support services for individuals affected by forced adoption practices," including "resources for the Australian Psychological Association to develop training for psychologists appropriate for adoptees and the mothers whose babies were taken" and methods to help reconnect mothers and children (14). But "full and universal" access to birth certificates and adoption records in Australia remains incomplete because policies vary by state (14).
6. The Eggleton et al. (2018) Senate report explains that "Beginning in the mid-1960's, the federal government committed to an annual investment of $25 million to permanently establish the Canada Assistance Plan (CAP), intended to help provincial social assistance programs. With respect to the forced adoption issue, the committee was told that federal funds, through CAP to the provinces and municipalities, specifically contributed to the maintenance of **maternity homes for unmarried mothers**, the provision of adoption and counselling services, and supporting the casework of social workers" (2; emphasis in original).
7. See Andrews (2018, 105–107) for a discussion of the "severe psychological impact" of separating mothers from their babies (106). Andrews notes that "There is ample evidence that social workers and maternity home matrons [among others] knew at the time that mothers would be affected for the rest of their lives. However, mothers were not advised of the adverse mental health effects that they and their children would suffer; instead, they were told they would forget about their babies" (106).

8. See Thearle and Weissenberger (1984), who note that "Lactation in non-paturient women has been recognized in many cultures over many centuries" but in "recent years, more publicity has been given to this technique for feeding adopted children" (283). The article, published in 1984, documents the use of drugs to facilitate lactation and also describes the increasing popularity of breast-feeding infants as part of the rationale for these efforts by adoptive parents (283).
9. See Stefánsson (2020), Gräslund (2006), and Bourns (2021) for some examples of the role of birds in Icelandic folklore, religion, and literature.
10. See Squires (2013) for insightful discussions regarding the Canadian government's stance regarding the American participation in and funding of the Vietnam War; the terminology used to describe those who tried to come to Canada as a "war resister," "draft dodger," or "deserter" (ix–x); and the ways in which the narrative of resistance was used to perpetuate a version of Canadian exceptionalism that is far more complex and contradictory.
11. See Poole (2007, 300–304).
12. See Brockmann and Barnard (1979) and Burger and Gichfield (1981) for explanations of kleptoparasitism in birds.
13. See Paumgarten (2015) for a detailed examination of Iceland's volunteer search-and-rescue system and the unique physical and climatic perils that Iceland poses for visitors and residents.
14. See Gorman (2019), who notes that there are "three good things about gulls: They are devoted parents. Males share child care equally with females. ... And they have figured out a way—actually many ways—to survive in a harsh and unforgiving world."

References

Andrews, Jennifer. 2020. Transnational Revelations: Forced Adoptions, Dispossession, and Legacies of Icelandic Immigration to Canada and the U.S. *Comparative American Studies* 16 (3–4): 174–186. https://www.tandfonline.com/doi/abs/10.1080/14775700.2020.1727639?journalCode=ycas20.

Andrews, Valerie. 2017. "White Unwed Mothers: The Adoption Mandate in Postwar Canada." MA thesis, York University.

———. 2018. *White Unwed Mothers: The Adoption Mandate in Postwar Canada.* Toronto: Demeter Press.

Balcom, Karen. 2015. *The Traffic in Babies: Cross-Border Adoption and Baby-Selling Between the United States and Canada.* Toronto: University of Toronto Press.

Bourns, Timothy. 2021. The Language of Birds in Old Norse Tradition. *The Journal of English and Germanic Philology* 120 (2): 209–238.

Braidotti, Rosi. 2011. *Nomadic Theory: The Portable Rosi Braidotti*. New York: Columbia University Press.

Brockmann, H. Jane, and C.J. Barnard. 1979. Kleptoparasitism in Birds. *Animal Behaviour* 27 (2): 487–514.

Burger, Joanna, and Michael Gichfield. 1981. Age-Related Differences in Piracy Behaviour of Four Species of Gulls, Larus. *Behavior* 77 (4): 242–266.

Calarco, Matthew. 2003. The Question of the Animal. *Electronic Book Review*, March 31. https://electronicbookreview.com/essay/the-question-of-the-animal/.

Coleman, Daniel. 2006. *White Civility: The Literary Project of English Canada*. Toronto: University of Toronto Press.

Comacchio, Cynthia R. 1999. *The Infinite Bonds of Family: Domesticity in Canada, 1850–1940*. Toronto: University of Toronto Press.

Derrida, Jacques. 1995. 'Eating Well,' or the Calculation of the Subject. In *Points...: Interviews, 1974–1994*, edited by Elizabeth Weber and translated by Peggy Kamuf et al., 255–287. Stanford: Stanford University Press.

Eggleton, Art, et al. 2018. *The Shame Is Ours: Forced Adoptions of the Babies of Unmarried Mothers in Post-war Canada*. Standing Senate Committee on Social Affairs, Science and Technology. https://sencanada.ca/en/info-page/parl-42-1/soci-adoption-mandate/.

Gorman, James. 2019. In Defense of Sea Gulls: They're Smart, and They Co-Parent, 50/50 All the Way. *The New York Times*, August 23. https://www.nytimes.com/2019/08/23/science/seagulls-behavior.html.

Gräslund, Anne-Sofie. 2006. Wolves, Serpents, and Birds: Their Symbolic Meaning in Old Norse Belief. In *Old Norse Religion in Long-Term Perspectives*, ed. Anders Andren et al., 124–130. Lund: Nordic Academic Press.

Greenspan, Jesse. 2015. The History and Evolution of the Migratory Bird Treaty Act. *Audubon.org*, May 22. https://www.audubon.org/news/the-history-and-evolution-migratory-bird-treaty-act.

Kunzel, Regina. 1993. *Fallen Women, Problem Girls: Unmarried Mothers and the Professionalization of Social Work 1890–1945*. New Haven, CT: Yale University Press.

Lee, Charles T. 2016. *Ingenious Citizenship: Recrafting Democracy for Social Change*. Durham: Duke University Press.

Maiti, Krishanu. 2013. The Animal That Therefore Derrida Is: Derrida and the Posthuman Critical Animal Studies. *Bhatter College Journal of Multidisciplinary Studies* 3: 92–99.

Paumgarten, Nick. 2015. Life Is Rescues. *The New Yorker*, November 2. https://www.newyorker.com/magazine/2015/11/09/life-is-rescues.

Poole, Leslie Kemp. 2007. The Women of the Early Florida Audubon Society: Agents of History in the Fight to Save State Birds. *The Florida Historical Quarterly* 85 (3): 297–323.

Pope, Alexandra. 2016. Mesmerizing Map Shows Bird Migrations Throughout the Year. *Canadian Geographic*, January 22. https://www.canadiangeographic.ca/article/mesmerizing-map-shows-bird-migrations-throughout-year.

Stefánsson, Hjörleifur Helgi. 2020. *Icelandic Folk Tales*. Cheltenham: The History Press.

Stevens, Emily E., Thelma E. Patrick, and Rita Pickler. 2009. A History of Infant Feeding. *The Journal of Perinatal Education* 18 (2): 32–39.

Squires, Jessica. 2013. *Building Sanctuary: The Movement to Support Vietnam War Resisters, 1965–1973*. Vancouver: University of British Columbia Press.

Stone, Ken. 2017. Judges 3 and the Queer Hermeneutics of Carnophallogocentricism. In *The Bible and Feminism: Remapping the Field*, ed. Yvonne Sherwood, 261–276. Oxford: Oxford University Press.

Sunley, Christina. 2009. *The Tricking of Freya: A Novel*. New York: St. Martin's Press.

Thearle, M.J., and Rolf Weissenberger. 1984. Induced Lactation in Adoptive Mothers. *Australia and New Zealand Journal of Obstetrics and Gynaecology* 24: 283–286.

CHAPTER 6

Escaping to Canada: Gambling on Northern Salvation in Stewart O'Nan's *The Odds*

> *[Canada] is a real-world, real-time example of a banking system in a medium-sized, advanced capitalist economy that worked. Understanding why the Canadian system survived could be a key to making the rest of the west equally robust. (Freeland 2010)*

> *Household debt in Canada, a nation generally known for moderation, has reached levels that could be qualified as excessive. Canadians owe $2.16 trillion—which, as a share of gross domestic product, is the highest debt load in the Group of Seven economies. (Fournier and Hertzberg 2019b)*

> *When credit works, it lives only in the future, transfixing in its seemingly magical power to move itself ever forward. But when it fails, credit is pulled back into its own uncanny past, back into the reality of labor and production that it so desperately attempted to disavow, confronted with the material limits it thought it had overcome.*
> *(McClanahan 2017, 133)*

In the opening pages of Stewart O'Nan's 2012 novel, aptly titled *The Odds*, a bankrupt middle-class white couple, Art and Marion Fowler, take a weekend vacation in Canada. They use a "Valentine's Day Getaway Special" to Niagara Falls to smuggle across the border a gym bag of cash, which they hope to use in the local casinos to gamble their way out of crushing debt in the US while evading legal repercussions (2012, 2). The novel takes place over a single weekend, interspersing both spouses'

© The Author(s), under exclusive license to Springer Nature Switzerland AG 2023
J. Andrews, *Canada Through American Eyes*,
https://doi.org/10.1007/978-3-031-22120-0_6

recollections of the past with the realities of a last desperate attempt to find a resolution to their impending separation and declaration of bankruptcy. *The Odds* explores the uncertain future of many apparently affluent white Americans in the wake of the Great Recession.

Through the Fowlers, who are haunted by the ghosts of their respective affairs and "prey to the tyranny of appearances" (O'Nan 2012, 1), O'Nan explores one seemingly privileged population affected by the fallout from the first post-millennial recession, provoked in large part by subprime mortgages, which enabled Americans to purchase homes they could not afford only to watch their investments disappear as the housing bubble burst. While Annie McClanahan's *Dead Pledges: Debt, Crisis, and Twenty-First Century Culture* probes the "overt risks, phantasmatic realities, and incalculable debts that a debt economy can no longer redeem" primarily in a US context (2017, 4), this chapter uses O'Nan's novel to explore Canada's overlooked role as a place of perceived escape within North America from what has been characterized as a predominantly American narrative of greed and economic failure. *The Odds* raises questions about how Canada functions as a place of sanctuary for Americans looking to get away from their lives, even temporarily.

At first glance, *The Odds* fails to offer the explicit critique of narratives of Canadian exceptionalism that so pointedly shape the novels by Duffy and Sunley. O'Nan is careful to foreground the relatively low level of risk experienced by the Fowlers during the Great Recession. They are a white well-educated American couple with grown children who have been downsized from their mid-level corporate jobs yet still apparently have the means to put a roof over their heads if or when their house is repossessed. However, through the story of Art and Marion's visit to Niagara Falls, O'Nan offers an intimate exploration of one American family's struggle to deal with the Great Recession through a carefully planned journey north of the Canada-US border. *The Odds* invokes a repeated motif within American narratives about Canada that Canada can provide a legal, cultural, political, economic, and psychological escape from the strictures of American law. These kinds of stories, as I have argued in previous chapters, have been used to bolster Canadian exceptionalism on both sides of the border. In doing so, however, *The Odds* raises questions about the Fowlers' efforts to embrace some aspects of Canadian exceptionality and exploit others to justify their illegal behavior.

This chapter argues that, through the voices and experiences of Art and Marion, O'Nan's book can be read as asking Americans and Canadians to re-examine dominant ideas about Canada as a kind and benevolent nation defined by the same pillars of "stability, security, and plenitude" that shape Northrop Frye's notion of the peaceable kingdom in Chap. 2. I suggest that *The Odds* provokes readers to think much more carefully about how national myths bolster narratives of exceptionalism that ultimately overlook critical truths about the Canadian economy, Canada's banking system, and its vulnerability to exploitation particularly through foreign investments and money laundering. The novel also gestures toward the government's efforts to keep key urban housing markets inflated regardless of the risks this strategy poses to some often racially marginalized Canadian households.

The White Experience of the US-to-Canada Border Crossings

In an ironic twist, O'Nan's novel begins with Marion Fowler telling her sister Celia that the Cleveland, Ohio-based couple are ostensibly fleeing the country by following the Underground Railroad "North, to Canada … Like the slaves" (2012, 1) to salvage their relationship and their finances. Fowler, of course, is appropriating a historical narrative familiar to many Canadians and Americans, particularly those living in Ohio: that of the fugitive Black enslaved person seeking refuge by crossing the Canada-US border, which was done most frequently by water. This symbol functions metaphorically in *The Odds*, primarily through the Fowlers' increasing recognition that their finances are about to plummet over the edge of the Falls.

Water crossings have served as a critical part of the narrative of slaves escaping from the US to Canada. As Alyssa MacLean explains, "the visual motif of Blacks boarding a boat, crossing from Ohio to Upper Canada on Lake Erie, and celebrating their newfound freedom … on Canadian shores, became the most popular image of border-crossing in mid-nineteenth-century abolitionist print culture" (2010, 163). Moreover, MacLean highlights the centrality of such images in the famed abolitionist novel, Harriet Beecher Stowe's *Uncle Tom's Cabin* (first published in 1852). The text documents the family's passage northward to Cleveland, where the Harris family takes a ferry to Canada, before securing the "reunification" of what was a "destroyed" family and the promise of a brighter future. Yet, the Harrises, as I note in the "Introduction" to this study, eventually leave Canada for France and then Liberia (235). For the

Harris family, colonial Canada does not answer their prayers. Likewise, the Fowlers may be looking for financial salvation and, Art hopes, for marital reconciliation as they move northward, but Canada offers only a temporary escape, even if it is not the matter of life and death faced by fleeing enslaved Black people seeking their freedom.

Nor are Marion and Art compelled to conceal their trip northward, despite the historical resonances of their hometown of Cleveland, which functioned as a critical part of the Underground Railroad. Geographically, Cleveland sits on the southern shore of Lake Erie. Lake Erie flows into the Niagara River, passing by the three sets of waterfalls that span the border between New York State and Ontario, Canada: Horseshoe Falls (or the "Canadian Falls" which literally straddles the Canada-US border), the American Falls, and the Bridal Falls, the latter two of which sit entirely on American soil. What MacLean describes as the "Lake Erie Passage" has become a "key part of the imagined geography of the Canada-US border" (2010, 163), serving as a "border zone" and a vital setting for narratives of "political emancipation, … personal transformation, and … literary convergence" in the mid-nineteenth century (163). While there are historical accounts of slaves using the Niagara Falls Suspension Bridge, "a recently opened rail link between the two countries" at the time (Foner 2015, 168), MacLean notes that water crossings were favored because they did not involve "passage through a tollbooth and … [the] inspection of passengers and baggage" (2010, 163).

In contrast, Art and Marion rely on these border checks as part of their cover when they travel from Cleveland to Niagara Falls, Canada, by bus a century and a half later. Art even laments the fact that the Canadian agent does not stamp his passport, which would provide an official memento of his travels northward. The Fowlers may perceive themselves as risk-takers, "'opting out' of the US" temporarily in the hopes of illegal financial gain (MacLean 2010, 161), but their appearance enables them to cross the border without incident.

Their whiteness and apparent affluence ensure seamless movement across nation-state borders. It affords them a veil of invisibility and trust on the part of the border guards, which is bolstered by their "gray middle age" status (O'Nan 2012, 3), even though they are carrying a gym bag full of illegal cash. Art also decides to have the couple travel as part of a "tour" to ensure that they "[m]ost likely wouldn't be searched anyway" (14). This strategy pointedly reinforces his efforts to ensure that they do not get caught. As Art has explained to Marion, "[l]egally, … you were allowed to bring as much as you wanted. The crime was not reporting it. The law was really about money laundering and funding terrorism, not what they were doing" (14). For Art, the deception of border authorities and violation of Canadian laws is justified by the small scale of the smuggling and the fact that he has not generated the money through illicit activities. He is merely trying to conceal remaining funds from his American creditors, in the hopes of changing his luck once across the Canada-US border. So, despite the post-9/11 institution of the "Cross Border Currency Reporting Regulations," which requires everyone crossing the Canada-US border to declare "currency and monetary instruments valued at $10,000 or more," including jewelry (Beare and Schneider 2007, 26), neither Art nor Marion includes the bundles of cash, or the diamond ring Art has purchased to upgrade Marion's engagement ring without her knowledge in their respective declarations. In this instance, Art plays the odds and wins, at least temporarily. He escapes the possibility of confiscation and the reality that, once the funds are claimed by Canada Customs, the onus is on Art to prove that he is not profiting from a crime.[1]

Moreover, in contrast with the Black enslaved people to whom she equates herself, Marion and her husband Art spend the weekend walking freely between Canada and the US as part of their vacation plans, revisiting past haunts and assessing their life together with virtually no impediments or concerns about their health and safety. They exercise a freedom of movement and visibility (through the repeated taking of tourist photos and selfies) that directly contrasts with the circumscribed and treacherous conditions of Black enslaved people who attempted to escape bondage, regardless of direction, or the Indigenous populations living on both sides of the border who have experienced racist "patterns of filtered bordering" for centuries (Helleiner 2016, 80).

Even when the Fowlers cross the bridge linking Canada to the US on foot on the Saturday afternoon of their weekend getaway to visit the observation tower on the "American side," honoring a tradition from their honeymoon, the only real challenges they face are cold weather, a weak bladder, and hangovers from the night before (O'Nan 2012, 123). The search for a public toilet leads Marion to utter "God Bless America" when she reaches the American entrance, having had no luck at the Canadian exit, which lacks such amenities (128). What they do see, looking from the American side, is telling: "a Canadian skyline, the futuristic sixties towers and bland seventies hotels, a testament to the perils of overdevelopment, doubly unfair since the view from there was so pristine"

(129). Clearly the tourism trade, in large part fueled by Americans, has overridden any desire to preserve the natural beauty of the Falls. Instead, profits and access to the right viewpoint to satisfy visitors and their wallets drive construction. Nonetheless, Marion's invocation of Canada's legacy as a place of refuge from American prejudice and exploitation and the couple's decision to smuggle funds into Canada in the hope of gambling their way back to solvency raise questions about Canada's deliberate self-positioning as a haven from the immediate impacts of the Great Recession and a globally attractive locale for those wishing to hide or convert assets from one form or currency to another.

Indigenous Border Crossings

Marion associates Niagara Falls with the legacy of US slavery—and Canada's role as a haven—but *The Odds* complicates this portrait through visual stereotypes. The historical injustice of imposing nation-state borders on Indigenous communities that straddle the Great Lakes and the reality that the Canada-US border's Niagara port continues to function to some degree as a site of criminal enterprise disguised as a tourist destination reveals a history that is far less savory. O'Nan pointedly gestures toward these two aspects of the border in his novel to raise questions about Canadian (and American) exceptionality and to demonstrate the ways in which both nations continue to cultivate narratives of superiority in relation to the other country without scrutinizing the complexities and contradictions of both. For instance, during the bus-trip to the Falls, Art carries the large sum of cash in a Cleveland Indians baseball team gym bag, replete with the "Chief Wahoo" logo, "the cartoonish image of a big-toothed First Nations man with a scarlet face and single feather in his headdress" (Strong 2018). Marion and Art initially feel out of place on the bus, "surrounded by much younger couples—including, … a fleshy pair in Harley gear necking directly across the aisle," whose public displays make them wish they had driven. However, the male biker's recognition of the Chief Wahoo logo proves comforting when the bus slides on ice, dislodging the bag of bundled bills (O'Nan 2012, 2). The biker not only returns the shifted bag to Art with the words, "Go Tribe," he even jokes about the bag's weight. He asks Art, "Whatta ya got in there—bricks?" (9), offering a prescient reminder of the purpose of the Fowler's trip: to win back the bricks-and-mortar home that they are about to lose.

In the case of the Cleveland Indians, journalist Gregory Strong explains that the Cleveland logo became the subject of "controversy during the 2016 Major League Baseball playoffs in Toronto" when "Indigenous activist Douglas Cardinal [based in Canada] filed a human rights complaint federally and provincially against the Indians … to stop Cleveland from using the logo during the [series]" (2018). The lawsuit was settled quickly, and the Cleveland team removed the racist logo from its jerseys during the playoffs, marking the beginning of the logo's demise. But the logo's presence on the bus serves as a critical reminder of the ways in which Americans like the Fowlers—and white Canadians—benefit from a legacy of settler colonialism that dates to the 1783 Treaty of Paris. That agreement ended the war between Britain and the American colonies, in part by using the "Niagara River as the boundary between Upper Canada and the United States, [and] thereby imposing a contested colonial border-scape on [the] First Nations … living on both sides of the river" (Helleiner 2016, 18). Despite the 1794 Jay Treaty, which is designed to facilitate "[f]ree movement and exemption from duty at the boundary line for 'Indians'" (18), Jane Helleiner points out that "uneven fulfilment of these and other treaty rights has been highlighted by long-standing Indigenous activism in the region" (18). She notes that the practice of "filtered bordering at Niagara" commonly discriminates against BIPOC border-crossers (80). The exception is when Indigenous people are rendered in clichéd and highly commodified forms, like the logo on a gym bag carried by a lifelong white Cleveland resident. The result is a suppressed history of "colonial and racialized violence" that has "produced the putatively white geography of Canadian Niagara, while simultaneously revealing patterns of racialized segregation" and "the 'absented presence' … of the non-white populations of the region" (Helleiner 2016, 85). Canada may represent the promise of inclusivity, yet the Canada-US border and the Niagara region come to embody the constructed nature of this supposed reality, which continues to allow for products that capitalize on dehumanizing stereotypes of Indigenous people like Chief Wahoo to flow freely between the two countries.

Cross-Border Criminal Financial Activities and Canadian Immigration Policies

The presence of the Harley-clad biker in *The Odds* also offers a pointed reminder of the ways in which "outlaw motorcycle gangs" in particular continue to rely on and benefit from the movement of "cross-border traffic" (Nicol 2015, 204) to facilitate their own illegal activities. The comradery that Art develops with the biker over the course of the novel serves another purpose by offering a distraction from the reality of global-scale money laundering in Canada that extends far beyond a single port of entry at the Canada-US border. Biker gangs are undoubtedly one sizeable source of illegal activity across Canada and the US, including the Niagara Falls region.[2] But in *The Odds*, the bikers who appear in this novel pose no actual threat to Art. For instance, when he first exchanges bundles of cash for chips and takes a turn into a deserted part of the hotel, he fears being robbed. The only person he encounters is the biker, who is chatting on his cell phone and gives Art a friendly "thumbs-up" before turning back to his conversation (O'Nan 2012, 43).

However, as Art and Marion's observations over the weekend on who frequent the casinos suggest, Canada's vulnerability to financial exploitation and related criminal activity is vast and multi-directional, most prominently shaped by "[o]rganized crime groups from Asia" and the movement of money by "wealthy Chinese into safe assets abroad" (Douglas 2019; Campbell and Obiko Pearson 2018). As Campbell and Obiko Pearson describe in "The City That Had Too Much Money," Canadian urban centers (most prominently Vancouver and Toronto) have become some of the "world's largest sluices for questionable funds moving from Asia into Western economies" (2018), primarily through casinos and real estate. Their work suggests (and *The Odds* hints) that there is a direct link between organized crime from Asia and Canada's immigration policies. Canada is known as a country that welcomes immigrants, roughly 300,000 "new permanent residents a year," which is considerably higher proportionally than the US (2018). The influx of wealth to Canada has resulted in huge increases in property values in key urban centers "[t]hanks ... to purchases by wealthy foreigners" (2018). Campbell and Obiko Pearson note that "Canada's immigration regime is weighted heavily toward applicants with marketable skills, and it offers other advantages to the better-off," including citizenship "after as little as three years of residence" and inconsistent "taxation on income earned abroad," conditions that have led to the "proliferation of 'astronaut' families" with a primary breadwinner overseas, while "a spouse and children live in Vancouver or Toronto" (2018).

Determining the source of wealth that is imported into Canada can be extremely challenging, as O'Nan's text suggests through Art's smuggling and the populations that Art and Marion observe in the casinos, hotels, and restaurants. In "Dirty Money: It's a Canadian Thing," Jason Kirby explores the difficulties of tracking funds brought in by under Canada's "immigrant investor program," a program designed to "lure the world's wealthy to Canada's shores with the promise of a passport" which ended in 2014 (2019). Kirby, for example, focuses on the example of a Chinese couple who acquired "$9.3 million" dollars' worth of real estate in the Toronto region, only to then fund the husband's "gambling activities" totaling nearly $6 million dollars through the "sale of properties" (2019). Yet neither spouse "had any employment or business interests in Canada beyond real estate investing" (2019). Kirby raises questions about the origins of such large amounts of money "and how [it] was … moved to Canada" (2019). He notes that only through better tracking and reporting of money laundering can the impact of these "ill-gotten gains" be understood, particularly with respect to soaring housing prices in Canada's urban centers (2019). Kirby specifically suggests that casinos offer an initial vehicle for money laundering that then can be used to purchase real estate, and Canada is an especially easy country for "homebuyers, domestic or foreign, to obscure their identities by using numbered companies, offshore trusts and nominee owners to conceal who ultimately owns a house or condominium" (2019). The result is a "flow of proceeds from crime into the housing market" (2019). Yet it is essential to recognize the complexity of money laundering and tax evasion in Canada, which may provide benefits for some wealthy racialized immigrants, while making other racialized immigrants more vulnerable to financial peril as they try to participate in overheated housing (or even rental) markets.

Race, Immigration, and Wealth (for Some)

As O'Nan demonstrates through the Fowlers in *The Odds*, the couple's interaction with and observations of various visible minorities throughout the course of the weekend signal their own racialized assumptions and stereotyped perceptions of Canada and Canadian inclusiveness. Marion, for instance, first notices the plethora of "elderly Chinese men" who populate the buffet the morning after their first night at the Niagara Falls hotel (O'Nan 2012, 57). She describes them as "grim and silent," suggesting that they are "losers" (like Art) who have come to "refuel" after a grueling night of gambling (58). Such racialized perceptions on Marion's part continue to the end of the novel, when during their final efforts to recover their losses through gambling, the couple find themselves sharing a croupier table with "an older Chinese man" who eventually loses and leaves the table "in disgust" (170, 175).

Niagara Falls is a well-known tourist mecca, drawing visitors from all over the globe. Yet, concurrently, Canada has a long-standing "official policy of multiculturalism," with its major urban centers, like Vancouver and Toronto, ranking "among the world's most racially and ethnically diverse" (Simone and Walks 2019, 287) and making it increasingly difficult to differentiate citizens from visitors. Art struggles to distinguish between Canadians and groups of visitors when he visits the casino on the first night of their trip and observes the "sheer variety of people" ranging from "young African couples in formal eveningwear" and "[s]izable Chinese and Indian contingents, less well dressed," along with "a flock of tall blondes who looked like models, tended by security detail in ill-fitting suits" (O'Nan 2012, 39). He laments the difference between himself and those he regards as "jet-setters" who have come to gamble for fun, a situation to which he no longer has access as someone who "before he'd wagered a penny ... was already a quarter million in the hole" (39). Here, Art seems to resent anyone with disposable wealth.

Nonetheless, when the Fowlers finally venture into the high-stakes tables of the hotel casino on Valentine's Day, they discover, much to their surprise, that the "stage set" of the "exclusive businessman's club" is "jammed with older, chain-smoking Asian men in suits" (O'Nan 2012, 107). At this moment, Marion comes to understand, rightly or wrongly, "that she and Art were the foreigners here" (107), a revelation that highlights both their relative class and race privilege and her sense that they are merely pawns in a global market that is far beyond their control. Marion's observation is telling. Yet, it also needs to be contextualized through her willingness to liken her own financial situation to that of a fleeing Black enslaved person, a claim that is itself deeply problematic. Nor does she consider the much more brutal forms of indebtedness faced by immigrant and racialized communities in both the US and Canada, during and after the Great Recession, who do not have the luxury of taking a vacation (even with an alternate agenda) or knowing that they will have a place to live and food to eat when they return. Marion's efforts to see their escape northward for the weekend as tied to a legacy of Black racial oppression offers a way to deflect individual responsibility for the family's situation and to ignore their continued relative affluence, despite their precarious financial state.

The Sheltering of White Privilege

So, while the Great Recession poses a fundamental threat to their wealth in terms of "financial assets" (Petev et al. 2011, 176), the Fowlers belong to a "relatively sheltered segment of the population—whites, the middle-aged and elderly" who find themselves in "[a] worse asset position" post-recession (176). They do not face immediate homelessness, and both seem certain that, even if they do divorce, each partner will be able to support themselves, albeit modestly. They may toast jokingly to a future of "Burger King" dinners when dining at several upscale restaurants in Niagara Falls over the course of the weekend, but each can imagine a viable (although potentially unappealing) reality (O'Nan 2012, 27). Art contemplates the possibility that he will live as a bachelor, sending "his laundry out … belonging to the legions of aging, unloved men buying frozen dinners and six-packs at the grocery store, or, worse, working there" (23). Although this is a less-than-ideal outcome from Art's perspective, primarily because Art believes that "without Marion he would not know what to do or even who he was," there is no threat of his living on the street or being unable to maintain a single-person household (23).

Marion appears even less concerned about her future. She finds relief in unloading the perceived burden of the house and her marriage: "[S]he didn't care about the money. She was sad about the house and sorry for Art, but the children were gone and they could live anywhere. Secretly, as horrible as it sounded, she was actually looking forward to moving into a smaller place and starting over" (O'Nan 2012, 7). Marion goes so far as to contemplate the division of furniture from the marital home during their trip, proposing to Art that she take their daughter's old bed. Not surprisingly, Art objects to Marion's offer. Marion soon recognizes Art's objection as the desire to ensure that his wife remains "the keeper of the marital bed" (60), a role that she has become increasingly tired of occupying in the two decades since Art's affair with Wendy Daigle, a fellow insurance broker.

The analogy between "marital betrayal" and "financial infidelity" in *The Odds* directly links "sexual and economic trespasses" (McClanahan 2017,

23) in O'Nan's novel, creating an added layer of complexity to the couple's relationship with money. The situation is further complicated by the fact that Marion knows about Art's affair with Wendy Daigle, but Art is unaware of Marion's relationship with another woman. Nonetheless, the story of Art and Marion Fowler is primarily shaped by race and class privilege. In contrast with Black American and Hispanic populations in the US during the Great Recession who faced the most dramatic losses in home equity and biggest decreases in "purchasing power" because of increasing unemployment and worsening debt levels (Petev et al. 2011, 176), whites were far less likely to be left with negative home equity or become delinquent on their mortgage due to lack of income.[3]

Moreover, despite feelings of sadness and anger about their current financial predicament, when the Fowlers learn over the course of the weekend that their daughter Emma has become engaged, Art contemplates "how to pay for" an upcoming wedding, recognizing that "[i]t would be too obvious if they waited until after the wedding to declare bankruptcy" (O'Nan 2012, 146). The financial burden of a wedding places added pressure on the couple as they embark on their plan to pay off their debts through gambling winnings. But it never occurs to Art not to commit to financing the wedding, suggesting that their race and class privilege, combined with their sense of obligation to traditional Western middle-class social responsibilities, still can and must be fulfilled for the sake of appearances. Even when, during their weekend getaway, Art has moments of uncertainty about what he perceives as the radical and desperate nature of their plan to try to gamble their way back to solvency, he recognizes that they are still in better financial shape than most: "He thought of the house, locked and dark, the realtor's sign a public admission in the yard. ... They could ride it out another six months if they had to" (92). While Art laments, "I never thought we'd lose money on that house" (93), Marion maintains that "[i]t was a good house. ... It was the right house for us" and assures Art that their grown children will not suffer greatly from the sale of their childhood home (93). She suggests that, despite the financial setbacks such a situation poses, her family is not doomed to unrelenting poverty.

In contrast, McClanahan notes that, in the US, those most dramatically impacted in real life by the subprime mortgage bubble were single Black American mothers, leading the "child advocacy group First Focus" in 2008 to predict that "nearly two million children would be directly affected by the housing crisis" because of mortgage defaults and "renter evictions" (2017, 147). Furthermore, the "[l]osses in wealth were worst within communities of color: every cent of wealth accumulated by African American households in the post-civil-rights era was lost as a result of the collapse of home and investment values" (9). This situation ensured that Black Americans, who were already financially disadvantaged because of long-standing racial prejudice, were further marginalized. Even "those too poor for mortgage debt" suffered as "foreclosure significantly increased the rate of family homelessness, since many of those evicted were renters who lived in buildings owned by landlords or property developers who had defaulted on their mortgages" (9). As McClanahan explains, "the financial markets of the early twenty-first century were in fact predicated on the selective deployment of uncontrollable risk and on the transfer of much of this risk to the most vulnerable economic subjects" (10), namely, poor Black and Hispanic American families, including those whose ancestors were enslaved in the US (and Canada).

Studies done in the aftermath of the Great Recession caution that the economic situation of Black Americans remains disproportionately bleak, with vast differences in household income based on race that existed prior to 2008 increasing substantially over the last decade. Black Americans now make 61% of a white, non-Hispanic income in the US, down from 64%, and home ownership levels sit at 42% in 2019 (as opposed to 73% for whites), leading to dramatic declines in measures like the median wealth of Black households and the average net worth of this same group (Adejumo 2019). However, as I argued in the Introduction and Chap. 3, Black racism is not isolated to the US. These statistics reveal the ironic—and deeply problematic—dimensions of Marion Fowler's claim that she and Art are traveling from the US in search of Canadian freedom. O'Nan's novel conveys the foibles of his characters and their desire to see Canada as a panacea for their problems, despite the reality that this kind of racially inflected financial precarity also exists north of the Canada-US border, but without the same levels of documentation or scrutiny.

In her study of "Racialized Precarious Employment and the Inadequacies of the Canadian Welfare State," Nicole Bernhardt argues that data collection regarding the workforce tends to replicate "Canadian color-blindness" (2015, 9), presuming that "issues of race" are only relevant to "culture" and that "racial conflict" should be confined to the "United States" (10). Nonetheless, Canada shares a history of removing "original native inhabitants" from their land (Simone and Walks 2019, 286). While its tradition of multicultural inclusion suggests a more "racially and ethnically diverse" population (287), the divide between immigrant and racialized household incomes and that of non-immigrants is increasingly stark, with the highest "debt-service ratios greater than 40 percent of disposable income" (Walks 2013, 161) growing most rapidly in racialized and immigrant "lowest-income households," especially as these groups find themselves in a "negative net equity position" (160–161). As Meh et al. explain, "poor debtors who fail to meet their obligations out of income may have trouble making up the difference through asset liquidation" (qtd. in Walks 2013, 161), such as the selling of property as O'Nan depicts the Fowlers doing with their home, which may force the couple to take a loss if it sells at all.

The Recession, Housing Costs, and Racism on Both Sides of the Canada-US Border

Canada was positioned as a much safer and more secure banking system throughout the Great Recession, in contrast to its neighbor to the south. Quoting Chrystia Freeland (represented as the first epigraph to this chapter),[4] Kevin Lynch explicitly lauds the Canadian banking system for its prudence in weathering a disastrous financial situation. He notes that "The vast majority of Canadians [sic] mortgages are originated by banks to be held … providing a 'front-line' incentive not to lend where there is a high risk of default; unlike the U.S., where the majority were originated to be sold" (Lynch 2010). However, in the decade since the Recession, "Canada's real estate bubble" has continued to grow and housing prices have become "severely unaffordable" in major Canadian cities, far outpacing the US, which remains in the "seriously unaffordable" category (Fleming 2018). Moreover, while Canada may wish to be seen as better than its American counterparts with respect to its financial stability, Simone and Walks see this as deeply problematic. Canada has "joined a select group of global nations where private debt levels and degrees of household debt-based vulnerability" have exceeded those found in the US before "the global financial crisis" (2019, 287). This situation has only grown more serious with the COVID-19 pandemic.

Simone and Walks note that there is no Canadian equivalent to the "significant amount of … research on the geography of subprime mortgage lending, household debt burdens, and foreclosures in the US," which has focused extensively on "race and immigrant status" (2019, 287). What little has been done often implicates "housing demand from wealthy foreign buyers from Hong Kong, China, and other Pacific Rim nations in driving up local real estate values" (287), without considering that "some immigrants could actually be recipients of aggressive and/or targeted mortgage lending" (287). Simone and Walks contend that there "has been rising antagonism against foreign buyers, and Chinese buyers in particular" in Canada, leading to the "implementation of a foreign homebuyers tax, … first in … British Columbia, and then in Ontario" (287). Andrea Yu describes "[t]he enduring legacy of Canada's racist head tax on Chinese-Canadians" (2019, 1), which resulted in a 2006 apology by then Canadian Prime Minister Stephen Harper and compensation payments for the head tax imposed from 1883 to 1923. The Exclusion Act subsequently prevented Chinese people from moving to Canada until 1947.

Canada's history also has been shaped by the Japanese-Canadian internment and other sustained patterns of race discrimination against Asian populations. Thus, any analysis of the presence of "Asian men," whether in the buffet lines or in the Niagara casino where the Fowlers try their luck, must recognize the contradictory history of racial discrimination in the US and Canada, much of which, in the case of Canada, remains unacknowledged (O'Nan 2012, 107). My reading suggests that through the Fowlers in *The Odds*, O'Nan alludes to the ways in which Canada continues to perpetuate a false narrative of racial inclusivity. The scene also demonstrates the country's exploitability for Art's small-time gambling, concealing a much more complex and contradictory portrait of the US' northern neighbor, which has become the target of large-scale money laundering and asset acquisition by foreign investors.

Moral Failure or Economic Miscalculation?

Central to the preservation of core national narratives of identity is the ability of both the Canadian and US governments to redirect institutional blame for the recession to individual citizens. Despite the reality that the "global financial system" is "impossibly complex, massive, and impenetrable," McClanahan contends that "personal failings" and "individual folly" have become a central part of narratives about the Great Recession, shifting blame from collective large-scale actions to the consequences of microbehaviors (2017, 22). Behavioral economists have ensured that the imposition of "restraint or accountability" in the case of "markets and market actors" remains untouched (McClanahan 2017, 28). This strategy accords with key principles of American individualism while supporting the ballooning wealth of a small segment of the population. It is a narrative that also resonates north of the Canada-US border, particularly in the case of racialized communities that may be demonized for artificially inflating urban Canadian housing prices through their efforts to move money abroad (as Simone and Walks describe), regardless of whether the behavior is criminal or not or may simply be perceived as aspiring to achieve too much.

Part of McClanahan's project involves examining how, in a handful of recent American novels, "fiscal irresponsibility" is understood to be as much "a failure of moral character … as an economic miscalculation" (2017, 23). This story is also reflected in *The Odds* through the overlapping narratives of Art's affair with Wendy 20 years ago, and the Fowlers' gradual progression over the watery falls of accruing and compounding debt, a metaphor that both Art and Marion return to repeatedly throughout the weekend to make sense of their precarity. In this respect, although Art and Marion are not literally putting their lives at risk fleeing to Canada, the Falls come to embody the impossibility of a return to their previously comfortable lifestyle. The relationship between Marion and Art, much like the house the Fowlers are on the brink of losing, is itself a reflection of Art's "one great shortcoming" (O'Nan 2012, 70), namely, his refusal to "accept and therefore have any shot at changing his fate even when the inevitable was clear to him" (70). For Art, the acquisition of the much sought-after house signals the beginning of a metaphorical journey toward the watery falls of financial ruin.

At least initially, Art Fowler believes that buying a much-desired home offers the promise of a better relationship with his spouse, Marion, a woman he has aspired to impress since first meeting her as a young man, although he has often fumbled along the way. Even when he first proposes marriage to Marion, he does so by looking at apartments on behalf of the couple without her knowledge. Art who is employed at the time by a non-profit organization and making a modest salary, lives in a "roach-infested studio" he deems unsuitable for Marion (O'Nan 2012, 87). She is sharing a "nice apartment" with her "old college roommates, trust fund babies" (87). So, in his eagerness to demonstrate his intentions, he searches for a place in a safe neighborhood, committed to getting Marion "away from" her affluent friends, who consider "him boring and unworthy of her" (87). Yet, when Art announces this plan to woo her, she responds quite differently than he expected. Marion is angered by the fact "that he'd taken her answer for granted" and challenges him to let her have a "say in her own life" (88). The result is that Art falls into a sustained pattern, often striving to please and impress Marion materially, conduct that reflects his own insecurity in relation to his spouse.

Not surprisingly then, when Marion finds a home that she loves years later, Art feels compelled to buy it: "The strength of her desire surprised him. He wanted to fulfill it, as if, out of gratitude, she might transfer that ardor to him" (70). Here, Art confuses the promise of love with the acquisition of a larger and more dignified home, one that reflects his vision of Marion. The purchase of the house marks the beginning of a series of "bad financial decisions" that, as McClanahan explains, raise questions about the irresponsibility of consumers and suggest the need for characters like Art to "atone for both sexual and economic trespasses" (2017, 23), potentially by facing the economic consequences of these aspirational actions.

Key to Art's desire to please his wife is his belief that buying the right home will ensure their mutual happiness. McClanahan notes that the "housing bubble" of "the late 1990s until 2007" marked "a unique period in the history of US housing," fueled in part by the recasting of homes as "simultaneously a fetish object and a savvy investment" (2017, 99). She explains that "[t]he home was no longer regarded simply as a consumer good but as a financial asset imbued with an aura of erotic desirability," most explicitly depicted in the explosive growth of television network shows focused on home renovations and makeovers (99). In the case of the Fowlers, marital infidelity and poor financial decision-making become conflated, ensuring that blame can be placed squarely with individual modes of conduct and unrealistic lifestyle goals rather than with banking systems and economic structures that encourage and support the leveraging of debt, regardless of the consequences for individuals and their families.

While this kind of dissociation between nation-state economic structures and the lives of citizens may be most explicitly foregrounded in the US context with situations like the Great Recession, there is no doubt that similar challenges continue to arise for homeowners north of the Canada-US border. A variety of business journalists and scholars have expressed deep concern with the rising debt loads and inflated housing markets that continue to shape the Canadian economy. This situation is fueled by easy access to unusually low interest rates, the increasing popularity of Home Equity Lines of Credit (HELOCs)—with balances growing from $35 billion in 2001 in Canada to $186 billion in 2010—and the growing availability of other forms of credit that may put families into debt forever. In May 2019, the Bank of Canada began to require the reporting of data on HELOCs from lenders in Canada because of the rapid evolution of HELOC products over the past decade.[5] This data demonstrated the steep growth of hybrid products that allow borrowers to combine HELOCs with mortgages. By combining the two, owners can access "as much as 80% of the home's value" rather than the traditional rate of 65% (Fournier and Hertzberg 2019a). Moreover, HELOCs are frequently used to service other forms of debt, making it challenging to identify what one credit rating analyst described as "emerging credit problems" (2019).

Notably, the language of debt is all too often a discourse of judgment, even in the case of Canadian journalist Rob Carrick, who in a January 2019 personal financial advice column about HELOCs in the national newspaper *The Globe and Mail* suggests a moral distinction between those who applied for a Home Equity Line of Credit but have never used it and those who are deeply in debt by "grading" their behaviors: "19 percent had not used their credit line. Kudos to that latter group—they have a powerful borrowing tool at their disposal, but the discipline not to use it" (2019, B1). In contrast, Carrick notes that, for some, "HELOCs" could rightly be compared to "drugs—helpful to many and dangerous or even addictive to a significant minority" (B1). He specifically argues that, despite the temptation to use lines of credit as "a blank cheque," "many people deserved good grades for the way they handled their credit line," including the one-third of "HELOC holders in the FCAC [Financial Consumer Agency of Canada] survey" who "planned to pay off their debt in less than one year," prompting Carrick to give "these people … [a]n A-plus" (B1). But there are also those for whom debt is inescapable, among them the "[t]hirteen percent of HELOC holders … [who] frequently used their credit line to meet payments on other debts, such as mortgage or credit card" (B1). The result is a vicious circle because "HELOCs are secured by the equity of your home, … and offer interest rates that are much lower than loans or unsecured lines of credit" (B1). While they are "'demand loans' that can be recalled by lenders at any time, … they do not have a maturity date," meaning that "consumers can draw on and repay their HELOC over an indefinite period" (Financial Consumer Agency of Canada 2017). Finally, HELOCs offer the option of just paying "interest owing each month" (Carrick 2019, B1), a spiral that potentially enables the accrual of a debt that can never be paid off.

In the case of Art and Marion Fowler, the descent into financial precarity is a gradual one that begins when they purchase a house that exceeds their means, despite knowing from the outset that it "was out of their [price] range" (O'Nan 2012, 70). Art initially lays some of the blame on Marion. He explains that "[h]e only went along to the showing to make her happy" and notes that she is the one who perceives it as "a bargain," based primarily on the age and elegance of the home with its "woodwork[,] ... leaded glass, [and] ... actual plaster walls"—the same qualities that soon reveal the home's myriad structural problems, from "original knob-and-tube wiring" to a furnace that resembles an "octopus," and a leaky roof (70–71). But as the family's financial manager, Art also acknowledges the absurdity of the purchase: "Technically they shouldn't have qualified for the mortgage even with them both working. ... With the stroke of a pen their nest egg was gone, and they were the owners of a leaky old showplace" (70). Having come from a financially conservative household (shaped by a mother who counted every penny but died with a large estate), Art has been able to use the money left by her from the sale of a family home for the down payment. However, that decision too has serious consequences. Art has counted on the so-called guilty windfall he thought would help pay for the children's college (70) to leverage their acquisition of the house, ultimately guaranteeing that debt piles upon debt, as the Fowlers borrow even more money to fund their middle-class children's college education, one crucial way of securing their children's future.

The Fowlers participate in what McClanahan describes as "the rhetoric of the 'ownership society,' a discourse frequently invoked by President George W. Bush as justification for the vigorous pursuit of new home borrowers" (2017, 153). As President of the US from 2001 to 2009, Bush argued in the aftermath of 9/11 that "Owning a home is part of the American dream," equating "property ownership ... with economic independence ... [,] sentimental attachment, moral legitimacy, and freedom" (qtd. in McClanahan 2017, 153–154). For McClanahan, "Bush's emphasis on home ownership provided a ready metaphor for national exceptionalism in the insecurity of a post-9/11 world" by "fram[ing] US citizenship through the logic of consumption" (154). But "it also provided ideological cover for a set of institutional and economic transformations that actually made home ownership increasingly insecure and then turned that insecurity into a securitizable asset" (154).

A similar phenomenon emerged in Canada during the same period, with an emphasis on creating "increasing homeownership among underserved groups, particularly immigrants" through "Canadian housing policies and mortgage lending policies" (Simone and Walks 2019, 288). Simone and Walks argue that these policies "run the risk of producing polarized groups" that divide people based on the ability to enter or be excluded from the market, depending on the "timing of housing market entry" (2019, 288). Simone and Walks also note that "[e]very major bank in Canada still (as of time of writing) offers 'newcomer packages'" by giving "special rates for mortgages," providing "'preferred' rates for car payments" and "offer[ing] credit cards of infinite varieties" (289). Yet in their 2019 article, Simone and Walks pointedly question this strategy, given the outcome of these kinds of policies in the US during the Great Recession and the "subprime/foreclosure crises in the US," which had a much more brutal impact on racialized, middle-to-lower class, and immigrant populations (289). By over-including vulnerable groups in lending practices and ensuring that lenders rather than borrowers are well protected,[6] Canada continues to cultivate a myth of national economic "stability, security, and plentitude," while relying on a pattern of exploitation of specific populations within the nation to sustain an asset-based welfare economy.

In contrast with first-time and immigrant owners who relied on mortgage deregulation to access home ownership in any form, the Fowlers would seem to be more financially secure than most families in the US and Canada. They have long-standing careers in insurance and healthcare, a family inheritance that ensures a substantial down payment on the house, and a "buy-and-hold" stock portfolio that is "conservative and diversified" (O'Nan 2012, 72), following in the footsteps of Art's financially savvy mother. Yet, the burden for Art and Marion is huge. Throughout his insurance career, Art has been trained to minimize "risk" and cannot conceive of the kinds of chances being taken by "AIG and Countrywide" (72), companies that were revealed in the aftermath of the Great Recession as having bet on and sold risky mortgages that should never have been approved.[7]

The Odds depicts a situation in which the Fowlers, like millions of other Americans, are expected to be able to predict and absorb market trends in the manner of financial professionals. This is an impossible task even for a man like Art who, despite "thirty years managing corporate accounts," realizes years later, when he is laid off and reading job ads, that he lacks basic skills: "he wasn't a CPA. ... He couldn't weld, he didn't have his Class B driver's license [so] ... he couldn't even be a janitor" (O'Nan 2012, 75). As Simone and Walks explain, "asset-based welfare requires households to become financially literate," to possess "sufficient ability to predict long-term trends of asset values, [to] profitably manage risk and uncertainty in financial markets, ... and ultimately to absorb financial risk and manage their finances as if they were hedge funds" (2019, 287). The Fowlers' largest asset, the house, it quickly becomes apparent, requires substantial investment. Despite the "realtor's inspector," they soon find themselves cashing in "a mutual fund to redo their roof, screwing up their taxes" (O'Nan 2012, 71). Nor does the house purchase appear to strengthen Marion and Art's marriage. Art's affair with Wendy Daigle becomes co-mingled with house projects. As he looks back on the story of the couples' changed financial status, he recalls that, "[w]hen he was seeing Wendy, they were repointing the chimneys" (71), suggesting that Art's belief that the house will fix his marriage is, in fact, false.

The "logic of consumption" permeates the Fowlers' approach to housing (McClanahan 2017, 154), as they take on a number of home improvement projects that lead to a final tipping point: the kitchen, which they gut in the aftermath of their son's college graduation because "interest rates were so low" that they are able to negotiate a "home equity loan that amounted to a second mortgage" (O'Nan 2012, 71). While Art initially blames Marion for wanting to "gut the cramped fifties-era kitchen," he is seduced by the idea that money is cheap and that "breaking into their IRAs early" makes no sense if they can take out "a loan" to "bridge the gap" (71). For Art, the problem is one of "liquidity," which he sees as tied up in his "firm's generous stock option," and he successfully convinces himself that these projects will both boost their investment in their home and ensure they can enjoy it (71). What the Fowlers discover is their presumption—that the house into which they've sunk their lifesavings and a large chunk of debt is not the "illiquid, spatially fixed and immobile, relatively durable" asset they have counted on to justify overextending their borrowing (Kevin Fox Gotham qtd. in McClanahan 2017, 163).

Fixed Versus Speculative Asset

Instead, what has historically been understood as a "fixed asset" has been transformed in early twenty-first-century North America into a "speculative asset" (McClanahan 2017, 161). This is a direct result of "mortgage securitization," which makes it easy to convert homes "into collateral for securitized credit" just as the Fowlers have done repeatedly by renovating various parts of their home. Moreover, the promise of secure and permanent employment based on "the education premium—the increase in lifetime earnings that accrues to those with a college degree" in the US, which was historically used to justify the high costs of post-secondary education—is now "nearly identical to the national average rate of unemployment," with many college graduates in jobs that do not require a degree (193). In O'Nan's novel, both Marion and Art lose their jobs in quick succession at the height of their financial leveraging. Marion's hours as a healthcare worker are cut shortly before the facility is closed altogether. In a moment that foreshadows the couple's ambivalence about the Asians they later see at the casino (and blame for their predicament), Art's insurance company employer is sold to an Asian investment group, which searches out plummeting stocks and buy them cheaply. The description of this purchase in the novel is yet another fictional example of the increasingly global reach of asset acquisition (in the form of homes and businesses) on both sides of the Canada-US border and a reminder that the two countries are shaped by global financial forces, far beyond any individual's control. As *The Odds* depicts, Art's retirement nest egg, in the form of stock options, is rendered worthless and the new owners of the insurance company download health and retirement planning onto workers before laying off the most expensive senior staff, including Art.

Once unemployed, a fact he hides from his neighbors out of shame, Art is left wondering what he could have done differently. While Art recognizes that "he could blame … the banks for being greedy and overextending themselves, putting the country at risk and then socking away the TARP [Troubled Asset Relief Program] money"—bailout money provided by the US government to stabilize the economy[8]—he ultimately conflates his historical self-perception as an "underachiever" (O'Nan 2012, 76) with his failure to keep his home. Notably, O'Nan repeatedly invokes specialized financial language and acronyms throughout the novel to describe the challenges Art and Marion face, revealing the ways in which they are woefully unprepared to manage such challenges. Grateful that his mother is no longer alive to see the couple's current predicament and desperate to stave off financial ruin, Art resorts "to stopgap measures she [his mother] would have disapproved of, paying bills late or paying with credit cards," and "then paying just the minimum on the cards so each month their balance rose" (76). The daily arrival of mail becomes an especially dreaded ritual. Art continues to pay some bills promptly, "the mortgages, their health and home and auto insurance," but "[e]ven when they didn't spend anything, the money … [keeps] draining away" (76). Moreover, Marion sees their finances as "just money and not a true barometer of their worth" (76), and so, unwilling to "make her as unhappy as he was," Art continues what he calls "his crooked bookkeeping" to ensure that the household runs until he can no longer do so (77). As O'Nan's novel demonstrates, Art has played the odds and lost, making the trip to Niagara Falls especially poignant because it is symbolic of his desire to imitate just a little longer the luxuries of a lifestyle the Fowlers can no longer afford. Paradoxically, by choosing Niagara Falls and a casino as the site for his effort at redemption, Art once again falls prey to the liquidity of assets, turning cash into chips to play the roulette wheel—literally— with what is left of the couple's life savings.

SEXUAL BETRAYAL AND DEBT

Through Art and Marion, *The Odds* probes the ways in which the irresponsibility of individual American consumers becomes a means of displacing the perils of a "global financial system" and the participation of governments (including the US Federal Reserve) and investment firms onto people rather than structures, a shift in blame that becomes imbedded in the language the Fowlers use to talk about Art's past affair with Wendy Daigle (McClanahan 2017, 21). Certainly, this is the case for Marion, who does not disclose her own secret lesbian affair with Karen, but hypocritically continues to hold Art accountable. Over dinner, their first night at the Falls, Art expresses hope that "like bankruptcy, everything [will be] forgiven" to which Marion retorts, "Sorry, some debts you have to pay" (O'Nan 2012, 29). Although Art jokingly laments, "[i]t was worth a try" (29), what becomes clear is that each partner in the marriage carries some guilt over their financial state because of their inability to curb "short-term desires" (23), both financial and sexual. But Marion also continues to cultivate a more privileged presence on Facebook. She boasts about the weekend getaway as a nostalgia trip and lets Art take numerous pictures of their activities. Marion even poses "like a bride" at the end of a clichéd carriage ride by the Falls, which has happened only after waiting in line in the cold for over an hour, as part of what she recognizes as "[i]mpossibly" the desire "to go back and start over," to "find a way not to ruin things" (67). Her stance vacillates between wanting to return to a life of affluence that is no longer possible and moving on from a marriage and household situation that she recognizes to be bankrupt, both literally and figuratively.

ACCESS TO CREDIT

The Fowlers' trip is funded by the couple's easy access to a considerable amount of credit, which O'Nan highlights when he begins the fourth chapter of the novel with the following: "*Odds of a U.S. citizen being an American Express cardholder: 1 in 10*" (2012, 17). In this case, O'Nan pointedly stresses the numerical evidence of the Fowlers' income and affluence over the course of their married life, a position that has enabled them to maintain their lifestyle even in a state of unemployment. Annie Lowrey explains that "credit scores and access to credit—and all that means for a family's ability to buy a house, finance an education, get a job, and have a comfortable cash cushion during rough economic times" offers a critical cushion from "[t]he cumulative impact of ... financial calamities" (2017). American Express launched its first charge card in 1958 and has since positioned its card as exclusive and accessible only to "affluent, upscale adults who travel and entertain frequently for business and pleasure" (Kara et al. 1996, 211). American Express has been known for its long-standing practice of requiring cardholders to pay their bill in full each month. They also historically charged higher interchange fees to merchants than other major credit cards. As a result, American Express cards were not as widely accepted in the US and abroad, consolidating the link between American Express usage and establishments that could afford to cater to the "rich and affluent" (Campos da Silva 2013, 18).

In *The Odds*, O'Nan offers a detailed exploration of the relationship Art has with his American Express card, one cultivated through the history of the card's print advertising, which continues to sustain a veil of privilege despite the reality of Art's financial status. Campos da Silva explores in her thesis, aptly titled "My Life. My Card," the unique association of "prestige and status" with American Express cards cultivated through strategic advertising campaigns (including "Membership Has Its Privileges," which ran from 1987 to 1996 and "My Life. My Card" from 2004 to 2007). Campos da Silva explains that "[p]ossessing the American Express card does not just give access to immediate credit, but also to an exclusive club, full of advantages, glamour and prominence" (2), the same narrative that Art relies on to fund the trip to Niagara Falls. Indeed, when the Fowlers arrive at the hotel in Niagara Falls, Art offers his American Express to secure a bridal suite overlooking the Falls, complete with "roses," "champagne," and a "fruit basket with a note from the management" (O'Nan 2012, 3). The receptionist returns the card moments later, having successfully authorized payment, a handover that prompts Art to take stock of his marriage through the card: "in a masterstroke promoting brand loyalty, the raised date reminded him that he'd been a member since 1981, the same year he and Marion were married" (20). The card provides a nostalgic reminder of their past travels, including "England, Ireland, Hawaii" (20), juxtaposed with the reality that he is, at this moment, committing fraud: "Somewhere in a windowless room, he was on camera, flattening the receipt against the counter in lo-res-black-and-white" (20). For Art, the credit card becomes a poignant and tangible symbol of a life to which he will no longer have access once the weekend ends.

During their time in Niagara Falls, O'Nan notes that Art continually uses his American Express card to charge meals and accommodation. He relies on a long history of good credit as he already has to service "day-to-day expenses" (Walks 2013, 160) including household bills, as well as funding a last-ditch effort to change his family's odds by crossing the Canada-US border to gamble. He knows that he will never actually pay these bills but because of his loyalty and strong credit history up to this point (as a previously affluent consumer), he is confident that this debt, minor in comparison to that of the house, "would be forgiven" (O'Nan 2012, 20). His punishment for this act, Art is confident, comes with "no more serious repercussions than he would never again own an American Express card" (20). From the moment the couple arrive at the hotel, they are relying on credit to fund the weekend away, a reality that Art recognizes but finds ways to justify:

> Technically, since he had no intention of paying the bill, he was guilty of fraud, or could be once he filed for bankruptcy, but that was months away, and by then so many other charges would have accumulated that the trustee assigned to his case would rightly assume he'd mismanaged his finances so badly that, owing alimony and with a piddling income, he was forced to use his credit cards to live. (19–20)

Art exploits the familiarity of this narrative for his own purposes, recognizing the "increased normalization of consumer debt" (McClanahan 2017, 79). As previously described, Art may have initially hidden the truth from his neighbors after losing his job, relying on Marion to keep his secret. But with the virtual evaporation of middle-class wealth in the US from 2007 to 2010, during which the "median net worth of U.S. households fell by 47 percent, reaching its lowest level in more than 40 years" (Woolf qtd. in

McClanahan 2017, 113), Art realizes that, as a middle-class white man potentially facing divorce, his story is a familiar one. He thus decides to use his race and class privilege to manage a deteriorating financial situation to his advantage.

Financial Precarity: Nowhere to Run

However, even Niagara Falls cannot provide the Fowlers with sustained relief from what appears to be a new form of precarity fueled by housing foreclosures and credit card debt, from which there is no guaranteed escape, even north of the Canada-US border, a version of financial enslavement that allows established and new forms of segregation to flourish. As McClanahan points out in the third epigraph to this chapter, while those with good credit are perceived as able to move forward, individuals and families who face the burden of a debt that is seemingly insurmountable are confronted and haunted by a past that will unrelentingly limit their future. Art and Marion Fowler may not be racially enslaved but their financial situation demonstrates a deeply unsettled relation to "domestic property" (McClanahan 2017, 126), further highlighted by the reality that mortgages are etymologically "dead pledge[s]" that make housing "liminal" spaces while "the loan is still owed" (127). The result is that houses are no longer places "of comfort" but rather highlight the "unease and alienation" of impending dispossession and the potential reality of endless debt (127). Notably, in the case of Canada, the continued strength and growth of home values during and after the Great Recession in places like Toronto (a mere 90-minute drive from Niagara Falls)[9] and Vancouver stands in direct contrast with the more "subdued" increases in the US over the past decade ("Hard or Soft Landing" 2012), raising fundamental questions about whether home ownership is even possible for many residents in these urban locales—especially those who are part of economically, socially, and culturally marginalized groups, despite Canada's seeming desire to be perceived as inclusive and tolerant in its development of a civic nationalism.[10]

In the immediate aftermath of the Great Recession, Canada was held up as a model of prudence and restraint. But the growth of Canadians borrowing against the value of their homes using Home Equity Lines of Credit (HELOCs) has created its own set of problems. A good proportion of those with HELOCs, when facing increasing financial precarity, are relying heavily on the perceived worth of housing to cover other debts and thus setting a dangerous precedent. McClanahan argues in the conclusion to her monograph that this kind of "permadebt" becomes an "affirmation of debt's unpayability" (2017, 197), which she views as a potential form of radical resistance to the "quantifiable claim on the future earnings of [a] worker" (197). While theoretically such a stance reflects the rejection of the "good-life fantasy" of upward mobility, which has shaped capitalist economies around the globe, including the US and Canada, pragmatically, there is a real-life cost to taking those kinds of positions (McClanahan 2017, 196). Canada's self-construction as exceptional and thus safe from such economic peril has led to a false sense of security north of the Canada-US border that no longer aligns with the financial realities of many Canadians. In a recent *BNNBloomberg.com* article, "Drowning in Debt, Freaked Out Canadians Brace for a Reckoning," Fournier and Hertzberg note that the ratio of Canadian household debt to gross domestic product exceeds that of the US by nearly 25 percent, setting a course for potential economic disaster (2019b).

In the final chapter of *The Odds*, which is subtitled "Odds of a divorced couple remarrying: 1 in 20,480" (O'Nan 2012, 165) indicating the improbability of a reconciliation should Marion and Art separate, the Fowlers pay a final visit to the high stakes table to make a concerted effort to gamble their way out of their serious financial woes. Rather than being examples of ingenious citizenship, a concept that has been discussed in previous chapters, Marion and Art are "complicit with and contaminated … [by a] liberal structural order" (Lee 2016, 87) that they will do almost anything to preserve, despite their own downward financial spiral. Art, at least, continues to believe that the couple have a right to recover their assets, regardless of method. When Marion fails to make back her stake midway through the evening, Art laments that "[t]his redistribution of wealth is trickier than I thought" (O'Nan 2012, 177). But he insists that if they persist, they will recover what ought to be theirs as white middle-class Americans who have prospered for much of their adult lives.

The novel ends with the promise of a potential lucky streak using the "Martingale method," which Art has turned to because it involves "the nerve to lose big" (O'Nan 2012, 114). This is the same kind of risky strategy that Ziemba and Ziemba in *Scenarios for Risk Management* caution against using because while it may yield "small profits most of the time, the gigantic losses you suffer once in a while yield losses in the long run" (2017, 6). Perversely, Art participates in the type of behavior and logic employed by bankers that drove the subprime mortgage collapse. Marion may decide in the final pages to bet on Art, accepting that "if it was a mistake, she would have to live with it" (O'Nan 2012, 179). But there is no happy ending. Ultimately, the novel suggests that, if *The Odds* are in their favor, their luck will soon run out, just as Art and Marion are destined to run out of chips. The Fowlers continue both to align themselves with and to blame racial others, without scrutinizing the complexities of such assertions or the stereotypes that they perpetuate in doing so. The couple collapses the literal and figurative distinctions between their flight to Canada and that of the Black predecessors Marion invokes, thus ignoring the long and sustained history of racial and immigrant exploitation that continues to this day on both sides of the Canada-US border. At the same time, *The Odds* reinforces the same concerns raised by McClanahan that equate domestic strife and marital failure with "fiscal irresponsibility" without examining the intersectional contexts that shape these stories of the couples depicted in post-Great Recession novels, including O'Nan's (McClanahan 2017, 23).

While the northward-facing orientation of *The Odds* might be expected to invoke the legacy of the Underground Railroad that Marion references at the beginning of the novel, a narrative that champions Canada as a site of freedom, "tolerance, and benevolence" (O'Nan 2012, 26), what the Fowlers observe is a picture of the US' northern neighbor that suggests the border has never marked a space of safety or protection from the global spread of capitalism, whether it takes the form of slavery, human trafficking, or the profitability of big banks. Canadians might like to believe that they are exceptional, particularly in the realm of financial responsibility, both individual and collective, but O'Nan's novel can be read as a reminder that Canada's superior stance is an illusion—like Niagara Falls—designed to sell a fantasy of security and prosperity.

Notes

1. Friscolanti notes that most confiscated funds are "dirty" but that under Canadian law the "burden of proof lies with the individual" to demonstrate that the money is not the proceeds of a crime, a challenge that results in almost no one recovering their cash, even if it was earned legitimately (2007, 22).
2. See Sher and Marsden (2003) and Langton (2013) for detailed explorations of how the Hell's Angels moved into Canada in the last decades of the twentieth century.
3. See Grusky et al. (2011, 134) for Table 6.1 which depicts the "Share of Homeowners Who Have Negative Home Equity and Are Delinquent on

Their Mortgages, by Household Characteristic (Percentages)" up to and including 2009. The table differentiates African-American and Hispanic households from "Non-Hispanic white" households; in every category these former groups constitute a vast majority, whether in the case of those with "Negative Home Equity, 2009," mortgage delinquency, or those behind in their mortgage payments (134). They stand in stark contrast to the situation of "Non-Hispanic white" homeowners who saw decreases in property values but experienced far lower delinquency rates, meaning that they had other resources to support their households during the Great Recession.
4. See page 4 of "Home equity lines of credit" report from the Financial Consumer Agency of Canada, last updated in 2017 which notes that "[s]ince 2011, the number of Canadian households who have a HELOC as stand-alone product, without also having a term mortgage on their home, has declined by 40 percent. In contrast, the number of households that have a HELOC and a term mortgage secured against their home has increased by nearly 40 percent."
5. Freeland, who has since served as the Deputy Prime Minister of Canada under Justin Trudeau (2019–) and the governing Liberal's Finance Minister since 2020, paints a rosy picture of Canada's financial health, using the same kind of rhetoric that Trudeau employs when discussing *Come From Away* as described in Chap. 8.
6. See Simone and Walks (2019, 289).
7. See Pfeifer and Puzzanghera (2019).
8. See Lucas who notes that "the total direct cost of the 2008 crisis-related bailouts in the United States was on the order of $500 billion, or 3.5% of GDP in 2009," a conclusion that "stands in sharp contrast to popular accounts that claim there was no cost because the money was repaid" (2019, 87).
9. See Doskoch who argues that "[w]hen you look at GTA housing prices and sales statistics, it's almost like there had never been a recession" (2010).
10. See Mackey for a closer examination of "civic nationalism" (2002, 154–161).

References

Adejumo, Vincent. 2019. African-Americans' Economic Setbacks from the Great Recession are Ongoing—and Could Be Repeated. *The Conversation*, February 13. https://theconversation.com/african-americans-economic-setbacks-from-the-great-recession-are-ongoing-and-could-be-repeated-109612.

Beare, Margaret E., and Stephen Schneider. 2007. *Money Laundering in Canada: Chasing Dirty and Dangerous Dollars.* Toronto: University of Toronto Press.

Bernhardt, Nicole S. 2015. Racialized Precarious Employment and the Inadequacies of the Canadian Welfare State. *Journal of Workplace Rights* (April–June): 1–13.

Campbell, Matthew, and Natalie Obiko Pearson. 2018. The City That Had Too Much Money. *Bloomberg Businessweek*, October 20. https://www.bloomberg.com/news/features/2018-10-20/vancouver-is-drowning-in-chinese-money.

Campos da Silva, Fabiola. 2013. My Life. My Card.: A Textual Analysis of the Role of Print Advertising in the Sign Value Construction Process of the AMERICAN EXPRESS© Cards. MA Thesis in Media Studies, Faculty of Humanities, Department of Media and Communications (IMK). University of Oslo. https://www.duo.uio.no/bitstream/handle/10852/38052/Fabiola-Campos-da-Silva.pdf?sequence=1&isAllowed=y.

Carrick, Rob. 2019. For Some Canadians, a HELOC Is Debt That May Never Be Paid Off. *The Globe and Mail*, January 15: B1.

Doskoch, Bill. 2010. GTA Housing Market Quickly Shook Off the Recession. *CTV News*, January 2. https://toronto.ctvnews.ca/gta-housing-market-quickly-shook-off-the-recession-1.469427.

Douglas, Jeremy. 2019. To Disrupt Money Laundering, Canada Should Consider a Different Relationship with Asia. *The Globe and Mail*, March 29. https://www.theglobeandmail.com/opinion/article-to-disrupt-money-laundering-canada-should-consider-a-different/.

Financial Consumer Agency of Canada. 2017. *Home Equity Lines of Credit: Market Trends and Consumer Issues*. Government of Canada, June 7. https://www.canada.ca/en/financial-consumer-agency/programs/research/home-equity-lines-credit-trends-issues.html.

Fleming, David. 2018. Canada vs. America Since The 2008 Recession. *TorontoRealtyBlog.com*, December 12. https://torontorealtyblog.com/blog/canada-vs-america-since-the-2008-recession/.

Foner, Eric. 2015. *Gateway to Freedom: The Hidden History of the Underground Railroad*. New York: W. W. Norton.

Fournier, Chris, and Erik Hertzberg. 2019a. As HELOCs Morph, the Bank of Canada Asks Lenders for Details. *BNNBloomberg.com*, May 9. https://www.bnnbloomberg.ca/as-helocs-morph-the-bank-of-canada-asks-lenders-for-details-1.1256201.

———. 2019b. Drowning in Debt, Freaked Out Canadians Brace for a Reckoning. *BNNBloomberg.com*, March 26. https://www.bnnbloomberg.ca/businessweek/canadians-are-feeling-the-debt-burn-1.1234735.

Freeland, Chrystia. 2010. What Toronto can teach New York and London. *Financial Times*, January 29. https://www.ft.com/content/db2b340a-0a1b-11df-8b23-00144feabdc0.

Friscolanti, Michael. 2007. Sorry, No Refunds on Cash Seizures: If Customs Confiscates Your Undeclared Cash, Don't Expect It Back. *Maclean's* 120 (33, Aug. 27): 22.

Grusky, David B., Bruce Western, and Christopher Wimer, eds. 2011. *The Great Recession*. New York: Russell Sage Foundation.

"Hard Or Soft Landing: A Look at Canada's Housing Market from Boom to...". 2012. *Financial Post*, November 29. https://business.financialpost.com/business-insider/a-review-of-canadas-housing-market-from-boom-to.

Helleiner, Jane. 2016. *Borderline Canadianness: Border Crossings and Everyday Nationalism in Niagara*. Toronto: University of Toronto Press.

Kara, Ali, Erdener Kaynak, and Orsay Kucukemiroglu. 1996. An Empirical Investigation of US Credit Card Users: Card Choice and Usage Behavior. *International Business Review* 5 (2): 209–230.

Kirby, Jason. 2019. Dirty Money: It's a Canadian Thing. *Maclean's*, June 12. https://www.macleans.ca/economy/realestateeconomy/b-c-s-money-laundering-crisis-goes-national/.

Langton, Jerry. 2013. *Showdown: How the Outlaws, Hells Angels and Cops Fought for Control of the Streets*. Toronto: HarperCollins.

Lee, Charles T. 2016. *Ingenious Citizenship: Recrafting Democracy for Social Change*. Durham: Duke University Press.

Lowrey, Annie. 2017. The Great Recession Is Still With Us. *The Atlantic*, December 1. https://www.theatlantic.com/business/archive/2017/12/great-recession-still-with-us/547268/.

Lucas, Deborah. 2019. Measuring the Cost of Bailouts. *Annual Review of Financial Economics* 11: 85–108.

Lynch, Kevin. 2010. Prudent, Perhaps, But the Canadian Model Pays Off. *The Globe and Mail*, May 28. https://www.theglobeandmail.com/opinion/prudent-perhaps-but-the-canadian-model-pays-off/article1367737/.

Mackey, Eva. 2002. *The House of Difference: Cultural Politics of National Identity in Canada*. Toronto: University of Toronto Press.

MacLean, Alyssa Erin. 2010. *Canadian Migrations: Reading Canada in Nineteenth-Century American Literature*. PhD diss., University of British Columbia. https://open.library.ubc.ca/cIRcle/collections/ubctheses/24/items/1.0071502.

McClanahan, Annie. 2017. *Dead Pledges: Debt, Crisis, and Twenty-First Century Culture*. Stanford: Stanford University Press.

Nicol, Heather W. 2015. *The Fence and The Bridge: Geopolitics and Identity along the Canada-US Border*. Waterloo: Wilfrid Laurier University Press.

O'Nan, Stewart. 2012. *The Odds*. New York: Viking Press.

Petev, Ivaylo D., Luigo Pistaferri, and Itay Saporta-Eksten. 2011. An Analysis of Trends, Perceptions, and Distributional Effects in Consumption. In *The Great Recession*, ed. David B. Grusky, Bruce Western, and Christopher Wimer, 161–195. New York: Russell Sage Foundation.

Pfeifer, Stuart, and Jim Puzzanghera. 2019. Countrywide, AIG Units in Legal Battle. *The Los Angeles Times*, March 20. https://www.latimes.com/archives/la-xpm-2009-mar-20-fi-countrywide20-story.html.

Sher, Julian, and William Marsden. 2003. *The Road to Hell: How the Biker Gangs are Conquering Canada*. Toronto: Seal Books.

Simone, Dylan, and Alan Walks. 2019. Immigration, Race, Mortgage Lending, and the Geography of Debt in Canada's Global Cities. *Geoforum* 98: 286–299.

Strong, Gregory. 2018. Cleveland Indians Praised for Shelving Chief Wahoo Logo for Toronto Series. *The Canadian Press*, September 7. https://www.cbc.ca/sports/baseball/mlb/indians-chief-wahoo-toronto-1.4814728.

Walks, Alan. 2013. Mapping the Urban Debtscape: The Geography of Household Debt in Canadian Cities. *Urban Geography* 34 (2): 153–187.

Yu, Andrea. 2019. The Enduring Legacy of Canada's Racist Head Tax on Chinese-Canadians. *Maclean's*, March 1: 1–6. https://www.macleans.ca/society/the-enduring-legacy-of-canadas-racist-head-tax-on-chinese-canadians/.

Ziemba, Rachel E.S., and William T. Ziemba. 2017. *Scenarios for Risk Management and Global Investment Strategies*. Hoboken, NJ: Wiley.

CHAPTER 7

Turning Away, Going West and South: The Receding Promise of Canada in *Future Home of the Living God* and *The Underground Railroad*

> *Indeed, the struggle for reproductive rights for Native American women has always been one of not only being able to have children but also being able to keep them in their custody. ... This point could also be made when speaking of the experiences of Aboriginal women in Canada as well.* (Stote 2015, 6)

> *Canadians have long seen slavery in terms, above all, of the Underground Railway, that clandestine network of forest and waterside paths by which Quakers, black freedmen and other human rights advocates smuggled runaway American slaves northwards to liberty in the early nineteenth century. ... for some strange reason, while congratulating Canadians for offering refuge to these fugitives, generations of historians maintained a virtual conspiracy of silence about slaves owned and exploited, bought and sold, by Canadians themselves.* (Tombs, Translator's Preface to Trudel 2013, 7)

> *We should not be surprised then, that most people who slipped the bonds of slavery [in the US] did not look north. In fact, despite its popularity today, the Underground Railroad was perhaps the* least *popular way for slaves to seek their freedom. ... Most runaways did not head north.* (Schulz 2016)

In an essay titled "A Golden Age for Dystopian Fiction" published in *The New Yorker* in May 2017, Jill Lepore examines the emergence of a "new [American] literature of radical pessimism." She argues this body of

© The Author(s), under exclusive license to Springer Nature Switzerland AG 2023
J. Andrews, *Canada Through American Eyes*,
https://doi.org/10.1007/978-3-031-22120-0_7

literature was prompted by the November 2016 election of Donald Trump as US President, defeating the first female candidate for President, Hilary Clinton, and directly following Obama's two terms in office, as the first Black President in the history of a nation whose Civil War was fought over Black slavery (2017). Lepore notes that "'dystopia,' meaning 'an unhappy country,' was coined in the seventeen-forties" which coincided with the rise of nation-states and increasing imperialism and colonialism around the globe (Lepore 2017). The dystopian tenor of the texts Lepore surveys may be read as reflecting the fear and anger felt by many Americans as they witnessed the rapid institution of Trump's right-wing and racist policies, viewed as especially egregious by liberal and left-leaning women and those belonging to racially and sexually marginalized populations, including Black and Indigenous peoples.[1]

During his first 100 days as President, Trump signed a litany of divisive executive orders, including the notorious Muslim ban, designed to block Muslim travelers and refugees from entering the US. The ban was deemed unlawful by various American courts, leading to Trump's repeated efforts to institute revised versions of the same ban in the years that followed. His government dismantled domestic and global reproductive rights, slashed caps on the US refugee program, sought to end the Affordable Care Act, and aggressively reinforced immigration laws. These actions led to increased detentions, deportations, and the separation of family members seeking refuge in America, with young children being held in US shelters while their parents were deported back to their country of origin. Public outcry over the contemporary detention of minor children led advocates to recall "America's cruel history of separating children from their parents," exemplified by the practice of selling slaves and their offspring without warning to the highest bidder and the forcible removal of Indigenous children from their families to attend "Indian schools" (Brown 2018). Such government policies have spanned most of the country's existence.

In contrast, Canadian Liberal Prime Minister Justin Trudeau, whose 2015 election majority removed three-term Conservative leader Stephen Harper from office, reinforced the idea of Canada "the good" from the beginning of his time in office, particularly when it came to those seeking refuge in Canada (Austen 2017). Within months, his government launched Operation Syrian Refugees and, shortly after, in December 2015, Trudeau was famously photographed greeting Syrian families with young children who had just arrived at Pearson International Airport in Toronto as they disembarked, uttering the message, "'You're safe at home now' and handing them winter coats" (Austen 2017). This gesture reinforced long-standing perceptions of Canada as a nation known for its "pacificism, peacekeeping, and tolerance" (Blake 2010, 81). The scene also highlighted Canada's ability to teach newcomers how to survive and thrive, even in an unforgiving northerly location with distinct seasons, and weather shaped, for much of the year, by "snow and ice" (Allan 2009, 1). These images can be read as part of a sustained tradition dating back to British colonialism, which argued, as Daniel Coleman describes in *White Civility*, "how the trials of colonial settlement" in such cold weather functioned as "a kind of crucible," refining and displacing British civility with Canadian Britishness (2006, 24). The "Northern myth" of supremacy was a critical part of "this figuration of Canada" (24). In other words, Canada's "stern, unaccommodating climate demanded strength of body, character, and mind while it winnowed away laziness, overindulgence, and false social niceties" (24). The implication, of course, was that Canadians possessed a heartiness and stamina lacking in those living south of the border, particularly in warmer climates.

In addition, multiple photos and videos were circulated of the Prime Minister, himself a father of three, interacting closely with the children and parents of these newly arrived Syrian families. The images suggested that, unlike the US, Canada would not use the separation of children from parents or the division of family members to discourage asylum seekers. The subsequent election of Donald Trump as US President facilitated and amplified Trudeau's efforts to position Canada as a kinder, gentler nation and to reinforce the country's historic role as a utopian escape from the brutality of American racism.

But as *New York Times* reporter Ian Austen explains in a 2018 article, while Canada may look "better with how it treats asylum seekers after they arrive," it also continues to detain child refugees, both with and without relatives, in "immigration centers" that are comparable to "medium-security prisons" (Austen 2018). And, despite Canada's seeming receptivity to the plight of those escaping persecution, legal scholar Audrey Macklin is quoted in Austen's article claiming that "Canada is harsher and more effective at preventing asylum seekers from arriving" (2018). In other words, the search for and belief in a utopic alternative north of the Canada-US border offers both the promise of hope and the challenge of facing a reality (either imagined or embodied) that fails to offer a better life for all.

Previous chapters in this book have focused extensively on American-authored novels that trace untold stories of Canada, animating specific historical events that have been ignored or overlooked in the service of cultivating and reinforcing Canadian exceptionalism or exploring the parallels between Canada and the US, despite the long-standing efforts of many Canadians to differentiate themselves from their American neighbors. The previous chapter examines the ways in which a white middle-class couple embark on a weekend visit to Canada, and more specifically Niagara Falls, in a final effort to resolve their financial and marital challenges. As mentioned at the beginning of the chapter, Marion Fowler equates the Fowlers' efforts to recoup their financial losses through a gambling holiday on the Canadian side of the Niagara Falls with the historical narrative of the Underground Railroad as a path to Black liberation from slavery. Yet, the events of O'Nan's story demonstrate the absurdity of this comparison because of the relative privilege of the Fowlers even as they face financial constraints.

This chapter looks more closely at Canada's role as a receding mirage of promise for a better life in two recent dystopian representations of America: Turtle Mountain Chippewa writer Louise Erdrich's *Future Home of the Living God* (2017) and Black author Colson Whitehead's *The Underground Railroad* (2016). Both novels imagine an America in the near future that is wretched—to varying degrees—and initially offer up Canada as a potential place of escape, ultimately tempering this depiction. In doing so, *Future Home* and *The Underground Railroad* portray the far more brutal reality faced by BIPOC Americans who have been historically relegated to various forms of enslavement and genocide within both nations. While Erdrich and Whitehead seem to offer up Canada as one potential place of escape in their respective texts, they do so in a much more provisional and uncertain fashion than O'Nan. Erdrich's and Whitehead's novels implicitly explore the limits of Canada's ability to function as a destination of salvation for their BIPOC characters and families, who remain ostracized or excluded from full participation in the nation-state, (even) if they ever reach Canada.

Future Home of the Living God and *The Underground Railroad* both examine specific dominant myths of Canada, stories of nation that Erdrich's and Whitehead's Indigenous and Black protagonists, respectively, probe, but also trouble to varying degrees or reject altogether.

Critically, neither novel delivers on the promise of a better life in Canada for its main protagonists. *Future Home of the Living God* tells the story of Cedar Hawk Songmaker, a young Ojibwe woman adopted into an affluent white Minnesota family, who finds herself pregnant in America at a moment when unpredictable shifts in evolution have led American state and federal governments to seize control over BIPOC women's bodies to try to ensure the continuation of a recognizably human (and ideally white) population. Cedar uses firsthand diary entries, dated only by month and day, to track her pregnancy and to convey her hopes and fears regarding her own future and that of her baby. Canada, for much of the novel, is positioned as a potential place of refuge from the changes ravaging the US population and climate. But movement among the US, Mexico, and Canada is tightly controlled because neither of the US' neighbors "want" to deal with the conflict (Erdrich 2017, 111). Therefore, it is unclear whether, even if Cedar could reach Canada, she would be able to live a life of liberty, or, more important, keep possession of her (unborn) baby.

Colson Whitehead's *The Underground Railroad* also looks to but ultimately turns away from the promise of salvation represented by Canada for its main protagonist, a Georgia-born enslaved Black woman named Cora. The novel traces the journey she takes as she runs for her freedom with a bounty hunter on her tail, the same bounty hunter who had sought and failed to capture her mother years ago. Cora travels on a literalized and often brutal underground railroad with station stops in various states around a reimagined American landscape seeking freedom. Lacking agency in determining her destination and uncertain that she can finding lasting sanctuary, Cora eventually looks to the Western and Southern US to try to secure her liberation from slavery rather than trying to reach Canada, although she initially favors "running north," replicating a narrative that has been shared over multiple generations of slaves on her plantation (2016, 3). In both novels, Erdrich and Whitehead offer truncated representations of Canada, flashes of possibility that ultimately prove either undesirable and/or inaccessible to their protagonists. This chapter offers an exploration of how these works contribute to our individual and collective understandings of Canada, its relationship to the US, and its long-standing treatment of Black and Indigenous peoples, given the Canadian tendency to use the US as a yardstick for asserting its superiority.

Canada as a Safe Haven

One of the most prevalent and durable fantasies about Canada is that it continues to serve as a safe haven for marginalized populations from the US and their families. In a 2017 interview with Canadian writer Margaret Atwood, Louise Erdrich explicitly acknowledges that *Future Home of the Living God* may appear to reinforce the long-standing "tendency for Americans to view Canada as our better nature" (qtd. in Atwood 2017). Atwood concurs, noting that Erdrich's novel invokes the familiar trope of heading north "for the Canadian border, as many have in the past" to escape a "repressive, women-stealing [US] government" that is desperately trying to stop a dramatic evolutionary reversal by monitoring and controlling female reproduction. This story is all too familiar to Atwood as the author of *The Handmaid's Tale* (1985). Atwood's dystopian novel, partly inspired by the rise of the Christian right in America and the election of Ronald Reagan in 1980 (Young 2019), depicts the patriarchal, totalitarian, and Christian state of Gilead, which has overthrown the US government. The narrator-protagonist, Offred, shares her life as a handmaid who is forced to produce children for the white Christian ruling class; in the novel, Canada is referenced only peripherally as a place of potential refuge, modeling the country's absent presence in ways that intersect with and continue to perpetuate the view that America's northern neighbor can serve, at least in dystopian texts, as a viable and vital option for those seeking liberty (as is also the case in Atwood's sequel to *The Handmaid's Tale, The Testaments*, published in 2019). At one point, however, a group of Quakers who run an Underground Femaleroad in Gilead to smuggle escapees into Canada are caught and publicly executed, serving as a cautionary tale for anyone who dreams of reaching Canada.

Like Atwood, who penned her novel in response to the rise of the religious right, Erdrich began to write *Future Home of the Living God* in response to the election of American President George W. Bush, whom she viewed as a disaster for reproductive rights, both nationally and globally. She notes that as soon as Bush took office he almost immediately reinstated the "global gag rule, which cuts international funding for contraceptives if abortion is mentioned," in essence stopping women from exercising choice and addressing "overpopulation" (Atwood 2017). Pregnant herself at the time, Erdrich was also troubled by Bush's refusal to acknowledge and deal with climate change.

Following the 2016 electoral win of Donald Trump, who brought back the global gag order, she returned to the novel to explore "the biological equivalent of our present political mess" (Atwood 2017). Over the course of the interview with Atwood, Erdrich moves between praising Canada as a more progressive and egalitarian society, complete with socialized health care, and acknowledging how the US' northern neighbor possesses its own legacy of Indigenous exploitation and genocide, manifested through the residential schooling system and, recently, through the targeted environmental degradation of lands occupied by Indigenous populations. Having grown up taking field trips to the Canadian city of Winnipeg from her Indigenous hometown in rural North Dakota, Erdrich explains that she has primarily conceived of "Canada as a land of culture," a beacon of progressiveness and multicultural inclusivity, where access to "[b]allet, museums" is paired with "gorgeous art, people speaking French," and "First Nations speakers of Ojibwemowin" (2017). Pragmatically, she explains that her "home reservation ... is nearly on the Canadian border" and that she has "Turtle Mountain relatives in Canada" (2017).

While Atwood does not hesitate to deflate some of the "complimentary" qualities Erdrich attributes to Canada, including the lack of a "death-throttle struggle over reproductive rights" by pointing out the nation-state's "terrible record with First Nations," in the same interview, Erdrich herself takes aim at the "Catholic Church['s]" lack of oversight in administering the "Canadian residential school system for First Nations children" (Atwood 2017). Erdrich also critiques the Alberta tar sands for their impact on Indigenous peoples and lands. Nonetheless, Erdrich continues to present an all-too-familiar attitude about Canada by noting that she herself has considered "fleeing" or, more accurately in her case, "calmly relocating ... to the Great North" (2017). She sees the main impediment as having "to take 30 to 40 beloved family members and friends along," a sentiment that reflects the hesitancy of many Americans who may imagine a move to Canada but recognize the logistical challenges (2017).

Nor is Erdrich unfamiliar with the challenges posed by the Canada-US border for Indigenous peoples who move between and among the tribal communities that straddle this imposed line. In particular, she is acutely aware of how the bodies of women of color (as vessels for reproduction for nations, both recognized and erased) are racially policed by nation-states. Her *Books and Islands in Ojibway Country: Traveling through the Lands of my Ancestors*, first published in 2003 and reprinted in 2014, opens with a map of Ojibwe Country which visibly depicts the territory of her tribe with its various reservations dotted across the state of Minnesota and the provinces of Ontario and Manitoba. Erdrich also recalls a "border incident" that occurred when returning from traveling around this tribal territory with her 18-month-old daughter. She is "quizzed over the maternity of her infant child" (Stirrup 2013, 14) by an American border guard who asks for proof that she is the baby's mother. Having become unexpectedly pregnant at 47, Erdrich is certainly aware that her vast maternal age is unusual: "Still, I was dazzled. I felt like Mary at the Annunciation. ... I'd gone from perimenopausal to violently pregnant" (Erdrich 2014, 13). Despite Erdrich's band enrollment card, which under the Jay Treaty "guarantees Native People the right to cross the Canadian-U.S. border without hassle," she is repeatedly asked a series of repetitive questions designed to trip her up until she and her daughter pass "some [mysterious] mother/daughter test" (2014, 83–84). The incident leaves her "shaken" because the guard's response relies on criteria that ignore her rights as an Ojibwe woman and mother (2014, 84). Indeed, she notes that, had her infant daughter been in a "mother-rejecting" stage, "branching out adventurously, or growling at me, as she likes to do as a joke, right now," all appropriate aspects of child development, the outcome might have been very different (2014, 84). Erdrich's personal experience informs the themes woven throughout her novel, including the long history of removing Indigenous children from their Indigenous parents as part of the efforts of colonial nations, including both the US and Canada, to cull so-called undesirable populations through forced sterilization and gain control of land through assimilation and genocide, practices that continue to this day.[2]

As Karen Stote explains in the first epigraph to this chapter, the struggle for reproductive rights for Indigenous women in the US and Canada is not about being able to have children "but ... being able to keep them in their custody" (2015, 6).[3] While Erdrich's description of her experience at the Canada-US border offers a specific critique of US border guards and their treatment of Indigenous women and their children, Stote's work demonstrates the pervasiveness of fantasies of possession over BIPOC bodies in Canada and the US, regardless of what side of the border one is on. She explains that "[d]isproportionate numbers of Aboriginal children have been and continue to be taken from their communities" on both sides of the Canada-US border and placed in foster or state care (2015, 42). She adds that the child welfare system in Canada has long functioned "as an agent in the colonization of Aboriginal peoples" (43). While in 2021 the Canadian government announced a $40 billion settlement to compensate Indigenous children and their families "harmed by the on-reserve child welfare system" within Canada, "[c]ensus data shows that more than half of the children in Canadian foster homes are indigenous, despite them making up less than 8% of the country's child population" ("Canada reaches" 2022). The data indicates that this is a long-standing and systemic problem. Given these facts, the possibility that Cedar's child would remain with her once in Canada can be understood pragmatically as another fantasy grounded in exceptionalism.

Places to Hide

In *Future Home*, Erdrich invokes the presence of multiple Ojibwe communities in northern Minnesota, whose rural locations and proximity to the border make them apparently ideal places to hide from the centralized authoritarian nation-state regimes depicted in the dystopian novel. Cedar explains in a September 17th diary entry that "[t]he borders were sealed off years ago … between the United States, or whatever we are now, and Mexico and Canada" (2017, 111). Nonetheless, "Canada still functions as the escape hatch in the roof of this country, though the fence is well guarded and people are constantly hunted down and returned" (111). Her observations echo the long-standing perception of Indigenous people on both sides of the Canada-US border as an inconvenient impediment to the logics of settler sovereignty. Conversely, Erdrich's novel mocks the impossibility of sealing a vast physical border that remains porous and subject to rupture or erasure by populations whose fluid presence predates the imposition of any nation-state line. At the same time, it is worth noting that Canada appears to have miraculously evaded some of the impacts of climate change that plague the US in *Future Home*. Cedar observes that Canada still produces "expensive real maple syrup" (60), selling it to Americans at a premium because it can no longer be produced in Minnesota, and thus finds its own modes of profitability and exclusivity.

The language Cedar uses, at least initially in plotting her escape, weaves together references to both the historical legacy of the Underground Railroad and the Indigenous idea of the "medicine line" (LaDow 2001, 40). As Black Canadian historian and activist Robyn Maynard argues, the Underground Railroad "is perhaps the most well-known and widely celebrated part of Canada's history of race relations, seeming to set Canadians apart from the brutal and damning anti-Blackness of their American neighbours" (30). Cedar herself explains that "[t]here are still many ways to cross the Canada-US border, on foot or by boat" (111). Readers soon learn through Cedar's diary entries that paddling a canoe and hiding in the forested areas around the islands that dot the border between northern Minnesota and Manitoba is likely one of the best ways for Cedar and her adoptive family to elude American authorities. In doing so, *Future Home* can be read as participating in the long-standing Indigenous understanding of the Canada-US border as a "medicine" road (LaDow 2001, 40). Beth LaDow, in *Life and Death on a North American Borderland*, explains that the word "*medicine* amongst Northern Plains tribes applies to objects supposed to have magical influence or mysterious power" (2001, 40–41). In contrast with the settler colonial treatment of the borderline as a "frontier ... [and] a way of establishing law, where one declared and fortified one's political identity," some Indigenous folks in Erdrich's novel regard the Canada-US border as a potential "instrument of camouflage" (41) for those looking to escape the increasingly powerful oppressive white regime. Likewise, Cedar emphasizes that despite appearing to be closed to Americans, there are ways to access Canada that defy visibility, capture, or a return to what are modern forms of slavery, particularly through forced pregnancy (Erdrich 2017, 111).

Shortly after, Cedar's Ojibwe stepfather, Eddy, travels from their reservation in northern Minnesota at night to visit Cedar in Minneapolis. The authoritarian American government has started seizing pregnant women on the street, and her pregnancy is becoming more physically obvious, making her a perfect target. He recommends that she follow her white adoptive parents, who, with Eddy's help, have successfully traveled "north" by using a canoe, crossing the Canada-US border shrouded in darkness, and then hiding in the islands that pepper the border area (112). But before she can manage to gather the needed equipment, her home is raided by a "honey-brown"-faced version of Red Riding Hood, whose picnic basket contains a handgun (123). She finds herself confined to a government hospital in Minneapolis in late September, where she is to be detained until she gives birth. Even Cedar admits that she has been disarmed by the American authoritarian regime's strategic use of racialized women to bring in those females who are hiding their pregnancy.

During her time in the hospital, Cedar gains a clear picture of her future if she stays there: she may not survive the delivery and the baby will be taken from her to be studied. She will also likely be forced to join the "female draft" in which "[w]omen are being forced to try and carry to term a frozen embryo from the old in-vitro clinics" (Erdrich 2017, 159), indicating the increasingly desperate attempts by this authoritarian government to produce so-called normal babies. Unwilling to remain a handmaiden, Cedar and her pregnant Chinese roommate, Tia Jackson, combine traditional Indigenous practices with contemporary elements to access a contemporary version of the Underground Railroad. Using the traditional finger-braiding that Cedar has witnessed her Ojibwe Grandma Mary Virginia use to create "fancy sashes, wall hangings, belts, tumplines, and robes," Cedar and Tia weave the lengthy and robust sashes needed to climb down the side of the hospital building and escape (141). Cedar's adoptive mother, Sera, who is a trained midwife, has journeyed back from her hiding place in the islands on the Canada-US border to work with various drivers to transport the pregnant women on recycling and mail trucks, taking at least Cedar to her home reservation.

But paths to liberty in *Future Home* are not necessarily straightforwardly north. Before they head out on the mail truck, Tia goes into labor and delivers a still born girl in the subterranean caves of Minneapolis. Having lost the baby perversely allows the racialized Tia to take a different escape route. She chooses to reunite with her husband in a suburban parking lot by the highway. "Without a baby," she can make "a run for California" because she is not visibly pregnant (Erdrich 2017, 187, 188). Her character demonstrates that there are, in fact, multiple viable escape routes that do not necessarily involve the northern US or Canada, and instead look West or South, a reality that is also true, as we will see, of *The Underground Railroad*. So, the heavily pregnant Cedar, accompanied by Sera, may travel the rest of the way northward to her Indigenous reservation, hidden in the back of a mail truck, stocked with "hammocks, bottles of water," moving blankets, heavy jackets, boots, "[a] bag of food and a covered bucket" as a toilet (201), but their route is one of many. Moreover, traveling by truck, Cedar and Sera are much more fortunate than most contemporary refugees and migrants, particularly those who have made the trek across the Canada-US border and may suffer frostbite or the loss of limbs in cold weather due to extreme exposure.[4] In this case, the two women reach the reservation in good health, a result of the big-heartedness of strangers like Cedar's mail carrier Hiro, who explains, "You were on my route" (202). His response recalls the innovation and kindness of unexpected community alliances between and among vulnerable populations.

Unfortunately, the generosity of her Indigenous community proves to be Cedar's downfall. The reservation holds a massive Thanksgiving feast without limiting attendance to its own Indigenous population. During the event, Cedar is targeted and kidnapped by "random [white] pilgrims" (Erdrich 2017, 248) desperate to make money from her impregnated body. Eager to collect their financial reward, the pilgrims take Cedar to a former Minnesota prison, renamed ironically the "Stillwater Birthing Center." There, she delivers her son on Christmas Day, only to have him removed from her care (249). Before giving birth, she is made up and photographed as the "Blessed Virgin," in preparation to join "the wall of martyrs" displayed in the prison dining hall—that is, images of the women who have died ostensibly serving "the future" (254). This ominous display offers a reminder of how Christian and Catholic models of sacrifice—in this case, women as vessels for reproduction—are used to oppress a wide array of female prisoners, all in the service of the nation-state. Cedar realizes that "Nobody gets out of here at all" (255); she remains imprisoned and is valued exclusively for her ability to reproduce. Cedar, herself, remains confined to the birthing center/prison in rural Minnesota, unable to access a potential escape route to Canada, and the whereabouts of her son and family—both adoptive and biological—remain uncertain.

Canada, and the broader idea of moving North across nation-state lines, initially appears to offer the promise of freedom and escape from exploitation, forced separation from offspring, or death at the hands of a repressive government regime within the US. However, *Future Home of the Living God* refuses to sustain the fiction of Canada as more progressive than the US. Instead, the novel offers no definitive resolution about Canada's (presumed) superiority and raises critical questions about the potential to access liberty by physically crossing the Canada-US border. Her narrative also dismantles, albeit implicitly, dominant assumptions about Canada as a peaceable kingdom when it comes to the treatment of BIPOC populations who are fleeing government-sanctioned racism and sexism.

Erdrich includes the character of Phil, the white Christian man who is the father of Cedar's baby. He makes a final offer to take Cedar and the unborn baby northward to Canada by van, shortly before she ends up at the birthing center. He has collaborated with the repressive American government, led by the so-called Church of the New Constitution (Erdrich 2017, 222), and the omniscient Mother figures who keep watch through the Internet. Phil has learned that Cedar has been targeted by this government precisely because she possesses something that is highly desirable—"Just a regular baby" (245) who lacks the regressive development that seems to plague most pregnancies. As Phil explains to Cedar, if she goes with him, presumably to Canada, "We would be in charge of things. Rich. Super rich!" (246). Hoping to profit from the genetic normalcy of Cedar's unborn child, Phil, whether north or south of the Canada-US border, reveals himself to be just as self-serving as the government agencies trying to halt "biological chaos" (246). Money and profit know no boundaries, and they contaminate both sides of the border. Cedar, however, refuses his offer, deciding to take her chances with her Indigenous community, who, despite their best efforts, fail to protect her. Instead, Erdrich's Trump-era novel leaves the female protagonist at the end of the text to create her own version of the dystopian America in which she finds herself. And so, the possibility of Canada eludes her, receding into the background and providing a cautionary tale in response to the potentiality that Cedar and others in her community initially seem to attach to the US' northern neighbor.

In the closing images of *Future Home of the Living God*, Cedar has become a handmaid to the whims of a white-dominated autocratic government that wants only to ensure its genetic survival, offering a haunting repetition of the ways in which historical genocide and assimilation have continued to oppress Indigenous populations—and Indigenous women in particular. Yet, at the same time, Cedar's closing question to her son, "Where will you be, my darling, the last time it snows on earth?" accords with her Indigenous stepfather Eddy's belief in the resilience of Indigenous populations to the challenges that have been posed to these communities since the arrival of European settlers, which cannot be underestimated (Erdrich 2017, 267). The "where" that Cedar contemplates may be neither in the US nor Canada, but in a to-be-imagined future locale that refuses or re-envisions nation-state paradigms.

The Promise of the Underground Railroad

Colson Whitehead's *The Underground Railroad* portrays the life of a young enslaved Black woman, Cora, who has escaped the Georgia plantation where she was born and raised and is on the run. Her complicated memories of her own mother who ran years ago and was thought to have escaped to Canada accompany her on the trip. Moreover, the bounty hunter who failed to catch her mother and is close on Cora's heels remains a constant threat. Cora's quest for freedom initially places her on a real-life Underground Railroad to escape plantation-life horrors in Georgia, only to realize over the course of the novel that she has little to no ability to control where the railroad may take her. Station stops are vulnerable to discovery by those who support slavery and Cora learns that moving northward on the rail-line does not guarantee her safety or liberty.

Cora makes several stops along this subterranean network of tunnels built and run by Black hands. In doing so, she encounters a variety of communities in different American states, each with its own lessons to be learned about what liberty looks like and how underlying racism shapes even the seemingly most liberal of societies within the US. As Manisha Sinha explains, "Each state that Cora moves through maps the historical geography of enslavement and freedom," with Whitehead employing "literary license to tell a broader story" (2016). For instance, in Whitehead's novel, South Carolina is imagined to be an "antislavery haven where Cora" may find "shelter and education," yet she soon learns that "the good teachers and doctors in the state are ardent eugenicists and scientific racists," using the pseudoscience of race to justify "preventing the propagation of an 'inferior race'" (Sinha 2016). Likewise, in North Carolina, Cora finds herself hidden as a fugitive, much like the nineteenth-century Black writer Harriet Jacobs, in the attic of a white covert abolitionist and his Christian wife, where she witnesses firsthand, in the adjacent public square, a variety of horrifying measures (from minstrel shows to public lynchings) that are used to enforce the abolition of the Black race within state bounds. She barely escapes with her life, before eventually reaching "a black utopia set improbably in racist Indiana," run by an interracial leader, Elijah Lander, who embodies critical aspects of several historical abolitionist leaders, most notably Frederick Douglass (Sinha 2016), giving Cora renewed hope. However, while delivering a lecture to his community, Lander's farm is attacked by a "racist white mob," who raze the place and force Cora to run yet again (Sinha 2016).

The title of Whitehead's novel may invoke the promise of a better life for fleeing Black enslaved people because of the powerful role the Underground Railroad has played in the collective imaginations of America and Canada, with the latter presumed, "especially after 1850," to be "the only sure avenue to freedom" (Foner 2015, 144, 144–145). But the text's dystopian depictions of life in various states for fugitive Black enslaved people who travel the railroad expose, explicitly and implicitly, the tendency on both sides of the Canada-US border to manipulate this concept to bolster national and regional narratives of exceptionalism and redemption. Instead, Whitehead offers a sustained critique of the teleological structure of liberation narratives.

Erdrich has an explicit and tangible relationship to Canada, grounded in an Indigenous community of belonging that literally straddles the Canada-US border, foregrounding the imposed and unnatural dimensions of this belatedly created nation-state line. In contrast, Whitehead's *The Underground Railroad* relies on a presumed connection to Canada through the long-standing and powerful narrative of the Underground Railroad, with Canada as its ultimate destination, particularly in years immediately following the institution of the 1850 Fugitive Slave Act in America. In Whitehead's novel, Canada plays a peripheral yet notable role precisely because it serves as an imagined locale for competing fantasies about what the future may hold for Cora's ancestors and, in turn, for her own life beyond the plantation. At least initially, Canada is subsumed into a broader notion of the idea of North and specifically the northern US as places of potential safety. Throughout *The Underground Railroad*, Canada is referenced by name only a handful of times, most explicitly by the vengeful slave catcher Ridgeway, who is hired to pursue Cora's mother Mabel and then, decades later, Cora herself when they each flee from the same Georgia plantation. According to Ridgeway, Canada functions as the ultimate refuge for Black runaways and dispossessed Indigenous peoples, impeding the "divine prescription" of "the American imperative," which motivates his actions (Whitehead 2016, 222). This "imperative" legitimates the removal of Indigenous peoples from the lands on which they live, enslaves Black people by killing those who defy their subservient position in US society, and ultimately ensures white prosperity for the nation, all in the name of "[p]rogress" (205).

Proud of "his facility for ensuring that property remained property," Ridgeway is haunted by the realization that Mabel's disappearance and presumed escape to Canada undermine his widespread reputation as a successful slavecatcher. He has been praised for being able to recover so-called lost property even in northern US states like New York, where "antislavery sentiment" dominates (Whitehead 2016, 80, 78). As a result, the slavecatcher is even more determined not to let Cora escape and reach a location where he believes he possesses less authority: Canada (82).

As Maynard explains, officially, the American Fugitive Slave Act of 1850 was only enforceable within the US, allowing "American law enforcement officials and citizens to track down Black enslaved people who had escaped to the so-called 'free states' of the North" (2017, 29).

As a result, "[t]he period between the passing of the *Fugitive Slave Act* and the end of the Civil War saw the largest number of freedom runners entering Canada" to seek "reprieve from subjugation, bondage and brutal racist violence" (29). Maynard stresses that for Canada, the Underground Railroad functioned as a point of pride, by "seeming to set Canadians apart from the brutal and damning anti-Blackness of their American neighbours" (30) and establishing the basis for "[t]he formal appearance of racial tolerance—a major part of Canada's identity today" (30). Afua Cooper, in her essay "The Miracle of Ann Maria Jackson, Slave Fugitive and Heroine of the Underground Railroad," stresses the way in which "the image of Canada welcoming the fleeing fugitive has lodged itself in Canadian consciousness and has become part and parcel of Canadian national identity" (2022, 119). However, Maynard's book and Cooper's article stress that "freedom from formal bondage did not protect" Black people from "the violence of racist hostility or formal and informal segregation in post-abolition Canada" (2017, 30). Cooper notes the "tensions inherent in Canadian history" given that it was a "slave-holding and slave-rescuing country simultaneously" (2022, 121). Likewise, Jason Silverman notes in his 1985 study of Canadian media from the era of the Underground Railroad that British North America's tolerance of "black refugees" was rooted in a desire to "prove their moral eminence over American civil liberties" (1985, 35). This perspective enabled Canada to chide "the United States for perpetuating the institution of slavery" (35), without having to acknowledge or change its own racist practices.

Throughout *The Underground Railroad*, Ridgeway remains personally affronted by the possibility that Mabel has reached Canada, seeing it as a mockery of his skills, and thus, a form of "personal injury" (Whitehead 2016, 222). He even tells Cora when he recaptures her in North Carolina that her mother is "up in Canada, laughing at the Randalls and me" (222). His only recourse is to inflict revenge on her daughter by buying and making Cora wear a dress that evokes memories of her mother, facilitating a "performance" of her subjugation that leads the young woman to realize, perversely, that she and Ridgeway share a hatred of the mother she believes has abandoned her (222).

Resolute in his ambition to stamp out Mabel's legacy, Ridgeway reveals the threat that he believes her multi-generational female lineage poses to the slavecatcher: "People like you and your mother are the best of your race. ... But we can't have you too clever" (Whitehead 2016, 223). As vehicles for profitability and producers of the next generation of slave labor, Mabel and Cora fulfill what Ridgeway sees as their role as "subjugates" in the civilizing American experience (223). Mabel and Cora also come to represent the promise of "hope" and threaten to unravel the precarity of a system reliant on the belief that slaves have no right to liberty (223). Despite her resentment of her mother's absence, Cora recognizes that Ridgeway is trapped by his commitment to a model of nation-building that fails to understand the possibilities of ingenious citizenship, even within the borders of America. While she may feel ambivalent about her mother's supposed decision to leave her and the plantation, Cora is able to recognize the need to look beyond and outside of the framework that Ridgeway relies on to justify his profession and right to treat her as an object to be possessed: "The slave catcher was wrong. If she'd made it north she would have disappeared into a life outside their terms. Like her mother. One thing the woman had passed on to her" (222). Regardless of where Mabel has ended up, Cora uses the pragmatics of her mother's legacy to forge a version of the future that does not depend upon defining herself solely in opposition to Ridgeway or her mother.

Whitehead's text makes no explicitly negative references to Canada. Nonetheless, given the mythical role granted to America's northern neighbor as a place of sanctity and liberation for fugitive Black enslaved people, its role in a novel that fundamentally re-envisions the Underground Railroad from the perspective of an enslaved Black woman is also called into question. Having been born and raised in Georgia, doing agricultural labor in a relatively warm climate, and lacking a formal education, Cora assumes that she does not have the skills or physical constitution needed to find work in the northern US or even Canada, especially in an urban location: "She contributed to the life of the farm. This was labor she recognized.... She'd grown up with her hands in the dirt" (Whitehead 2016, 266). Her line of thought notably echoes the strategies used by Canadian politicians to dissuade Black people from coming northward before and long after the end of the Fugitive Slave Act. For instance, at the end of the nineteenth and early twentieth centuries, the Department of Immigration went so far as to pay "Black American doctors" to inform Black Americans seeking a new life in Canada that "the Canadian climate was dangerous" and potentially fatal to Black people in particular (Maynard 2017, 35). The extreme seasonal variations were just one of many tactics employed by the Canadian government to prohibit the official entry of immigrants (35).

So, while in *Future Home of the Living God*, Cedar holds onto the somewhat romantic belief that Canada may potentially be a place of hope—where the snow still falls—Cora's relationship to Canada remains deeply ambivalent and provisional, precisely because of its colder climate and links to Mabel, the mother who seemingly abandoned Cora for a chance at freedom. Indeed, when asking fellow residents on a farm in Indiana, intended to be a way stop and locale for fugitive Black enslaved people "between places," they speculate that Mabel "[m]ay be ... in Canada" but also note that "it's awful cold" (Whitehead 2016, 245). Their response takes another turn for Cora, who ironically notes that if Mabel is indeed there, her mother is getting what she deserves as an errant parent who has brought shame on her daughter: "Cold nights for the coldhearted" (245). Here, the Canadian climate becomes a reflection of Mabel's failure to protect her daughter and a symbol of her ability to reject her maternal responsibilities in favor of her own presumed survival. More broadly, the climate is unwelcoming, cold, and frigid; in other words, Canada is a frozen paradise, one that protects some (notably Mabel), but not others (such as Cora).

In *The Underground Railroad*, there is one marginal character who appears to have garnered freedom by fleeing to Canada. Justin is the single slave Cora knows who has joined his Black relatives in Montreal and found employment outside of the bonds of slavery. Justin sends Cora a letter during her time in Indiana attesting to his improved circumstances in Montreal. But as the work of Marcel Trudel has revealed, Montreal—and the province of Quebec—had, like many communities in Canada, a Black slave population for hundreds of years, despite the claim that "[s]lavery was formally abolished in 1834 throughout the British Empire" (2013, 15). The second epigraph to this chapter, written by Trudel's translator, George Tombs, notes that "generations of historians maintained a virtual conspiracy of silence about slaves owned and exploited, bought and sold, by Canadians themselves" (Trudel 2013, 7). So, Whitehead's choice of Montreal as the location for Justin's arrival—and access to a better life— must also be understood in the context of a city that was itself shaped by Black slavery. Justin appears to have found work at a "building company" (Whitehead 2016, 266) and is free to write and send letters as he pleases. However, it is impossible to know if he is a free man or simply able to access more liberties than during his previous life in the US. Nonetheless, in a playful demonstration of the opportunities afforded in making the risky journey to Canada, Justin's nieces have "signed their names [on the letter] in different-colored ink" (266). This gesture demonstrates the relative affluence and privilege of these presumably Black girls who are living north of the Canada-US border, at least when compared to Cora, who only learns to read and write as an adult in a class full of children.

Canada also supposedly houses Mabel, whom Ridgeway and Cora both believe has found refuge north of the Canada-US border, sacrificing her young daughter to save herself. This narrative is especially troubling for Cora, who believes she has been abandoned by her mother and, as a result, serves as the unrelenting target of Ridgeway's revenge. So, while Cora may initially favor heading north on the literalized underground railroad, in *The Underground Railroad*, she ultimately ends up traveling West and South across the US in search of liberty. This geographical shift punctures a long-held belief that Canada was the primary "safe haven for the enslaved Black Americans who had fled the United States through the Underground Railroad" (Maynard 2017, 4). Lacking the agency to control exactly where she journeys on the railroad and losing hope that she can access real sanctuary, Cora follows the tunnels without clear knowledge of where she will end up. The third epigraph heading this chapter, from a 2016 *New Yorker* article by Kathryn Schulz aptly titled "The Perilous Lure of the Underground Railroad," argues that despite the rhetorical prominence of the Underground Railroad as the primary route for Black enslaved people wishing to escape their bondage, historically "[m]ost runaways did not head north" (2016). In Whitehead's novel, the centrality of Canada as the primary and deeply desired destination for those traveling the Underground Railroad is presented as merely one of many treacherous paths to freedom. In addition, the story Whitehead tells offers a far more nuanced and provisional understanding of the grim reality that in "American slavery, almost no one ever escaped at all" (Schulz 2016), and those who did constituted a tiny fraction of the slave population, predominantly headed South or West, as Cora does in the closing pages of the novel.

Canada as (An)other Lie

The concluding sections of *The Underground Railroad* pointedly reorient whatever northward projection might have propelled Cora toward apparent locations of freedom. Here, Canada functions as a receding mirage, rather than the primary direction of escape that promises a form of salvation. The penultimate chapter in Whitehead's novel reveals the true story of Mabel's efforts to leave the plantation and the reality of her demise.

Mabel uses the "north star" to guide her journey by foot (Whitehead 2016, 291) and relies on the sustenance provided by the small plot of land she has inherited from her enslaved mother. Paradoxically, the will to "survive," which motivates Mabel to run from the farm, gives her a treasured "moment" of freedom, one that she perceives as a potential inheritance to be passed on to her daughter: "When she found the words to share it with Cora, the girl would understand there was something beyond the plantation, past all that she knew. That one day if she stayed strong, the girl could have it for herself" (294). However, Mabel is unwilling to abandon her child and so decides to make her way back to the plantation before the slave owners even realize she has escaped. However, she is bitten and killed by a cottonmouth snake while hiding in a swamp during her return journey, erasing any tangible evidence of her existence or intentions to go back to the plantation and Cora. Whitehead's narrative reveals that Mabel's presumed escape to Canada is an unfulfilled grand illusion. The fact that she did not get away nor gained her liberty serves as a reminder of this reality for most American slaves: Canada was more of a mirage than real—for Black people on both sides of the border.

Cora's and Mabel's experiences offer a reminder that liberation narratives are complex and unpredictable. Cora's last stop on the railroad does not take her to "Canada" or even anywhere beyond "America" (305). While waiting on the trail, Cora encounters three different wagons, each with its own driver: the first contains a white couple who ignore Cora altogether; the second, a "redheaded fellow with Irish features" who stops to admire her physically; and finally, there is "an older negro man," who offers food to Cora, which, along with his Southern accent, comforts her (Whitehead 2016, 305–306). Having learned whom to trust during her time riding the rails—with each wagon arguably representing a different stop on her previous travels among the US states—Cora accepts a ride from the third and final driver, whom she soon discovers has a "horseshoe brand on his neck" (306), indicating his own past legacy of enslavement. Moreover, she learns that he is headed to St. Louis, Missouri, and ultimately, following "the trail to California" (306), a journey that will take Cora West and South, the same directions that she initially resisted in her efforts to attain freedom. In doing so, Whitehead's novel portrays the contradictory reality of the Underground Railroad as an unpredictable and multi-directional network to aid the escape of Black enslaved people that is not readily framed and contained by either Canadian or American narratives of progress and enlightenment.

Future Home of the Living God represents the worst of dystopian America, with Cedar separated from her son and inevitably forced to become impregnated again in a world where fear of evolutionary regression necessitates using BIPOC women as handmaids. But Erdrich counters the bleakness of Cedar's incarceration with the promise that her Indigenous community—led by her stepfather, Eddy—will continue to "adapt" as they always have (Erdrich 2017, 28), in part by undertaking a sustained and aggressive "tribal clawback of treaty land" (215). Eddy seizes this moment of evolutionary chaos to begin a benevolent reclamation of lands that were removed from Indigenous communal ownership over the past two centuries. Rather than favoring a Canadian alterna(rra)tive as a response to the chaos of an American dystopia, the novel turns to and foregrounds the ingenuity of the Indigenous population that straddles the Canada-US border. When Cedar first travels northward on the highway from Minneapolis to her home reservation, she notes the doomsday attitude of several sermons she sees posted on church billboards along the route—messages that ironically promise salvation as the "Endtime" approaches (13). One, however, prompts Cedar to stop her journey and take a photograph: "In one enormous, empty field a sign is planted that reads *Future Home of the Living God*. It's just a bare field, fallow and weedy, stretching to the pale horizon" (13). The sign, which is also the title of the novel, of course, functions as a reminder of the absurdity of colonial and imperialist efforts to assert control over the universe through ownership of property and people along with the harm that comes from doing so, regardless of which side of the border one is on.

Cedar's Indigenous community has become its own savior by taking back power into its own hands. Nor is their salvation linked to an arbitrary border. Even Eddy, who absolutely wants to protect "our pregnant tribal members" and argues that "[o]ur women are sacred to us," demonstrates a sense of pragmatism as to what can be accomplished. He anticipates that "[w]hichever military entity comes out on top will probably remember about us," but cannot be sure who will lead such an attack (Erdrich 2017, 227), anticipating the reality that Cedar finds herself in at the novel's conclusion. But Eddy's efforts hint at one possible way that Cedar's tribal community may continue to find ways to adjust, survive, and ultimately thrive: relying on traditional practices—such as "finger-braiding" (141)—in combination with established aspects of capitalist enterprise, ranging from "gangsters growing seedlings in the grow-lighted aisles of casinos" to keeping the gas pumps well-stocked, steps to secure the tribe's return to self-sufficiency, "like the old days" (226, 227).

Likewise, in the final pages of *The Underground Railroad*, Cora focuses on the ingenuity of those who built the underground railroad in Whitehead's novel. She pays tribute to the "ones who excavated a million tons of rock and dirt, toiled in the belly of the earth for the deliverance of slaves like her" (Whitehead 2016, 303), and admires the enormity of the physical labor involved in its creation as she travels the underground railroad, arguing that the "up-top world must be so ordinary compared to the miracle beneath" (304). In doing so, Cora—like Cedar's Indigenous community—can be read as challenging readers to look again and differently at Canada's presumed prominence as the only or primary place of escape. Instead, both novels call on the imagination of their protagonists to look across, beneath, or around imposed nation-state borders to better understand and engage with BIPOC communities that find creative ways to survive and even thrive that are not unidirectional nor tied to a single narrative outcome. As a result, Erdrich's and Whitehead's texts problematize a long-standing inclination that may be shared by readers on both sides of the Canada-US border to view Canada as the only or ideal alternative to a dystopic America.

Notes

1. Lepore includes brief analyses of several novels that portray US-Canada relations, including most notably *Underground Airlines* by Ben Winters, a dystopian story of a Black man who works as a bounty hunter for the US Marshals Service in the hope of obtaining his freedom, ideally by taking a "flight to Canada" (Winters 2016, 188). But the promise of accessing freedom via the North is deflated as Victor uncovers the hypocrisy of co-operating "Clean Hands" states (9) and neighboring countries, like Canada, which claim to refuse to engage economically or politically with the four "Slave States" (vii) in the US by relying on organizations such as the "North American Human Rights Association" (located in Montreal) to inspect supply lines and ensure that they are not directly linked to the profits generated by slavery (9). As a result, Canada plays a decidedly ambivalent role within Winters' text. Obviously, Winters' novel could have been included in my study; however, I wanted to focus on books produced by Black and Indigenous authors to ensure that those voices were of primary concern in this chapter.

2. There have been substantive discussions regarding the use of the term "genocide" in relation to the treatment of Indigenous populations in Canada and the US. See, for example, MacDonald (2019), Woolford et al. (2014), Starblanket (2018), and Woolford (2015).
3. See also Flores (2020) for an examination of the long-standing practice of "forcibly sterilizing women" of color in the US; Prather et al. (2018) for a consideration of how historical contexts in the US have shaped equity through a study of "Racism, African American Women, and Their Sexual and Reproductive Health"; Lawrence's (2000) analysis of the Indian Health Service in the US and the forced sterilization of Indigenous women during the 1960s and 1970s; as well as Stote's (2015) book-length study. This should be residential school system and Sixties Scoop in Canada, the latter of which placed Indigenous children in non-Indigenous homes, also reveal Canada's long-standing efforts to colonize and assimilate Indigenous peoples. Notably, forced sterilization of Indigenous women continues in both countries to this day. See Longman (2018) and Talaga (2022) for articles that detail these issues.
4. See, for example, McKeen (2022) for coverage of the plight of four members of a family from India who flew to the US and then tried to cross the Canada-US border in January 2022 and froze to death, a phenomenon that has been happening since well before the election of Trump.

References

Allan, Chantal. 2009. *Bomb Canada and Other Unkind Remarks in the American Media*. Edmonton: Athabasca University Press.
Atwood, Margaret. 2017. Inside the Dystopian Vision of Margaret Atwood and Louise Erdrich. *Elle*, November 14. https://www.elle.com/culture/books/a13530871/future-home-of-the-living-god-louise-erdrich-interview/.
Austen, Ian. 2017. In Canada, Justin Trudeau Says Refugees are Welcome. *The New York Times*, January 28. https://www.nytimes.com/2017/01/28/world/canada/justin-trudeau-trump-refugee-ban.html.
———. 2018. Trudeau Doesn't Separate Refugee Families, But He Does Send Them Away. *The New York Times*, June 22. https://www.nytimes.com/2018/06/22/world/canada/trudeau-doesnt-separate-refugee-families-but-he-does-send-them-away-the-canada-letter.html.
Blake, Jason. 2010. *Canadian Hockey Literature*. Toronto: University of Toronto Press.
Brown, DeNeen L. 2018. "Barbaric": America's Cruel History of Separating Children from Their Parents. *The Washington Post*, May 31. https://www.washingtonpost.com/news/retropolis/wp/2018/05/31/barbaric-americas-cruel-history-of-separating-children-from-their-parents/.

Canada Reaches $31bn Deal in Indigenous Child Welfare Case. 2022. *BBC.com*, January 4. https://www.bbc.com/news/world-us-canada-59833123.

Coleman, Daniel. 2006. *White Civility: The Literary Project of English Canada*. Toronto: University of Toronto Press.

Cooper, Afua. 2022. The Miracle of Ann Maria Jackson, Slave Fugitive and Heroine of the Underground Railroad. In *Harriet's Legacies: Race, Historical Memory, and Futures in Canada*, ed. Ronald Cummings and Natalee Caple, 118–140. Montreal & Kingston: McGill-Queen's University Press.

Erdrich, Louise. 2014. *Books and Islands in Ojibwe Country: Traveling Through the Lands of My Ancestors*. New York: Harper Perennial.

———. 2017. *Future Home of the Living God: A Novel*. New York: Harper Perennial.

Flores, Jerry. 2020. ICE Detainees' Alleged Hysterectomies Recall a Long History of Forced Sterilizations. *The Conversation*, September 28. https://theconversation.com/ice-detainees-alleged-hysterectomies-recall-a-long-history-of-forced-sterilizations-146820.

Foner, Eric. 2015. *Gateway to Freedom: The Hidden History of the Underground Railroad*. New York: W. W. Norton.

LaDow, Beth. 2001. *The Medicine Line: Life and Death on a North American Borderland*. New York: Routledge.

Lawrence, Jane. 2000. The Indian Health Service and the Sterilization of Native American Women. *American Indian Quarterly* 24 (3): 400–419.

Lepore, Jill. 2017. A Golden Age for Dystopian Fiction. *The New Yorker*, May 29. https://www.newyorker.com/magazine/2017/06/05/a-golden-age-for-dystopian-fiction.

Longman, Nickita. 2018. End Forced Sterilization of Indigenous Women in Canada. *The Washington Post*, December 4. https://www.proquest.com/printviewfile?accountid=10406.

MacDonald, David Bruce. 2019. *The Sleeping Giant Awakens: Genocide, Indian Residential Schools, and the Challenge of Conciliation*. Toronto: University of Toronto Press.

Maynard, Robyn. 2017. *Policing Black Lives: State Violence from Slavery to the Present*. Halifax: Fernwood.

McKeen, Alex. 2022. My Heart Is Crying: Family Who Died of Cold Near Canada-U.S. Border Identified in Indian Press. *Toronto Star*, January 26. https://www.thestar.com/news/canada/2022/01/26/my-heart-is-crying-family-who-died-of-cold-near-canada-us-border-identified-in-indian-press.html.

Prather, Cynthia, et al. 2018. Racism, African American Women, and Their Sexual and Reproductive Health: A Review of Historical and Contemporary Evidence and Implications for Health Equity. *Health Equity* 2 (1): 249–259.

Schulz, Kathryn. 2016. The Perilous Lure of the Underground Railroad. *The New Yorker*, August 22. https://www.newyorker.com/magazine/2016/08/22/the-perilous-lure-of-the-underground-railroad.

Silverman, Jason. 1985. *Unwelcome Guests: Canada West's Response to American Fugitive Slaves*. Millwood, NY: Associated Faculty Press.

Sinha, Manisha. 2016. The Underground Railroad in Art and History: A Review of Colson Whitehead's Novel. *The Journal of the Civil War Era*, November 29. https://www.journalofthecivilwarera.org/2016/11/underground-railroad-art-history-review-colson-whiteheads-novel/.

Starblanket, Tamara. 2018. *Suffer the Little Children: Genocide, Indigenous Nations and the Canadian State*. Atlanta: Clarity Press.

Stirrup, David. 2013. *Louise Erdrich*. Manchester: Manchester University Press.

Stote, Karen. 2015. *An Act of Genocide: Colonialism and the Sterilization of Aboriginal Women*. Halifax: Fernwood Publishing.

Talaga, Tanya. 2022. Women's Rights Are Under Attack. *The Globe and Mail*, May 5. https://www.proquest.com/docview/2659539362?parentSessionId=%2FX5eeAgkdvUjQacZsCm3H71XfoCtLGDDk5yNtXq1GJ0%3D&pq-origsite=primo&accountid=10406#.

Trudel, Marcel. 2013. *Canada's Forgotten Slaves: Two Hundred Years of Bondage*. Translated by George Tombs. Montreal: Véhicule Press.

Whitehead, Colson. 2016. *The Underground Railroad: A Novel*. New York: Doubleday.

Winters, Ben H. 2016. *Underground Airlines*. London: Century/Random House.

Woolford, Andrew, et al., ed. 2014. *Colonial Genocide in Indigenous North America*. Durham: Duke University Press.

Woolford, Andrew. 2015. *This Benevolent Experiment: Indigenous Boarding Schools, Genocide and Redress in Canada and the United States*. Winnipeg: University of Manitoba Press.

Young, Cathy. 2019. Trump's America Is Not *The Handmaid's Tale*. *The Atlantic*, October 9. https://www.theatlantic.com/ideas/archive/2019/10/a-handmaids-tale-is-not-coming-true/599674/.

CHAPTER 8

The Limits of Canadian Exceptionalism: *Bowling for Columbine*, *Come From Away*, and *Nîpawistamâsowin: We Will Stand Up*

> *This is an American tradition.... If you're not armed, you're not responsible.* (a Michigan militia member in Moore 2003)
>
> *[I]n spite of the innocence of the story that Canada likes to tell about itself, that it is a place of immigrant and settler founding, that in this, it is a place that somehow escapes the ugliness of history, that it is a place that is **not** like the place below it, across that border ... [it remains] a settler society whose multicultural, liberal and democratic structure and performance of governance seeks an ongoing "settling" of this land.*
> (Simpson 2016, my emphasis)

Gillian Roberts argues in *Discrepant Parallels: Cultural Implications of the Canada-U.S. Border*, published in 2015, that "[d]espite the language of friendship and neighbourliness that characterizes the official discourse of Canada-US relations," Canadian citizens are also "positioned in multiple and often contradictory ways at the Canada-US border" (2015, 5). She notes that "Canadian cultural texts that examine the Canada-US border frequently touch on issues of hospitality, with border guards policing the passage of travellers" by either "officially welcoming citizens of each other's countries across the line, or refusing entry" (5). Roberts' study, as summarized in the Introduction, devotes considerable attention to the exploration of "Indigenous and ethnic-minority positions" within Canada that complicate predominant views of the nation and its border with the US (12). In contrast, most of this monograph has been devoted to close

© The Author(s), under exclusive license to Springer Nature Switzerland AG 2023
J. Andrews, *Canada Through American Eyes*,
https://doi.org/10.1007/978-3-031-22120-0_8

readings of American texts that observe, comment on, and contribute to an enriched understanding of Canada and Canada-US interactions by looking (or choosing not to look) northward. Rather than primarily investigating American-authored texts, my Conclusion examines a combination of American and Canadian cinematic and musical narratives to understand how Canadian exceptionality continues to circulate on both sides of the Canada-US border, even as racial and ethnic minority populations within Canada continue to experience relations with the nation-state that are fundamentally hostile rather than "hospitable" (14).

Drawing on Mireille Rosello, Roberts points out that "there is often a disjunction between an ethics of hospitality (or indeed a mythic hospitality upon which the nation might desire to pin its identity) and '[a] politics of hospitality, ... [which] involves limits and borders'" (2015, 14). Moreover, much as "the Canadian nation-state might point to moments in its history when it claims to be hospitable as part of its 'myths of ... benevolence,'" as previous chapters have shown, "the mere act of permitting 'guests' to cross the border into Canadian territory has not always been genuinely hospitable" (14). While Canada "claims to have offered sanctuary to border-crossers," entering the country has "not always ... resonated for ethnic-minority groups in the same way [as] ... for the white, Anglo, dominant group" (14). This chapter takes a provocative approach to exploring these issues by putting into conversation three texts that might, at first glance, constitute an unlikely trio.

The first, American documentary filmmaker Michael Moore's *Bowling for Columbine* (2003), explores the propensity for gun violence in the US in contrast with other nations, most prominently Canada. Moore suggests that racism and hatred of those perceived as "Other" is a historically rooted dynamic in America that has contributed to the epidemic of gun ownership and gun violence in the US. The second, the feel-good, Canadian-authored musical *Come From Away* (2013), depicts the experiences of the thousands of passengers who found themselves stranded in Gander, Newfoundland, in the days following 9/11 and affirms Canada's status as a peaceful nation. It demonstrates that, at least for most of the passengers (including Black and queer characters), Canada provides a welcoming haven from the divisive and violent forces that are so prevalent in America. The third and final work, *Nîpawistamâsowin: We Will Stand Up* (2019), created by Cree documentary filmmaker Tasha Hubbard, examines the aftermath of the execution-style killing of a young Cree man, Colten Boushie, in August 2016 by a white farmer, Gerald Stanley, in

Battleford, Saskatchewan. Hubbard graphically explores the reality of historical and contemporary Canadian racism toward Indigenous peoples and the hidden pervasiveness of gun violence in Canada.

Bringing these three works together in a single chapter highlights the popularity of Canadian stories of exceptionality and, conversely, serves as a reminder that Canada is a vexed nation that remains deeply invested in concealing its hidden histories. This chapter examines the precarity of Canadian claims to exceptionality, as well as the need to engage with the contradictory dimensions that continue to underlie such a stance in the twenty-first century, aspects of Canadian identity that are often helpfully probed by using the US as a lens through which to better understand life north of the border. In particular, Hubbard's film addresses the dangers of national claims to superiority by exploring the immediate and lasting impacts of racial hatred as manifested through gun violence. Including it serves as a reminder of the pervasiveness of colonial aggression aimed at clearing the land and consolidating colonization, regardless of what stories a nation-state chooses to tell itself or its neighbors.

Canadian Virtuosity in *Bowling for Columbine*

In a memorable set of scenes from *Bowling for Columbine*, which was filmed shortly after 9/11, Moore visits several central Canadian cities and interviews locals to understand better why the murder rate is so much lower north of the Canada-US border, even though guns are easily acquired in Canada, known as "a nation of hunters" (2003). The filmmaker "has long viewed America's northern neighbour as a more decent, humanitarian version of his home country" (Kane 2019), and this documentary is no exception. The footage shot in Canada provides a "temporary reprieve" from what critics have described as the "emotional onslaught" that shapes much of the movie (Ott and Sci 2015, 87). Moore sees himself as deeply connected to Canada through the legacy of his "grandfather [who] was a country doctor" (Johnson 2007) in Ontario. Moreover, he repeatedly describes Canada as a site of refuge, particularly just prior to the release of his 2018 film, *Fahrenheit 9/11*, which takes aim at the presidency of Donald Trump. While he notes that "Canada has a lot of problems," they are nowhere "near what we [Americans] have to take care of and correct" (Moore qtd. in "Michael Moore Plots Canadian Escape" 2018). Despite Moore's championing of Canada throughout his filmmaking career, and his plan after releasing *Fahrenheit 9/11* to "escape potential persecution in the U.S. ... [by] moving to Canada," he remains an American citizen to this day (2018).

Early in *Bowling for Columbine*, Moore meets with a group of white Michigan militia from his home state who, as noted in the first epigraph to this chapter, insist that "it's an American responsibility to be armed ... it's your job to defend you and yours," yet who also claim that "we're here to help" (2003). These militia, of course, are relying on the Second Amendment of the American Constitution, first adopted in 1791, which was envisioned by the architects of the Constitution as a "means to check tyranny"; it has become a justification, supported by the Supreme Court, for individual American citizens to carry and use guns (Goldberg 2000, 2). While one Canadian firearms manufacturer and dealer has tried to claim for Canada "a constitutional right to bear arms without government interference or regulation," that stance has been rejected by the Canadian Supreme Court and thus offers a fundamental difference between Canada and its neighbor to the south (Young 2010).

When Moore visits Ontario, the Canadians he interviews observe that Americans "must be afraid of your neighbour[s]" if they feel they must be armed (Moore 2003). He speaks with residents of Sarnia and Windsor, both of whom are in very close proximity to the Canada-US border and who confirm that they do not lock their doors, even though they have experienced vandalism of their homes and property. In a revealing experiment, Moore then walks from house-to-house in a downtown Toronto neighborhood, knocking on doors and opening them to demonstrate the perceived difference in culture. He is repeatedly greeted by the occupants in a welcoming and peaceful manner that fundamentally contradicts the expectation described by one Canadian resident that, in the US normally, the "first reaction is [to] pull the gun out. 'You're on my property'" (2003). Here, stereotypes abound, with Moore even visiting a so-called Canadian ghetto in downtown Toronto, which looks more like a middle-class neighborhood and appears to be relatively free from the gun violence that plagues similar American communities. In doing so, he once again affirms the notion that the US has a much more violent history than its northern neighbor. Conversely, when queried in an interview about whether his "utopian portrayal seems removed from Canadian reality," he counters these critiques by insisting that "this line of criticism" is "symptomatic of what he views as Canada's national complex: We're just too hard on ourselves" ("Michael Moore plots Canadian escape" 2018). Through his films, Moore creates and sustains a vision of Canada as better than the US, securing and reinforcing the long-standing narrative of Canada as a place of refuge for Americans that also provides a tempered and therefore sensible approach to gun laws and gun ownership.

In particular, Moore's observations about the propensity for gun violence in the US (unlike Canada) provide a useful framework for thinking about the limits of Canadian exceptionalism and shifting conceptions of neighborliness through a comparative analysis of the popular Canadian-authored musical *Come From Away* and *Nîpawistamâsowin: We Will Stand Up*. While a movie like Moore's may make it easy to view Canada as a "peaceable kingdom" (Andrews 2018, 361), it also demonstrates the ways in which some Americans, to subvert the long-standing claims of American exceptionalism, inadvertently continue to bolster Canadian exceptionalism and ignore the complexities of gun violence aimed primarily at BIPOC communities north of the Canada-US border.

Celebrating Canadian Exceptionality in *Come From Away*

The hit musical *Come From Away*, written by a Canadian couple living in New York, tells the story of the days following 9/11 when 38 planes carrying "6595 passengers and crew members" (DeFede 2002, 7) were unexpectedly diverted to Gander, Newfoundland. The passengers spent a week as guests of the local town and surrounding communities because of the sudden closure of US airspace following the airline hijacking and suicide attacks of four passenger planes in the US. Two planes hit the North and South Towers of the World Trade Center in New York, the third struck the Pentagon in Washington, DC, and the fourth crashed in a rural area adjacent to Pittsburgh. The "only option for most [planes travelling in US airspace at the time] was to land in Canada" (6). As Jim DeFede notes in *The Day The World Came to Town: 9/11 in Gander, Newfoundland*, "although officials in the United States were certainly justified in wanting to protect their own borders, they were effectively passing the potential threat posed by these planes onto their neighbor" (6). Yet, "[d]espite the risk, Canada didn't hesitate to accept the orphaned planes," a stance of generosity and neighborliness in times of trouble that provided the narrative framework for the musical (6).

Writers Irene Sankoff and David Hein based their musical on an extensive collective of interviews conducted with Gander residents and plane passengers around the tenth anniversary of 9/11.[1] In his foreword to the 2018 script of the musical, Canadian Prime Minister Justin Trudeau argues that *Come From Away* exemplifies "humanity at its best" by depicting how through tragedy, "residents and newcomers built relationships and became friends across languages and cultures," standing together "at a time when fear threatened to divide" people (2019, 5). Notably, he attributes the success of *Come From Away* to its Canadian roots, as a "Canadian musical, written by Canadians, about Canadians" that "brought Canadian creativity to Broadway, and showcased the Canadian spirit of compassion, resourcefulness, and generosity" (5). The prominence of Trudeau as a champion for *Come From Away* suggests that this musical has come to function as more than just an example of Canada's ability to produce desirable cultural content for audiences at home and abroad; it can also be read as offering a vision of Canadian propaganda that extends the Canadian government's efforts to sustain its exceptionality in relation to the US.

The musical's feel-good elements rely specifically on the fact that, while it is a story "rooted in … tragedy[,] … it's emblematic of what it means to be a neighbour and friend" (Trudeau 2019, 5) to folks from across the globe. Much of the musical chronicles the close relationships that develop between a selection of Newfoundland locals and those who have literally "come from away" and find themselves beholden to the unique hospitality of small-town life over a period of an event-filled five days. While there are moments of racial tension and uncertainty about, for instance, how some practices of Muslim faith will be received over the course of the musical, the story relies on and cultivates an acceptance of diversity. Artistic Director Christopher Ashley confirmed that this was something he grappled with carefully in the early days of the musical's development. Ashley explains that "Gander is such a white environment—but we … decided that we had to release that literalness" so that a small group of actors could play an array of characters of different ethnic and racial backgrounds as well as varied sexual orientations (Sankoff and Hein 2019, 86).

Ashley's observation accords with the historical and contemporary composition of Newfoundland and Labrador's provincial population. Although the province did not join Canadian Confederation until 1949, it was influenced by the Canadian trend to exclude seemingly undesirable ethnic and racial minorities up to the post-Second World War era and beyond. Even in the twenty-first century, the numbers of visible minorities living in the province, including Black and Arab people, remain low, religious diversity is "minimal," and recognition of Indigenous communities continues to be provisional (Tremblay and Bittner 2011, 334), The last is partly a result of the fact that the Newfoundland government adopted the view when the province joined Confederation that "no special status" would be "afforded to the Indigenous peoples of Newfoundland" (Grammond 2014, 471), a position likely fueled by the mythological status granted the Beothuk as an isolated Indigenous population that had resided in Newfoundland before becoming extinct. This narrative of tragic erasure has shifted over the past several decades as the Mi'kmaq have raised questions about the Beothuk extinction in relation to their own people.[2] At the same time, the federal government has begun to sign treaties, create bands and reserves, and then redefine those groups in the case of several Indigenous communities in the province in ways that have been damaging and divisive.[3] Yet, the play makes no mention of any Indigenous characters either residing in Newfoundland or as passengers and crew from the grounded planes.

Welcoming the (Queer or Black) Stranger

Nonetheless, *Come From Away* presents a series of scenes that reinforce a vision of openness and inclusivity regarding the sexual orientation and race of those who live in or are visiting Gander and the adjacent small towns portrayed in the musical. For instance, the American homosexual couple, Kevin T and Kevin J, who unwittingly out themselves in a rural Newfoundland bar, soon find themselves surrounded by locals who have queer relatives, providing a peaceful resolution to what they first anticipate may be an uncomfortable or even violent encounter. Kevin T explains, "We somehow ended up in the gayest town in Newfoundland" and share a laugh with the community as they speculate that "[t]here must be something in the water" (Sankoff and Hein 2019, 109). Likewise, in the scene that directly follows, the actor who plays Bob, a Black man and "eternal 'outsider' from Brooklyn" (206) and who is being housed by Derm Flynn, the Mayor of Appleton, is enlisted to help with a "big cookout for the whole community" to keep the passengers' "minds off of everything" (109). Derm tells Bob, "Right, m'son, do me a favor and start to round up some grills" (109), and suggests that "Yeah, just go to people's yards and take their grills" (110). Bob, however, is rightly hesitant to do so. In the notes about the ensemble cast, actor Rodney Hicks, who originally developed Bob's character for the show, decides to play him as a Black character and explains, "I could see Bob as someone who is never around white people, typically, someone who is removed. And his first instinct is to isolate himself, because if he crosses a line, if he moves anything he shouldn't, he thinks he's going to get shot" (206). For Hicks, the history of race relations and Black racism in the US fundamentally shapes Bob's cautionary attitude.

Not surprisingly, Bob is initially reluctant to take on such a task, presuming that, if he takes "their grills … Someone's gonna shoot me" (Sankoff and Hein 2019, 110). While Derm insists that that is not the case, Bob remains vigilant, expecting the whole time that, as he gathers barbeques, "someone is going to shoot me in the back" (110). Instead, he finds himself being repeatedly invited in for tea, presumably in stark contrast to his experiences in his home country of America. As Bob explains:

> I get offered a cup a tea in every single backyard—and most of them offer to help me steal their own barbeques. We bring them all over to the community center—no names on them. I don't know how they ever get 'em back. But that's how we have a big cookout—completely free. After that I stop worrying so much about my wallet. (110)

Here, the treatment of Bob reinforces the belief that Canada's "'idealized mythic identity'" is "'associated with willingness to welcome strangers'" (Rosello, qtd. in Roberts 2015, 14). Moreover, Roberts argues that "Canada's official multicultural policy, first introduced in 1971," has enabled the nation to create and reinforce the illusion that the nation has, from even before its inception, offered sanctuary to Americans seeking refuge, "from the Loyalists to the Underground Railroad to Vietnam War draft resisters" (14). This is a story that *Come From Away* continues to perpetuate.

In the musical, Bob's character shifts from that of a fearful Black American man to a visitor who, for the first time in his life, feels truly welcome rather than a target of racial hatred and distrust. Bob even volunteers to participate in the traditional Newfoundland screeching-in ceremony. He goes so far as to pass around his traditional "Sou'wester hat" (Sankoff and Hein 2019, 170), a key accessory of the screeching-in ceremony, when the flights begin to depart from Gander. Bob collects money to create a scholarship for the local population, an endeavor that is hugely successful. The safety and hospitality that Bob experiences while in Newfoundland, however, evaporate once he leaves Canada. As he flies over New York, re-entering US air space, he witnesses "smoke" rising in

"Manhattan," an experience that makes him "afraid all over again" (182). Arguably, this concluding moment of the musical can be seen as conflating the tragedy of 9/11 with the long-standing history of anti-Black racism by returning Bob to a location that he associates with fear for multiple reasons, while bolstering the idea of Canada as "kinder, gentler, [and] more accepting of others" (Brantley 2017).

This perception of Canada is strengthened by the commentary provided by Rodney Hicks, who played the character of Bob from the initial workshop in 2011 to Broadway, where the musical debuted in 2017. In the *Come From Away* book, Hicks describes the cast's 2016 visit to Gander to perform the musical there. Again, he emphasizes the hospitality and inclusivity shown by locals. Hicks explains, "There are practically no black people in Gander" and so when he arrives, he gives himself over to "being a foreigner … that was my aim for Bob—he's scared, he's just scared" (Sankoff and Hein 2019, 193). Even Hicks, however, offers a deeply romanticized view of Gander, Newfoundland, and, more broadly, Canada. Hicks notes that despite wanting "to pretend that I didn't really know any white people … I was personally so welcomed that the energy blew me away" (193). He goes so far as to claim, "I walked into the stores and I never felt like anyone was watching me—because they weren't. There was that honest welcoming" (193). What Hicks fails to consider is that he is there as an invited guest and a recognized celebrity as part of a cast of a musical that not only made Gander famous globally, but also secured Canada's place on Broadway, financially and commercially. As a Black man in Gander, he is, moreover, readily recognized as a visitor and thus can expect a warm reception.

What does not correspond to the "feel good" narrative—and what is therefore ignored—is the long history of "racialized surveillance, policing and incarceration [of Black people] in Canada" that continues to this day (Maynard 2017, 85) but remains unacknowledged. As Sherene Razack reminds us in her exploration of Canada's virtuosity as a peacekeeping nation, when Canadians hear stories "of police brutality or racial profiling [within Canada], we insist on the madness of those who make such claims" (2004, 165). But as Tanovich explains, the profiling of Black people as they circulate in stores or make their way through neighborhoods, especially those that are predominantly populated by Black people, is "a self-fulfilling prophecy. The more that a group is targeted, the greater the likelihood that criminality will be discovered" (Tanovich 2004, 916). Over-surveillance leads to more arrests, a reality that Hicks does not recognize or acknowledge as a fundamental part of Canada's justice system because of his uniquely privileged position, in spite of his skin color, when visiting Newfoundland.

The only character who encounters repeated experiences of racism and racial profiling in *Come From Away* is Ali, a Muslim chef living in the US who is a passenger on a flight from Paris to Dallas, traveling for business. He identifies himself as "Egyptian" upon his arrival in Gander, yet he is pulled aside for further scrutiny (Sankoff and Hein 2019, 74). When he is finally released by the customs officers and permitted to board a bus bound to local shelters, he is again targeted by fellow passengers as a "guy from the Middle East" (75). Ali is perceived as a security threat (75), an experience that reflects the targeted racism directed at Muslims particularly in the aftermath of 9/11 in both Canada and the US. In a 2021 news article, reporter Sean Boynton explains that "[s]ince 9/11, Islamophobia has been 'a constant feature' in Canada" (2021). The rate of anti-Muslim hate crimes has continued to grow over the past two decades and flourish, particularly between 2015 and the present in response to both federal denouncement of Islamophobia in 2016 and the Quebec government's 2019 secularism bill, which limits "public sector workers from wearing religious symbols" at their places of employment (2021).

The musical moderates this early scene by describing the discomfort that Ali and other practicing Muslim, Hindu, and Jewish passengers experience as they try to carry out their prayers in the shelters. This situation is ameliorated when locals suggest that "[t]he library's open—for anyone looking for some peace—and a quiet place to pray" (Sankoff and Hein 2019, 129). Nonetheless, the targeting of Muslims by passengers remains part of the plot, particularly in a section called "On The Edge," which takes place midway through the musical in an effort, as co-writer David Hein explains, "to find more tension" (130). Here, Ali is challenged by a fellow passenger when he speaks in a foreign language on the phone. The passenger accuses Ali of "telling your Muslim friends where to bomb next" (130), a scene that serves as a reminder that many of the stranded Muslim passengers are, in fact, born and raised American (and Canadian) citizens. It is only after a local Newfoundland teacher turned coordinator of food services, Beulah, stops to listen long enough to learn that Ali is, as he explains, "a master chef for an international hotel chain" who oversees "restaurants around the world," that he finally gets a chance to showcase his cooking skills and start producing food for those who are stranded (132). In doing so, Beulah secures Ali's legitimacy as a generous person, eager to help his fellow passengers, even in the face of their hostility toward him.

Despite these talents, Ali remains the target of racism to the end of the musical, with an unidentified airline attendant complaining to the character of Captain Beverley as the crew prepare to board and depart days later that "[t]here's a Muslim man on our flight— / I saw him praying—and he's been acting ... suspicious. He doesn't have a carry-on" (Sankoff and Hein 2019, 156). The flight attendant refuses to "get ... back on that plane" with Ali, and so, of course, when Ali arrives at the Gander airport to re-board the plane, he is quickly "pulled out of line" yet again by airport security (156). Beverley insists that she is "responsible for the safety of my passengers and my crew" (156); she has been told by security that "any perceived threats must be taken extremely seriously" (156). Beverley feels she has a duty to report the attendant's concerns, but later regrets having provoked the invasive process that is inflicted upon him.

Ali finds himself in a room with the female captain, who watches him being physically searched: "In my culture, there is a word—'awrah'—the area between your stomach and your knees. It is forbidden in my religion for anyone to see this but my wife. // To have a woman in the room, watching this. Watching me. // You can't understand" (Sankoff and Hein 2019, 156). Beverley offers her apologies, having realized that he has undergone "the most thorough body search I've ever witnessed" (156). Although she tells him, "I am so very sorry that happened," all Ali can do is ask if he is "free to go now," reflecting the reality that the captain does not truly comprehend the magnitude of this violation of Ali's religious beliefs (156). His story ends directly after this scene. There is no further reference to him in the script after he is released. Captain Beverley's plane presumably takes off with him on board, and he is ultimately allowed to re-enter US airspace and make his return to Dallas. Through the inclusion of this narrative strand in the plot, *Come From Away* displaces the reality of Canadian racism with a narrative that suggests this kind of anti-Muslim behavior is fundamentally an American phenomenon. Beverley, after all, is an American, so when her flight leaves Gander, presumably so do the prejudicial behaviors of the captain and her passengers. In crafting this storyline, which so abruptly vanishes from view, *Come From Away* reinforces the sense that Canada, or at least Gander and the surrounding towns, provide places of safety and acceptance for most of the people who find themselves stranded there, in deliberate contrast with Canada's southern neighbor.

Canada's Prime Minister did not hesitate to make the same kinds of claims for Canada's inclusivity when *Come From Away* opened on Broadway in March 2017, just days after then-US President Trump announced a ban on Muslim travelers to the country, which had prompted a "surge in asylum seekers fleeing from the United States to Canada" (Paulson 2017b). Trudeau responded by tweeting that "'Canadians will welcome you'" (qtd. in Cole 2020, 150). As mentioned in Chap. 3, Trudeau used Trump's announcement to showcase the idea that, for Canada, "the act of 'welcoming the stranger'" serves to "constitute the nation" (Roberts 2015, 14) in stark contrast to the immigration and refugee policies advanced by Trump's government. Of course, the premiere of *Come From Away* in New York proved to be a particularly useful vehicle for Trudeau, who delivered "remarks to the audience before the show" and spoke to reporters afterward (Paulson 2017c, A6). He employed the musical to mobilize "Canadian soft power" and reinforced a narrative of Canadian exceptionality and neighborliness to the world, which was well received (A6).

In *Broadway North*, Mel Atkey explains that Canada's long history as a British colony located adjacent to the US has fundamentally shaped what constitutes success for a Canadian musical, which is, "without question, the most popular form of live theatre" (2006, 5): "'The only road to applause of a Toronto theatre audience is by way of Broadway'" (Sandwell qtd. in Atkey 2006, 1).[4] Atkey notes, however, that the Canadian relationship to Broadway is complicated precisely because Canadian-authored musicals typically lack certain marketable traits: "what American musicals do exude—and this is something to be emulated—is a terrific sense of confidence" (7). While Canada has a reputation as a "peacekeeper" nation that avoids the "flag-waving triumphalism" exhibited by some Americans, he also recognizes that "Canadians are … capable of a smug superiority, especially … regarding their southern neighbours" (7, 10). The narrative of *Come From Away*, as I have suggested above, exemplifies and reinforces the legitimacy of this contradictory stance: when performed on Broadway, it becomes a powerful cultural vehicle for circulating key narratives about Canada directly to American audiences.

As journalists later revealed, the Canadian federal government used *Come From Away*'s arrival on Broadway as an opportunity for strategic cross-border diplomacy. Trudeau's government purchased a total of 502 tickets to the Broadway premiere at a cost of nearly "$23,000 Canadian," inviting over 700 "VIPs" to attend, among them "125 United Nations ambassadors," "business people, lawyers, consultants and government officials" (Smith 2018), although only 276 actually agreed to come. Perhaps the most famous guest, despite being absent from the official guest list—which is heavily "redacted"—was Ivanka Trump, who attended the event with Nikki Haley, the American ambassador to the United Nations, and who was seated directly behind former Prime Minister Jean Chretien (Smith 2018). Further, Trudeau used his pre-performance speech to reiterate the importance of "the deep friendship between Canada and the United States," leaving the musical to communicate more explicitly Canada's seeming commitment to diversity and its policy of "welcoming … refugees" in contrast to the US (Paulson 2017c, A6). As *The New York Times* reporter Michael Paulson noted over several days of coverage of the premiere of *Come From Away*, the audience was populated in part by Canadians who had immigrated to the US and who did not hesitate to clearly articulate what they viewed as the musical's main message. For instance, Sophie de Caen, a Canadian who lives and works in New York for the United Nations, helping to aid Syrian refugees, told Paulson, "As we can see in this show, Canadians have a generosity of spirit. We accept diversity" (A6). Other Canadian attendees shared similar messages, noting that "The contrast between the U.S. and Canada is so stark. … Nothing is solved unless we have dialogue" (A6). The premiere became a public relations success story for the Canadian federal government and Canadians more broadly, one that reinforced the narrative of exceptionality and secured, once again, the need for talk rather than action to resolve differences, following the same trajectory as that modeled in Moore's depiction of Canada in *Bowling for Columbine*.

Debunking Canadian Exceptionality in *Nîpawistamâsowin: We Will Stand Up*

Both Moore's movie and *Come From Away* overlook or ignore what I have been describing throughout this study as the hidden histories of Canada. These storylines expose and subvert the predominant stories of Canadian identity and belonging, displacing them with a more nuanced and contradictory vision of the nation, particularly in relationship to the US. While on the one hand the US has proved to be a useful foil for justifying and protecting descriptions of Canadian exceptionalism, on the other hand, probing both American and Canadian stories that problematize (or sustain) exceptionality on either side of the border provides a means of scrutinizing and reconfiguring long-standing narratives that cultivate and reinforce such a stance of inclusivity and hospitality. Hubbard's documentary *Nîpawistamâsowin: We Will Stand Up* is far less familiar to Canadian or American audiences than Michael Moore's films or *Come From Away*.

Nîpawistamâsowin: We Will Stand Up premiered in April 2019 as the opening film at Hot Docs, marking "the first time the festival had ever selected an indigenous-themed film" ("*Nîpawistamâsowin*" 2022) for this honor, followed by a commercial premiere at the Roxy Theatre in Saskatoon a month later. Described on the National Film Board (NFB) site as a "profound narrative encompassing the filmmaker's own adoption, the stark history of colonialism on the Prairies, and a vision of the future where Indigenous children can live safely on their homelands,"[5] Hubbard notes that the film has garnered much more attention than she ever expected, within Canada and beyond. It went on a national tour in May 2019, including "a run of showings" at the Toronto International Film Festival's "Lightbox summer programming" (Braat 2019); premiered on the Aboriginal Peoples Television Network in a "full 98-minute runtime" in September 2020 with a "community engagement guide … [and] links to support resources" (Short 2020); and was subsequently released for free public viewing on the NFB site with a learning guide for Grades 7–12[6] through the free Canadian streaming service CBC Gem, and at a nominal cost on Amazon Prime in the US.

While Eleanore Sunchild, one of the Boushie family's lawyers, "thinks all Canadians should watch the film," especially those "who don't want to see it" to prompt much-needed conversations about "'racism, discrimination, stereotypes and reconciliation'" in Canada (Braat 2019), Hubbard's movie remains outside of the larger commercial venues that would substantially increase viewership. The documentary has primarily circulated in recent years through screening events and panel discussions at Canadian universities, including the Indigenous Law Students' Association at the University of Alberta in February 2020 and University of Calgary's Werklund School of Education in March 2021. When I attended a daytime screening of the film at TIFF's Lightbox during its six-day run (from May 31 to June 5, 2019), I was one of two viewers in a theater that seats roughly 45 people, one of two smaller theaters in the venue. This experience stood in stark contrast to the full-to-capacity crowd I was part of a day earlier when attending *Come From Away* at Toronto's Elgin Theatre, a 2100-seat venue, which has previously been used for TIFF's opening-night screenings.

Nîpawistamâsowin: We Will Stand Up offers a pointed challenge to Canadian narratives of exceptionality by documenting the trial of Gerald Stanley for the shooting death of Colten Boushie, Stanley's subsequent acquittal, and the community efforts that follow to seek "Justice for Colten" (Hubbard 2019). This phrase is used throughout the film to highlight the violent settler colonial history of Canada, which, as the movie demonstrates, still shapes Canadian society. In particular, the film probes the ongoing legitimation of settler killings of Indigenous people in Canada "in the name of protecting private property for white settlers," a set of narratives that underpin the national myth of the "proletariat farmer who broke the prairie sod to make way for the settlement and moderniza- tion of the new agricultural base of the Canadian national economy" (Morton 2019, 437, 440). Hubbard's film provides an alterna(rra)tive understanding of Indigenous-settler relations that demonstrates how Canada continues to foster these "founding national mythologies" based on "white settler superiority" (Morton 2019, 440). More specifically, her documentary examines how "prairie farming is [treated as] a meritocracy built on individual work ethic" by erasing the prior existence of Indigenous peoples on that same land (Morton 2019, 440). Focused on "the histories of white settler colonial violence in Treaty 6 territory," the land of some of Hubbard's Cree ancestors, the movie probes the ways in which national narratives about the "formation of Canada" continue to justify "anti-Indigenous violence and the settler killing of Indigenous peoples today" (Morton 2019, 437).

As Audra Simpson explains in the second epigraph to Chap. 8, "in spite of the innocence of the story that Canada likes to tell about itself ... that it is a place that is not like the place below it, across that border," Canada continues to differentiate itself from its American neighbor precisely because the Canadian government has "apologized" for past wrongdo- ings, while continuing to carry out what she describes as "an extractive and simultaneously murderous state of affairs" (2016). In other words, by offering contrition for historical actions, whether in the form of a federal apology for residential schooling (2008), the hanging of Métis leader Louis Riel (1998, 2017), or provincial apologies for the Sixties Scoop by Manitoba (2015), Alberta (2018), and Saskatchewan (2019),[7] Canada remains "a settler society whose multicultural, liberal and democratic structure and performance of governance seeks an ongoing 'settling' of this land" that is far from innocent (Simpson 2016).

In *Nîpawistamâsowin: We Will Stand Up*, Hubbard demonstrates that access to justice remains limited or nonexistent for BIPOC communities in Canada and fundamentally shaped by settler beliefs. It also foregrounds the propensity for white settler farmers to continue to use gun violence to support "a killing state and its armed citizens" who perceive themselves as the "rightful inheritors of land and labour from … [their] settler kin" (Morton 2019, 437–438). Yet, as Morton notes, the brutality inflicted by farmers like Stanley is deliberately severed from "past [acts of] imperial violence" to justify such behaviors and suggest the (relative) innocence of those who are seen to be merely reinforcing their right to own and defend their land from unwanted intruders (438).

The film begins with Hubbard, her son, and her nephew reflecting on the development of Prairie lands prior to and during Canada's colonization by settlers. Cree director Hubbard also notes her own adoption by a "homesteading" settler family before turning to the events surrounding the death of Colten Boushie, a member of the Red Pheasant Cree Nation, a reserve located 33 kilometers north of Battleford, Saskatchewan. In the opening scene, Hubbard and the two boys walk across the vast Prairie landscape near her childhood farm and immediately encounter a barbed wire fence that they carefully climb through to avoid being injured. One child takes pictures of the vista with a camera and asks the other child if he wishes he could turn back the clock to a time "before the settlers came" (Hubbard 2019). Hubbard recalls that the land on which they are standing had not been developed when she was a child. The film makes clear that it is being cultivated, as evidenced by the fence and the plowed lands. This initial scene is juxtaposed with a view of her settler grandfather planting seeds in his garden plot; Hubbard's son sits beside him, helping him with the planting process. As with the farming lands they have just walked through, a fence separates the garden from the adjacent street, marking her white grandfather's ownership of the land. While Hubbard describes her non-Indigenous grandfather as always making "us feel that we're part of his family," she also emphasizes that the "Prairies have a complicated history" and that "Indigenous peoples are often at the receiving end of racism" because they are perceived as trespassers on their own territory (2019).

Having been separated from her Indigenous birth family until she was a teenager, Hubbard describes in the film how she has committed to making "things different for my son" by instilling in him the belief that "we belong here, even if people try to make us think we don't," and ensuring that he "not accept … [or] internalize" the long history of racism and exclusion directed at Indigenous peoples (Hubbard 2019). Moreover, as Hubbard explains in the voiceover that accompanies these initial images of her son and nephew on the Prairie, in Cree culture, children do not belong to their parents. Instead, they "belong to themselves" and their relations "are responsible for keeping them safe." The shooting of Colten Boushie at close range in the back of the head by a farmer in August 2016 demonstrates that it is impossible to do so, given the ways in which settler violence on the Prairies is not only permitted but supported by the legal system: Stanley's trial and subsequent acquittal are evidence of that. For Hubbard, Colten's death prompts the brutal realization that, even if she teaches her son and nephew "how to protect themselves as they grow into men," Hubbard cannot guarantee their safety (2019). Neighborliness has been displaced by what Sunchild describes as "vigilante justice," with non-Indigenous farmers casting themselves as victims protecting their property from criminals (Hubbard 2019). By pairing her examination of Stanley's trial and its aftermath with historical materials and narratives that Hubbard shares with her son and nephew, her documentary foregrounds the historical and contemporary impact of Canadian racism on multiple generations of Indigenous people and the pervasiveness of gun violence directed at those same communities.

Central to *Nîpawistamâsowin: We Will Stand Up* is the brutal execution-style death of Boushie by shotgun on Gerald Stanley's property. In a voiceover narrated by Hubbard, the documentary describes the events that occurred on the day of the shooting: "Colten's girlfriend, her cousin, and two other friends picked Colten up. They drank, swam, and then headed home" (2019). Hubbard notes that, while they were driving back home, "Colten was sleeping in the back of the SUV." The "other two young men" stopped the vehicle and tried to break into a truck unsuccessfully. Finally, the group decided that, because one tire on the SUV was losing air and could potentially damage the rim, they would stop at Gerald Stanley's farm. Stanley "was known for fixing cars, and his farm was close by" (Hubbard 2019). However, when they entered Stanley's property, one of the Indigenous men departed the SUV and jumped onto a quad in the yard, causing Stanley and his son to start yelling and smash the SUV taillight and windshield. Gerald Stanley also went to retrieve a gun. Because they were driving with a flat tire, several of the other occupants of the SUV were unable to see where they were going and ended up crashing into a parked vehicle on the property. They left the SUV and fled on foot. Colten, who finally woke up, was left to try to protect the woman who was still in the vehicle. He hopped into the front seat, intending to drive off the property, but could not escape. Stanley fired three shots—the third one, which was discharged at close range, killed Colten.

Hubbard's documentary explains that Colten's death was caused by a single shot in close proximity, with the bullet entering the back of Colten's head by his left ear. As Colten's mother, Debbie Baptiste, argues in the film, Stanley did not have to shoot at anyone. He "could have shot … the gun in the air," made the passengers exit the SUV, and waited for the RCMP to arrive. Instead, "he took it upon himself to do justice. … He figured … 'they're on my land'" and so he "walk[ed] right up behind my son and … [shot] him in the back of the head" (Hubbard 2019). Hubbard's voiceover mentions that Colten's girlfriend and cousin later testified that, after Colten was killed, they heard Stanley's wife say, "That's what you get for trespassing." Not surprisingly, the Royal Canadian Mounted Police (RCMP) responsible for investigating the incident were quick to describe the shooting as a "theft" investigation, a strategy that explicitly displaced blame onto the Indigenous youths who had entered Stanley's yard (Hubbard 2019). In doing so, they turned Colten's gun death into a by-product of what was characterized as criminal activity on the part of Boushie and everyone else in the SUV. By "criminalizing Indigenous peoples on white property," the RCMP enabled Stanley and his family to rely on "the connection between white fears of Indigenous 'trespass' and 'theft' and fatal gun violence in the name of protecting white property" (Morton 2019, 441). This strategy "frames [white] occupation as peaceable," which "justifies citizen violence on behalf of the state, and reimagines Canada['s] … state systems as just and benevolent" (2019, 441).

THE REALITY OF GUN VIOLENCE IN CANADA

To challenge the veracity of the RCMP's case, *Nîpawistamâsowin: We Will Stand Up* includes clips of the emotional reactions of family and community members to Colten's sudden death. The film pays special attention to the words of Debbie Baptiste and Jade Tootoosis, Colten's cousin. Jade, a young Cree woman prompted by her grandmother to take on the role of primary spokesperson for Colten's family and the Red Pheasant community, becomes a critical voice in the efforts to achieve justice for Colten.

For example, Jade outlines in detail the sustained and vitriolic hatred toward Indigenous peoples expressed online in the immediate aftermath of his death. Tootoosis describes how gun violence is justified as a legitimate and even necessary response to the perceived threat Indigenous populations pose to farmers and their property, a reality that Hubbard reminds viewers is a long-standing practice, dating back to the colonization of Canada. The RCMP's search of Stanley's farm uncovers 12 guns, including a restricted handgun; despite this evidence, Stanley is released on $10,000 bail. As the documentary demonstrates, any hope of getting justice for Colten is eroded over the course of the trial because of the power and persistence of long-standing Indigenous stereotypes that ensure "a continuum of historic oppression" (Mullen 2019).

Hubbard's movie deftly weaves together the legacies of colonialism in Treaty 6 territory, providing a summary of past injustices that frame the Stanley trial. The documentary catalogues the introduction of the Indian Act in 1876 with the institution of reserves and the subsequent creation of the pass system to limit Indigenous travel off reserve beginning in 1885. Hubbard acknowledges the harm done by residential schools, first created in the 1880s; the last one was closed in 1996. She also references the Sixties Scoop, which placed Indigenous children and babies, including Hubbard herself, with non-Indigenous families. These events document the long-standing racial hatred that informs the unfolding narrative of the trial held at the Court of Queen's Bench in Battleford, Saskatchewan, from January 30 to February 9, 2018, located close to the farm where the shooting occurred. She argues that the historical efforts of the Canadian government to starve the Indigenous peoples off the land in the Battleford area resulted in a hostile relationship between settlers and Indigenous peoples that continues to shape contemporary relations.

The film juxtaposes an emotional visit Hubbard makes with her son and nephew to the RCMP Heritage Centre exhibit "Maintaining Law and Order in the West" and its colonial archives with footage of the trial. *Nîpawistamâsowin: We Will Stand Up* includes media questions posed outside the courthouse, sketches from the trial, and interviews with Boushie family members and supporters about Colten, along with comments made by lawyers on both sides of the case. Concerned about achieving justice, Boushie's family hires its own lawyers, rather than relying on the Crown prosecutor, and asks the community to petition for an out-of-province prosecutor. The province, however, decides to keep the prosecutor already in place. As a result, the family has little to no ability to shape the Crown's case, replicating the historical practice of shutting Indigenous peoples out of participation in legal processes.

Moreover, by using pre-emptory challenges to veto potential jurors "without giving any reason why," Stanley's lawyer ensures that there are no Indigenous people on the jury (Hubbard 2019). *Nîpawistamâsowin: We Will Stand Up* argues that the Indigenous witnesses to the crime are "the ones [put] on trial" instead (Hubbard 2019). The audience in the small courtroom is visibly divided, with Boushie's family seated on one side and Stanley's family on the other, separated by the media. The trial reveals that examination of the evidence was delayed and ruined by rain. Blood spatter experts used photographs taken in the aftermath of these delays, rather than the scene itself, to make their determinations. Additionally, before the trial even begins, Stanley's lawyer, Scott Spencer, asserts that the trial is "not a referendum on race" (Hubbard 2019). While presenting Stanley's case, Spencer uses photographs of Colten Boushie after he had been murdered as part of his questioning of Indigenous witnesses in the courtroom, which is a gross violation of Indigenous protocols.

Most importantly, Stanley's lawyer claims that the shooting of Colten was an accident. His defense rests on the theory that Stanley, whom he characterizes as a hard-working farmer, experienced a "hangfire [or malfunction of the gun], a delay between pulling the trigger and the bullet firing," which is described in Hubbard's film as the "magic gun defense" (2019). Although it is a very rare occurrence that relies on defective ammunition and does not fit the facts of this case, Spencer calls upon several so-called expert witnesses during the trial who describe similar malfunctions with their guns, although these guns are not the same make or model as Stanley's (2019). Despite the unlikeliness of this defense, Gerald Stanley is found "not guilty," a verdict that for Colten's brother suggested that "you could shoot people in the back of the head and get away with it" (2019).

Searching for "Justice for Colten"

The remainder of the documentary probes the steps that Colten's community takes after the trial in their quest to deliver much sought-after "Justice for Colten" (Hubbard 2019). Their efforts are fueled by the recognition that he has been shot to protect the rights and property of white settlers. This is not unlike those who killed off the buffalo over a century ago to starve the Cree who were living on the land that the federal government wanted to colonize as part of its expansion westward. As Hubbard's birth father, who was one of the first Cree lawyers in Saskatchewan, explains to Hubbard's son, the Cree word for "justice" is fundamentally tied to respect, a respect that is lacking when it comes to Indigenous peoples in Canada: "When a government is not fair with the subjects, or when two parties of an agreement, like Treaties, are not living up to what they agreed to, that's not fair, so then you don't see justice" (Hubbard 2019). Public outrage following the acquittal prompts a meeting 20 hours later that the film documents between Saskatchewan Premier Scott Moe, Don Morgan, Saskatchewan's Justice Minister, and Colten's family. In it, Jade Tootoosis describes the systemic racism they have experienced ever since Colten's death and the RCMP's neglect in processing the crime scene evidence.

They then travel to Ottawa to appear on CBC's television show *Power and Politics*, followed by in-person meetings with a variety of federal politicians, including the first Indigenous Justice Minister, Jody Wilson-Raybould, Indigenous Senators Murray Sinclair and Lillian Dyck, NDP leader Jagmeet Singh, and Prime Minister Justin Trudeau, along with three Conservative members of parliament (MPs). Conservative leader Andrew Scheer, despite being from Saskatchewan, declines to meet with them. Again, Hubbard's documentary creates a montage of moments from these various meetings, including Sinclair's promise that the Liberal government is putting forward a bill to end the pre-emptory challenges used by Stanley's lawyer to secure an entirely non-Indigenous jury for the trial, a bill that finally succeeds in changing the law in 2019.

Nîpawistamâsowin: We Will Stand Up highlights the relative lack of action taken to change the long-standing pattern of prejudice aimed at Indigenous peoples in Canada. For instance, the meeting with Trudeau is largely symbolic. While it may give visibility to Colten's wrongful death, Hubbard notes that the Prime Minister listens but does not offer to take concrete action. Throughout their time in Ottawa, the film repeatedly returns to the family's desire to have the provincial and federal governments directly address the "structural racism in the [Canadian] legal system" that has led to Stanley's acquittal (Hubbard 2019). Jade Tootoosis asks the three Conservative MPs what they are "going to do, as human beings" to change what is going on in Saskatchewan, particularly given the flourishing of online racial hatred directed toward Boushie's family in the aftermath of the verdict (Hubbard 2019). The situation is exacerbated when, a month later, Saskatchewan's Justice Department—representing the Crown's case—declines to appeal Stanley's not guilty verdict and proceeds to "strengthen trespass laws" (Hubbard 2019). The RCMP subsequently holds town halls across Saskatchewan, including one in Stanley's neighborhood, where local farmers continue to advocate for the right to bear arms to protect their property, prioritizing the defense of land over a person's right to safety.

GOING SOUTH TO SEEK JUSTICE

Out of options in Canada, Colten's family ultimately turns to an international body, the United Nations Permanent Forum on Indigenous Issues, to provoke change, knowing that this body has advocated for the rights of Indigenous peoples globally and demonstrated the legitimacy of historic and modern treaties between Indigenous nations and federal governments, including Canada's agreements with various Indigenous communities. This forum promotes respect for and the application of the provisions of the UN Declaration on the Rights of Indigenous People, which Canada's Liberal government finally agreed to endorse in May 2016, a mere three months before Colten was killed. Notably, Canada, along with three other settler-invader nations (Australia, New Zealand, and the US), originally voted against the declaration in 2007 (see "United Nations"), fearful of the expectation that the nations who signed it would be obliged to "obtain ... free, prior and informed consent [from Indigenous groups] before adopting and implementing legislative or administrative measures" that may affect those populations (Office of the High Commissioner 2013).

Nîpawistamâsowin: We Will Stand Up tracks the family's trip to New York City, home of the United Nations. Jade has been chosen to speak on behalf of the family. Tension builds throughout these scenes because, despite having gotten a seat at the forum for the day through the Federation of Saskatchewan Indigenous Nations, she must secure a spot on the speaker's list. Throughout their brief visit to the UN, Debbie Baptiste, who sits beside Jade on the floor of the forum meeting, keeps lifting her arm to show a photo of Colten, offering a persistent and visible reminder of the reason for the family's presence. Finally, at 6 pm, as the forum is about to end and Colten's mother fears that they will not get a chance to speak, the chair of the forum grants Jade special dispensation to tell the story of Colten's death and the resulting acquittal of Stanley.

In one of the most poignant scenes of the film, Jade Tootoosis delivers a brief yet pointed speech to the forum, which calls on the international

8 THE LIMITS OF CANADIAN EXCEPTIONALISM: BOWLING... 221

body and its delegates to undertake a study of racism against Indigenous peoples within the "judicial and legal systems in Canada" and produce "recommendations" (Hubbard 2019). In doing so, the Boushie family hope that the UN will compel Canada to undertake a Royal Commission that can conduct an independent investigation of Boushie's death because, in Canada, a Royal Commission has the authority "to fully and impartially investigate issues of national importance" ("Commissions" 2022). It has the power "to subpoena witnesses, take evidence under oath and request documents" with a mandate to enact change in situations of injustice (2022). Her speech garners thunderous applause and Jade, overwhelmed by the experience of speaking to hundreds of UN delegates, starts crying as soon as she leaves the building. Unlike the Canadian tourists and diplomats discussed earlier on in this chapter—including the Prime Minister of Canada—who come to New York to see a Broadway show like *Come From Away*, Colten's family are not there to champion positive accounts of Canadian exceptionality and virtuosity. Rather, they have come to the UN to expose a fundamental problem with the stories Canada chooses to tell about its national identity and values, a set of narratives that have legitimated the existence of the nation by inflicting settler violence against Indigenous peoples for centuries. The gun violence that has led to Colten's death is part of a larger set of nation-state mechanisms that prioritize the protection of non-Indigenous farmers and property owners and legitimate the use of guns against Indigenous peoples in the name of progress and national unity.

The closing segments of the documentary return Hubbard to Saskatchewan, offering yet another perspective on gun violence by demonstrating how supportive relationships between and among Indigenous and non-Indigenous peoples may start to shift long-held racist beliefs and actions. Hubbard, her son, and her birth father visit her white adoptive parents on a family farm in southern Saskatchewan where she lived until she was 11. During the visit, her adoptive father and birth father decide that Hubbard's son is old enough to learn how to discharge a pellet gun. The scene that unfolds demonstrates the care that these two men take in educating the young Indigenous man on how to safely use a pellet gun for target practice; in this case, the target is a set of tin cans. Her adoptive father begins by telling their grandson, named Quannah, that he should "always assume the rifle is loaded—always" (Hubbard 2019). The settler grandfather insists that any gun should "always point ... away from people or animals or buildings or anything you don't want to shoot" (Hubbard

2019). This word of caution stands in direct contrast to Gerald Stanley's decision to point his gun at Colten Boushie, shoot him, and then claim that his gun malfunctioned. Quannah follows his grandfather's advice and holds the gun steady, despite the wind that might change the pellet's trajectory. He hits several targets, earning the praise of his grandfathers, before the film switches to a conversation among Hubbard, her white settler grandfather, and her son sitting at a farmhouse table with a pile of stones.

Viewers learn that her grandfather kept the stones, markers for teepee rings, which he uncovered decades before while breaking up his land for farming; he wondered if he should farm the land, but he admits that he did it anyway, eventually giving the stones to Hubbard and her son as contrition for what he has done (Hubbard 2019). The dialogue moves between two aspects of the film: Hubbard's explanation of why she has made *Nîpawistamâsowin: We Will Stand Up* and her adoptive grandfather's effort to try to find a middle ground between land ownership and Indigenous presence on the Prairies. Hubbard's adoptive grandfather argues for the importance of protecting one's hard-earned property, while recognizing that there are "always going to … [be] some people [who] are going to be racist…. It's always been that way." Yet as Quannah points out, conflicts over land ownership should not be resolved "by shooting someone" (Hubbard 2019). Hubbard's adoptive grandfather agrees, but predicts that any kind of reconciliation will take a long time to happen, providing a vivid reminder of the legacy of colonialism on the Prairies and its deep-seated roots.

In a 2020 interview about her film, Hubbard explains that having watched the Boushie family advocate for transformative changes to Canadian society, she chose the word *nîpawistamâsowin* for the film title because it is a Cree word that describes "a small group of people standing up on behalf of a larger group" (Frank 2020). The subtitle provides "the English shorthand" for viewers. The documentary gives voice to the reality that "the Canadian justice system" was designed "to eradicate Indigenous life" (Nixon 2019) and that Boushie's death needs to be understood as part of "a continuum of historic oppression" (Mullen 2019). Hubbard's film revisits and complicates the issues Roberts raises as fundamental to her examination of Canada-US relations by highlighting the hostility that Indigenous peoples have encountered and continue to experience within Canada. This hostility stands in contrast to the ways in which Canada is championed as a "kinder and gentler nation," committed to inclusion for BIPOC populations. Instead, *Nîpawistamâsowin: We Will Stand Up* offers a tangible example of how narratives of Canadian exceptionality have erased a fundamental reality: the prior presence and continued existence of Indigenous peoples on the very same land that has been stolen to secure the existence of this colonial nation-state. Hubbard, as well as Boushie's family and community, refuse to be silenced, exposing the fact that Canada, like its neighbor to the south, relies on violence and hostility to achieve and maintain the country's veneer of hospitality and inclusivity, whether for visitors to the nation or populations whose existence pre-dates colonization. Yet as both *Bowling for Columbine* and *Come from Away* attest, Canadian exceptionalism remains, in many cases, a critical tool for demonstrating the shortcomings of American patriotism and its own narratives of exceptionality, while celebrating Canadian inclusivity, tolerance, and sanctuary.

In seeking justice for Colten, Hubbard's documentary also searches for justice on a larger scale by recognizing the violence done to Indigenous peoples across Canada who have been wronged by a nation built on lies. It is an uncomfortable truth, one that dismantles Canada's national and international reputation as a "peaceable kingdom" while championing the potential to achieve justice by traveling from Canada to the US to plead for changes to rights of Indigenous peoples. It is integral to capping this study, throughout which I have traced examples of ingenious citizenship—moments in a variety of texts that portrays how BIPOC populations have challenged and continue to subvert pervasive stereotypes of what constitutes national belonging. These characters insist upon forging their own paths and identities in relation to the nation-state, whether it be Canada or the US or both. The concluding chapter complicates how readers and viewers may understand or recognize examples of Canadian exceptionality and focuses on texts that both reinforce and undermine dominant narratives to make clear who those stories serve and to what end.

In the final section of *Ingenious Citizenship*, Charles T. Lee describes the concept of "ingenious futurity" (2016, 254), a strategy that he argues enables individuals and communities to "continuously work on and recraft the present to reshape and reorient it" (254). Rather than looking for an ideal form of purity in the past, present, or future, ingenious futurity acknowledges the "already tainted cultural script" of white liberal democracy by attending to the realities of settler colonialism while insisting on the possibilities that "abject improvisations of nonexistent citizenship" can offer to those individuals who take up the task of "ingenious appropriation" to whatever degree is possible (254, 255). As several of the texts examined in this monograph suggest, there is value in attending to instances of "human creativity" that disrupt the democratic script of exceptionalism that has shaped Canada's self-construction as a "disinterested non-colonial power" at home and abroad (Razack 2004, 34). I have focused on works and characters that can be read as challenging Canada's narrative of "national goodness" (35) and refusing to allow Canadians to "take refuge behind the stock phrases about how nice we are" (165), but I have also highlighted moments in which such ingenious appropriation can and does fail. Texts like Hubbard's documentary foreground the potential for transformation in how viewers see and understand Canada by providing ways to look to the future that do not merely replicate familiar dominant histories, but also acknowledge that change is never easy, especially for those who have benefited from and continue to benefit from settler colonialism.

By paying attention to American depictions of Canada, I have argued that Canadians may learn a great deal about their history and national identity. The shifts in perspective that I have traced in this book offer new and different ways of looking at Canada and Canadian values. They affirm that American literature remains fundamentally engaged in investigating Canada's significance as the US' northern neighbor, trading partner, and friend, while probing and reframing its long-standing historical positioning as a place of escape from American bigotry. *Nîpawistamâsowin: We Will Stand Up* brings this book full circle by suggesting that the US as home to the UN may offer a reprieve, albeit only temporary, from the pervasive racism that shapes daily life on the Saskatchewan prairies—and in Canada more generally. In *Where Is American Literature*, Caroline Levander contends that "American authors consistently turn to the nation's vanishing points, edges, and the blurry boundaries between nations to resist and recreate as well as articulate national imperatives" (2013, 8). *Canada Through American Eyes* extends and refashions Levander's claim to demonstrate the value of attending to what American (and Canadian) eyes see and what stories they tell. Only by examining these perspectives can we start to understand better the ways in which Canada has perpetuated its own stories of exceptionality to its benefit and detriment. Looking south of the border reveals valuable information about Canada and Canadians, offering lessons that we cannot afford to ignore.

Notes

1. See Paulson, "A Broadway Musical" 2017c, A6 which explains that "most of [the musical's] … pre-Broadway development took place in the United States, and the vast majority of the show's $12 million capitalization was raised" in the US, "though there are a number of Canadian investors."
2. See Polack 2018 for a discussion of the Miawpukek First Nation's chief, Mi'sel Joe's refutation of "European assumptions that the Beothuk ceased to exist in 1829" (7).
3. See Grammond and Memorial University's "Primer on Indigenous Peoples and protocols in Newfoundland and Labrador" (https://www.mun.ca/research/Indigenous/primer.php) for descriptions of the status of various Indigenous communities in Newfoundland and Labrador.
4. See Paulson, "Prime Minister" 2017a, C4 for a brief history of which Canadian-authored musicals have premiered on Broadway. *Come From Away* is "only the fifth musical with a Canadian writing team to reach Broadway," following in the steps of "'Rockabye Hamlet' in 1976, 'Billy Bishop Goes to War' in 1980, 'The Drowsy Chaperone' in 2006, and 'The Story of My Life' in 2009. All but 'The Drowsy Chaperone' were considered flops."
5. See https://www.nfb.ca/film/nipawistamasowin-we-will-stand-up/.
6. See http://www3.nfb.ca/sg2/NFB-We-Will-Stand-Up-EN.pdf.
7. See Ka'nhehsì:io Deer 2020 for details of the efforts undertaken in recent years to obtain an apology from Canada's Prime Minister to the survivors of the Sixties Scoop.

References

Andrews, Jennifer. 2018. The Missionary Position: The American Roots of Northrop Frye's Peaceable Kingdom. *The Journal of Canadian Studies* 52 (2): 361–380.

Atkey, Mel. 2006. *Broadway North: The Dream of a Canadian Musical Theatre*. Toronto: Natural Heritage/Natural History Inc.

Boynton, Sean. 2021. Since 9/11, Islamophobia Has Been "a Constant Feature" in Canada, Experts Say. *Global News*, September 13. https://globalnews.ca/news/8174029/9-11-islamophobia-canada/.

Braat, Taylor. 2019. "Canadians Should See This Film": Colten Boushie Doc Sets Out on National Tour. *Global News*, May 22. https://globalnews.ca/news/5302394/colten-boushie-documentary-national-tour/.

Brantley, Ben. 2017. Review: "Come From Away," a Canadian Embrace on a Grim Day. *The New York Times*, March 12. https://www.nytimes.com/2017/03/12/theater/come-from-away-review.html.

Cole, Desmond. 2020. *The Skin We're In: A Year of Black Resistance and Power.* Toronto: Doubleday Canada.

"Commissions of Inquiry". 2022. *Government of Canada.* https://www.canada.ca/en/privy-council/services/commissions-inquiry.html. Accessed 7 June 2022.

Deer, Ka'nhehsì:io. 2020. Group Petitions PM for National Apology to 60s Scoop Survivors. *CBC News,* October 26. https://www.cbc.ca/news/indigenous/60s-scoop-national-apology-petition-1.5772768.

DeFede, Jim. 2002. *The Day the World Came to Town: 9/11 in Gander Newfoundland.* New York: HarperCollins.

Frank, Mary. 2020. "*nîpawistamâsowin:* We Will Stand Up" Highlights Racism in Canada's Judicial System. *The Gateway: The University of Alberta's Official Student Newspaper,* June 21. https://thegatewayonline.ca/2020/06/nipawistamasowin-the-gateway/.

Goldberg, David L. 2000. Commentary: A Well Regulated Militia, or a Volatile Militancy? *Criminal Justice Ethics* 19 (1): 2, 55.

Grammond, Sébastian. 2014. Equally Recognized? The Indigenous Peoples of Newfoundland and Labrador. *Osgoode Hall Law Journal* 51 (2): 469–499.

Hubbard, Tasha, Director. 2019. *nîpawistamâsowin: We Will Stand Up.* National Film Board.

Johnson, Brian D. 2007. They Love Me, They Love Me Not. *Maclean's,* June 25. https://archive.macleans.ca/article/2007/6/25/they-love-me-they-love-me-not.

Kane, Laura. 2019. Filmmaker Michael Moore Weighs in on Canadian Politics in VIFF Appearance. *CTV News,* October 5. https://bc.ctvnews.ca/filmmaker-michael-moore-weighs-in-on-canadian-politics-in-viff-appearance-1.4625791.

Lee, Charles T. 2016. *Ingenious Citizenship: Recrafting Democracy for Social Change.* Durham: Duke University Press.

Levander, Caroline. 2013. *Where is American Literature?* Chichester: Wiley-Blackwell.

Maynard, Robyn. 2017. *Policing Black Lives: State Violence in Canada from Slavery to the Present.* Halifax: Fernwood.

"Michael Moore Plots Canadian Escape Ahead of New Documentary Taking Aim at Trump". 2018. *The Canadian Press,* September 19. https://www.cbc.ca/news/entertainment/michael-moore-plots-canadian-escape-1.4829810.

Moore, Michael. 2003. *Bowling for Columbine.* MGM Home Entertainment.

Morton, Erin. 2019. White Settler Death Drives: Settler Statecraft, White Possession, and Multiple Colonialisms Under Treaty 6. *Cultural Studies* 33 (3): 437–459.

Mullen, Pat. 2019. Justice for Colten. *Point of View: Canada's Documentary Magazine,* April 20. https://povmagazine.com/justice-for-colten/.

"Nîpawistamâsowin: We Will Stand Up". 2022. *Wikipedia.* https://en.wikipedia.org/wiki/Nîpawistamâsowin:_We_Will_Stand_Up. Accessed 22 June.

Nixon, Lindsay. 2019. nîpawistamâsowin: We Will Stand Up. *Canadian Art,* May 1. https://canadianart.ca/reviews/nipawistamasowin-we-will-stand-up/.

Office of the High Commissioner for Human Rights. 2013. Free, Prior and Informed Consent Of Indigenous Peoples. September. https://www.ohchr.org/sites/default/files/Documents/Issues/IPeoples/FreePriorandInformedConsent.pdf.

Ott, Brian L., and Susan A. Sci. 2015. The Many Moods of Michael Moore: Aesthetics and Affect in *Bowling for Columbine.* In *Michael Moore and the Rhetoric of Documentary,* ed. Thomas W. Benson and Brian J. Snee, 74–100. Carbondale: Southern Illinois University Press.

Paulson, Michael. 2017a. Prime Minister to See Canadian Broadway Musical. *New York Times, March* 6: C4.

———. 2017b. Justin Trudeau Brings Ivanka Trump to Broadway Show on Welcoming Outsiders. *New York Times,* March 15. https://www.nytimes.com/2017/03/15/theater/justin-trudeau-ivanka-trump-broadway-come-from-away.html.

———. 2017c. A Broadway Musical Brings Out Soft Power. *New York Times,* March 17: A6. https://www.nytimes.com/2017/03/16/theater/a-broadway-musical-brings-out-canadian-soft-power.html.

Polack, Fiona. 2018. Introduction: De-islanding the Beothuk. In *Tracing Ochre: Changing Perspectives on the Beothuk,* ed. Fiona Polack, 3–29. Toronto: University of Toronto Press.

Razack, Sherene. 2004. *Dark Threats and White Knights: the Somalia Affair, Peacekeeping, and the New Imperialism.* Toronto: University of Toronto Press.

Roberts, Gillian. 2015. *Discrepant Parallels: Cultural Implications of the Canada-US Border.* Montreal & Kingston: McGill-Queen's University Press.

Sankoff, Irene, and David Hein. 2019. *Come From Away: Welcome to the Rock.* New York: Hachette Books.

Short, Amanda. 2020. Full-Length Colten Boushie Documentary Airing on TV for the First Time. *The Star Phoenix,* September 12. https://thestarphoenix.com/news/local-news/full-length-colten-boushie-documentary-airing-on-tv-for-the-first-time.

Simpson, Audra. 2016. The State is a Man: Theresa Spence, Loretta Saunders and the Gender of Settler Sovereignty. *Theory & Event* 19, no. 4. https://www.muse.jhu.edu/article/633280.

Smith, Marie-Danielle. 2018. When Justin Trudeau Invited Guests to See *Come From Away* on Broadway, a Couple of Hundred Didn't Even Bother to RSVP. *National Post,* March 12. https://nationalpost.com/news/politics/when-justin-trudeau-invited-guests-to-see-come-from-away-on-broadway-a-couple-of-hundred-didnt-even-bother-to-rsvp.

Tanovich, David M. 2004. E-Racing Racial Profiling. *Alberta Law Review* 41 (4): 905–933.

Tremblay, Reeta Chowdhari, and Amanda Bittner. 2011. Newfoundland and Labrador: Creating Change in the Twenty-First Century. In *Integration and Inclusion of Newcomers and Minorities across Canada*, ed. John Biles et al., 325–353. Montreal & Kingston: McGill-Queen's University Press.

Trudeau, Justin. 2019. Foreword to *Come From Away: Welcome to the Rock*, by Irene Sankoff and David Hein, 5. New York: Hachette Books.

"United Nations Declaration of the Rights of Indigenous Peoples." 2007. *United Nations*, 1–29. New York. https://www.un.org/development/desa/indigenouspeoples/wp-content/uploads/sites/19/2018/11/UNDRIP_E_web.pdf.

Young, Jim. 2010. Ontario Court Confirms No Right to Bear Arms in Canada; Supreme Court Will Not Hear Appeal. *Centre for Constitutional Studies*, October 5. https://www.constitutionalstudies.ca/2010/10/ontario-court-confirms-no-right-to-bear-arms-in-canada-supreme-court-will-not-hear-appeal/.

Index[1]

A
Acadia, Acadians, 18, 55, 58, 59, 61–68, 70–73, 76, 77, 78n3, 78n9, 86
  communities, 56, 57, 66–68, 71, 79n13
  Deportation, 14, 54–57, 59, 61, 69, 70, 78n3, 78n7, 87, 100
  francophone, 15, 53
  and Mi'kmaq, 79n13
  See also Louisiana
Adoption, 111, 112, 136n4, 212, 214
  and baby formula, 116–117
  Canadian government and, 116
  consequences of, 118, 120, 127–128
  cross-border, 11
  forced, 18, 109, 112, 113, 116, 124, 126, 132–134, 136n5, 136n6
  mandate, 114, 117, 123
Ambassador Bridge, xii
American Dream, x–xi, 159
American studies, 4–7, 12
  inter-, 1, 6
Amherst (NS), 18, 85–87, 89–92
  See also under Camps, internment
Anastakis, Dimitry, 48n8
Andrews, Valerie, 113–117, 134–135, 136n4, 136n7
Anti-Blackness, 103, 181, 188
  See also Racism, anti-Black
Art, folk, 10, 17, 29, 33, 34, 45, 47n5, 105
Ashley, Christopher, 204
Assimilate, assimilation, 61, 93–94, 122, 124–126, 131
  Indigenous, 56, 180, 185, 195n3
Atkey, Mel, 210
Atwood, Margaret, 178–179
Austen, Ian, 175

---

[1] Note: Page numbers followed by 'n' refer to notes.

© The Author(s), under exclusive license to Springer Nature Switzerland AG 2023
J. Andrews, *Canada Through American Eyes*,
https://doi.org/10.1007/978-3-031-22120-0

229

B

Balcom, Karen, 111
Baptiste, Debbie, 216, 220
Barker, Adam, 8
Basque, Maurice, 78n7
Bates, Robin, 63
Battleford (SK), 201, 214, 217
Becker, Kurt, 91
Becoming-animal (Braidotti), 113, 119–120, 124, 125, 129, 134
  See also Braidotti, Rosi
Beecher Stowe, Harriet, 12, 15, 143
Bentley, David, 47n5
Beothuk, 53, 205, 225n2
Berlant, Lauren, x, 106n2
Bernhardt, Nicole, 153
Bible, biblical, 28, 30, 34, 45, 75
  allegories, 33, 34, 45
  stories, 35
  typology, 36
BIPOC: Americans, 176
  bodies, 177, 180
  communities, 194, 203, 214
  people, 14, 147
  populations, 2, 9, 19, 184
  women, 177, 193
  writers, 5, 12
Birds, 109, 112–113, 118–124, 130–132, 134, 137n9
  as Freya (goddess), 125
  imagery, 128
  migration of, 112, 135–136n2
Bismarck, Otto von, 96
Black: Americans, x, 18, 34, 104, 153, 191
  authors, 5, 9, 176, 194n1
  Canadians, 53
  enslaved people, 9, 15, 19, 143–145, 150–151, 174, 176, 177, 186–191, 200, 204–207
  liberation, 176
  Loyalists, 53
  people, 2, 11, 168, 174, 189, 192
  populations, 103, 152
  salvation, 20n13
  single mothers, 113, 152
  unwed mothers, 113
  visual stereotypes, 102–104
Border crossing, xii, xvii, 6, 7, 57
  Canada-US, 18
  stations, 2
  white experience of US to Canada, 143–146
  Indigenous, 146–147
Boushie, Colten, 200–201, 213–216, 221, 222
  family of, 212, 217–219, 221–223
Bowling for Columbine (documentary), *see under* Moore, Michael
Boynton, Sean, 208
Braidotti, Rosi, 112–113, 118–119, 125
Bryant, Rachel, 9–10, 45
Bush, George W., 159, 178
Butler, Judith, 17, 21n16

C

Caen, Sophie de, 211
Calarco, Matthew, 118
Campbell, Matthew, 148
Campos da Silva, Fabiola, 164
Camps, internment, 85, 91, 97
  Amherst Internment Camp, 84–92
  prisoners' artworks in, 87–88
Canada Post Corporation, 78n3
Canadian First World War Internment Recognition Fund, 85, 106n3
Cardinal, Douglas, 147
Carlson-Manathara, Elizabeth, 8
Carnophallogocentrism (Derrida), 118–119
  See also Derrida, Jacques

INDEX 231

Carrick, Rob, 158
Cartographer of No Man's Land, The (novel), see under Duffy, P.S.
Catholic, 59, 60, 65, 70, 79n13, 179
 francophone, 15
 French, 95, 99, 114
 models of sacrifice, 184
Charyn, Jerome, 20n13
Chester, Philip, 31
Chinese, 148–150, 155, 183
 head tax, 53, 55, 155
 immigrants, 53
Christian, Christianity, 30, 34, 43, 94, 125, 184, 186
 anglophone, 114
 belief, 28
 charity, 40
 models of sacrifice, 184
 right, 178
Church, Frederic, xi, xii, xvn3 (Pref.)
Church of England, 43
Ciarlo, David, 103
Citizenship, 73, 95, 116, 223
 American, 11, 15–17, 159
 Canadian, 17, 135, 148
 ingenious xiv, 17–19, 76–77, 118, 167, 189, 223
 liberal, 17
Civility, 55–56, 70, 72
 white, 56, 62, 64, 70
Civil War, American, 13, 14, 31, 62, 174, 188
 post-, 15, 122
Class, x, 11, 84, 98, 113, 150, 152, 160, 178
 middle, x, 141, 152, 159, 165–167, 176, 202
 women and, 113–116, 123
 working xi
Cobb, Jasmine, 104
Coleman, Daniel, 46, 55, 175

Colonial, colonialism, 10, 13, 57–59, 70–71, 77, 103, 120, 174, 201, 222, 223
 British, 70, 71, 96, 175
 and Canada, 8, 9, 13, 14, 18, 30, 32, 54, 55, 68, 144, 195n3, 214, 217
 German, 97
 histories of, 2, 212
 justice, 73
 settler, 8, 32, 147, 183, 213, 223, 224
 values, 110, 130
Comacchio, Cynthia, 115
Come From Away (musical), 11, 19, 200, 203–212, 221, 223, 225n4
Confederation, 84, 103, 204, 205
 post-, 13–15, 64, 86
 pre-, 76
Cooper, Afua, 188
Coulson, Ray, 87
Cree, x, 213–217
Cultural studies, 6, 7
Culture and the Canada-U.S. Border (CCUSB), 7
Cumberland County Museum (Amherst NS), 87

D

Davies, Gwen, 48n10
Debt, 11, 152, 154, 156–159, 161, 163, 165–167
 credit card, 166
 household, 141–142
 mortgage, 153
Declaration of Independence, 44
Declaration on the Rights of Indigenous People, 220
DeFede, Jim, 203
Delvoie, Louis, 48n9
Derrida, Jacques, 118–119

INDEX

Doskoch, Bill, 169n8
Douglass, Frederick, 186
Doyle, James, 12–15
Dryden, OmiSoore H., 20n11
Duffy, P.S., 11, 18, 83–84, 92, 94–97, 100–102, 104, 105, 110, 111, 142
  Cartographer of No Man's Land, The, 4, 18, 84, 85, 92, 95–97, 101–102, 104, 105, 110, 111
Dyck, Lillian, 219

E
Erdrich, Louise, 4, 11, 18, 19, 176–187, 193–194
  Future Home of the Living God, 4, 18, 176–178, 181, 185, 190, 193
Eugenics, 114, 186
Evangeline (Longfellow), 15, 18, 57–62
  and marketing, 62–67
  popularity of, 58
  publication of, 54
  See also Longfellow, Henry Wadsworth
Evangeline, A Novel, see under Farmer, Ben
Exceptionalism, exceptionality, 5, 7, 18, 19, 54, 143, 146, 159, 181, 186, 224
  American, xiii, xiv, 3, 9–10, 12, 64
  Canadian, 8–10, 18, 20n11, 28, 45, 55, 76, 84–85, 87, 105, 135, 137n10, 142, 176, 200–204, 210, 211, 224
  in *Come From Away*, 221
  discourses, 77
  in *Nîpawistamâsowin*, 211–223
Exclusion Act, 155

F
Faragher, John, 56–57
Farmer, Ben, 4, 11, 17, 18, 53–54, 57, 67–77, 77–78n1, 79n13, 110
  Evangeline: A Novel, 53–54, 67, 71–77
  See also Evangeline (Longfellow)
Field, Erastus Salisbury, 17, 29, 34–36, 45, 46, 48n12
First World War, 53, 85, 86, 92, 93, 97, 102, 105
Ford, Richard, ix–x, xiii–xiv, svn2 (Pref.), 3, 4, 11, 12, 135
  Canada (novel), ix–xiv, xvn2 (Pref.)
Fournier, Chris, 167
Freyja (Norse goddess), 125–126
Friscolanti, Michael, 168n1
Frye, Northrop, 11, 48n12
  background, 30–31, 45–46
  beliefs, 28–30, 47n5
  "Conclusion" (essay), 10, 28–29, 31–33, 36, 40, 43–47
  Literary History of Canada, 10, 28, 33, 40, 43, 45
  and the peaceable kingdom, 10, 17, 28, 29, 31, 33, 36, 38–39, 47n1, 48n8, 53, 143
  See also Hicks, Edward
Fugitive Slave Act (1850), 187–189
Future Home of the Living God (novel), see under Erdrich, Louise

G
Gander (NL), 200, 203–209
Genocide, 64, 67, 78n7, 176
  Herero and Namaqua, 103
  Indigenous, 13, 179, 180, 185, 195n2
Giles, Wenona, 66
Gimli (MB), 130, 134, 135n1
Gorman, James, 133, 137n14

Grand-Pré (NS), 62, 63, 65, 70,
  71, 78n9
  development of, 64
  National Historic site, 56, 66,
    67, 78n3
  See also *Evangeline* (Longfellow)
Great chain of being, 38
Grewal, Inderpal, 10, 64
Grove, Frederick Phillip, 46

H
Haley, Nikki, 211
Haliburton, Thomas Chandler, 58
Hawthorne, Nathaniel, 57
Healey, Robynne, 43
Hein, David, 203, 208
Helleiner, Jane, 147
Hell's Angels, 168n2
HELOC (Home Equity Line of
  Credit), 157–158,
  166–167, 169n4
Hemisphere, hemispheric studies, 1–3,
  5–8, 14, 16
Hertzberg, Erik, 167
Hicks, Edward, 17, 35, 47n5
  "Peaceable Kingdom, The"
    (painting), 29, 33, 35–43, 45,
    46, 48n8
  and religion, 35–38, 40, 46
  See also Frye, Northrop;
    Quakers
Hicks, Elias, 37–39
Hicksites, 37, 43
  See also Quakers
Hicks, Rodney, 205–208
Hicksites, *see under* Hicks, Elias
Hispanic Americans, 152, 153,
  168–169n3
Home Equity Line of Credit,
  see HELOC
Hot Docs (film festival), 212

Housing, 154–155,
  159–161, 166–167
  bubble, 142, 157
  crisis, 152
  markets, 143, 149, 157
  prices, 149, 154, 156, 169n9
Hubbard, Tasha, 11, 19, 200–201,
  212–219, 221–224
Hughes, Robert, xvn3 (Pref.)
Hutcheon, Linda, 96
Hyndman, Jennifer, 66

I
Ibbitson, John, 32–33, 45
Iceland, Icelanders, 109–112, 116,
  118, 120, 123, 126, 128–133,
  135, 137n13
  communities, 110
  language, 122, 127
  literature, lore, mythology,
    121, 125
  New Iceland, 118, 122, 125, 126,
    128, 132, 133, 135
  Reykjavik, 131
  See also Gimli
Identity, 20n13, 43, 54, 123,
  126, 200
  Acadian, 64, 78n9
  American, 14, 15
  Canada and, 28, 29, 45–47, 78n7,
    90, 102, 105, 188, 201,
    206, 211
  cultural, 12
  and gender, 21n16
  national, 15, 32, 57, 155, 188,
    221, 224
  political, 182
Imperialism, 5, 7, 174, 193
  American, 14
  British, 65
  cultural, 6

Inclusivity, xiv, 7, 55, 94, 100, 103, 135, 147, 179, 205, 207, 210, 212, 223
  racial, 10, 155
Indian Act, 217
Indigenous
  and border crossings, 146–147
  children, removal of, 56, 174, 180, 181, 195n3, 212, 217
  Cleveland Indians controversy, 146–147
  communities, 59, 183, 185, 187, 193, 194, 204–205, 220, 225n3
  peoples, 2, 8, 11, 14, 18, 34, 69, 76, 78n7, 174, 177, 179, 181, 187, 195n3, 201, 205, 213–223
  populations, 8, 13, 76, 145, 179, 183, 185, 193, 195n2, 205, 217
  unwed mothers, 113
  women, 60, 68, 69, 73, 77, 180, 185, 195n3
  See also Sterilization, forced
Isaiah (biblical prophet), 35–37, 39–41, 46
  See also Hicks, Edward

J
Jacobs, Harriet, 186
Japanese Canadians, 55–56
  internment of, 155
Jay Treaty, 147, 180
Jewishness, Jews, ix, x, xiv, 53, 94, 208

K
Kirby, Jason, 149
Kitchener (ON), 94
Klaus, Fritz, 91

Klinck, Carl, 33
Kokotailo, Philip, 47n5

L
LaDow, Beth, 182
Lamay, Pamphile, 67
Lawrence, Charles, 58, 66
Laxer, James, 79n13
LeBlanc, Barbara, 64, 65
Lecker, Robert, 28–29
Lee, Charles, xiv, 17, 21n16, 77, 118, 223
Leni-Lenape (Indigenous people), 38, 39, 46, 48–49n14
Lennon, Suzanne, 20n11
Lepore, Jill, 173–174, 194n1
Levander, Caroline, 3, 224
Levecq, Christine, 20n13
Lincoln, Abraham, 34
Literary History of Canada (scholarly work), *see under* Frye, Northrop
Longfellow, Henry Wadsworth, 12, 14, 17–18, 54, 56, 110
  and Acadians, 56–57, 59, 62
  and Americanness, 61
  and *Evangeline*, 57–62
  monument to, 65
  and Nathaniel Hawthorne, 57
  translation of work, 57, 67
  See also Acadia, Acadians; *Evangeline* (Longfellow)
Louisiana, 56, 61, 73–75
Lount, Elizabeth, 43, 44, 46, 54
Lount, Samuel, 43, 44, 54
Loyalists, 2, 30, 62, 92, 206
  Black, 53
Lucas, Deborah, 169n7
Luciuk, Kassandra, 105–106n1
Luciuk, Lubomyr, 88–89
Lynch, Jim, 4
Lynch, Kevin, 154

M
Mackey, Eva, 8
Macklin, Audrey, 175
MacLean, Alyssa, 15–16, 143, 144
Maiti, Krishanu, 119
Manifest destiny, 6, 60
Matthews, Heidi, 78n7
Maynard, Robyn, 11, 181, 187–188
Mbembe, Achille, 70, 73
McClanahan, Annie, 142, 152, 153, 155—156, 157, 159, 166–168
McGill Institute for the Study of Canada, 9
McGill, Robert, 31
McIntyre, John, 43
McKay, Ian, 63, 104–105
Medicine line/road, 181, 182
Melting pot, 93–94, 105
Mercer, Greg, 78n9
Methodism, Methodists, 30, 31, 45, 47n5, 48n6
   American, 42
Mi'kmaq, 9, 66
   and Amherst area, 86
   and Beothuk, 205
   possible intermarriage with Acadians, 67–68, 79n13
Minnesota, 177, 180–182, 184
Moore, Michael, 10, 19, 200–203
Bowling for Columbine, 10, 19, 200–202, 211, 223
Morton, Erin, 88, 214
Mothers, unwed, 18, 113–116, 124, 130, 134–135, 136n6
   sterilization of, 114
Mullins, Richard F., 77–78n1
Multiculturalism, 55, 66, 92, 94, 95, 150, 153, 179, 199, 206, 213
Muslim, 174, 204, 208–210

N
Nancy, Jean-Luc, 119
National Film Board, 212
Nation state, 15, 55, 57, 65, 70, 72, 77, 134, 157, 174, 176, 181, 185, 200, 201, 221, 223
   American, 54, 134
   and borders, 5, 15, 57, 73, 112, 135, 144, 146, 187, 194
   Canadian, 31, 54, 64, 65, 100, 134, 184, 200, 223
   and Indigenous people, 146, 179
   power, 64
   settlers,' 56
Necropolitics, 64, 72
Nelson, Dana, 10
Niagara Falls, xi–xii, xvn2 (Pref.), 18, 141, 142, 144, 146, 148–151, 163–166, 168, 176
   See also Church, Frederic
9/11, 2, 3, 54, 56, 159, 200, 201, 203, 204, 207, 208
Nîpawistamâsowin: We Will Stand Up (documentary), 11, 19, 200, 203, 219, 220, 222–224
   and Canadian exceptionality, 211–216
   and gun violence, 216–218
   See also Boushie, Colten
Nischik, Reingard, 16
Nova Scotia Highlanders Regimental Museum, 87, 90, 91, 102

O
Obiko Pearson, Natalie, 148
Odds, The (novel), *see under* O'Nan, Stewart
Ojibwe, 177, 179–183
O'Nan, Stewart, 4, 11, 18, 141–143, 146, 149, 152–155, 162–165, 168, 176
The Odds, 4, 16, 141–168

P

Paulson, Michael, 211, 225n1
Peaceable kingdom, *see under* Frye, Northrop; Hicks, Edward
Pearson, Lester B., 31
Pelletier, Pierre-Yves, 78n3
Penn, William, 38–40, 46, 48–49n14
Phelan, Peggy, xii–xiii, 16
Phillips Casteel, Sarah, 5
Pontiac Herald (newspaper), 44
Poole, Leslie Kemp, 122
Privilege, 135, 142, 164, 176, 191, 208
 class, 150, 152, 166
 economic, 119
 race, 150, 152, 166
 white, 151
Propaganda
 anti-German, 94
 Canadian, 204
 war, 10, 87, 97, 98
Protestant, 95, 98–99, 114

Q

Quakers, 29, 35, 39, 40, 47–48n5, 54, 173, 178
 beliefs, 36, 39
 Hicksites, 37, 43
 Inward Light, 36, 37
 migration to Upper Canada, 42
 Orthodox, 36–38, 41, 43
 Primitive, 37, 38
 schism in, 36–37, 42–44, 46
 Yonge Street settlement, 42–43
 See also Hicks, Edward; Rebellion of, 1837

R

Racism, racist, x, 2, 8, 11, 66, 84, 96, 98, 123, 145, 154–155, 184, 186–187, 208, 209
 anti-Black, 104, 153, 206, 207

 Canadian, 9, 11, 18, 84, 100, 103, 105, 155, 201, 209, 212, 214–215, 219–221, 224
 and Donald Trump, 174
 systemic, 55, 219
 tropes, 102–103
 in the United States, 32, 175, 200
Raynal, Guillaume Thomas, 59
Razack, Sherene, 31–32, 207
Rebellion of, 1837, 43–44
Recession, Great, 142, 146, 150–155, 157, 160, 166, 168, 169n3
Red Pheasant Cree Nation, 213, 216
Reed, Ishmael, 12, 14, 20n13
Refugees, 2, 9, 20n11, 32, 70, 72–74, 174, 183, 211
 Black, 188
 child, 175
 policies, 77, 210
Renan, Ernest, 54
Reproduction (human), 178, 184, 195n3
 Acadian, 71
 and mental handicap, 114
 rights, 173, 174, 178–180
 See also Women
Revolution, American, 2, 12, 15, 31, 34, 38, 46
 post-, 60
 pre-, 13, 60, 72, 76
Revolution, Industrial, 62, 63
Riel, Louis, 213
Roberts, Gillian, 199, 200, 206, 222
Rowe, John Carlos, 4, 6
Royal Canadian Mounted Police (RCMP), 98, 216, 217, 219, 220

S

Sacrifice, 54, 59, 119, 124, 129, 191
 Catholic and Christian, 184
 self-, 39, 69
 structure, 118
 symbolic, 119

INDEX   237

Sankoff, Irene, 203
Savoie, Donald, 86
Scheer, Andrew, 219
Schoolcraft, Henry, 60
Schools, residential, 46, 56, 179, 195n3, 213, 217
Schulz, Kathryn, 191
Second Amendment (U.S. Constitution), 202
Second World War, x, 53, 55, 94, 115, 204
Sexism, 11, 18, 47n2, 184
Shawnee, 60, 68–69
Siemerling, Winfried, 5
Silverman, Jason, 188
Simone, Dylan, 154–156, 160–161
Simpson, Audra, 213
Sinclair, Murray, 219
Singh, Jagmeet, 219
Sinha, Manisha, 186
Sixties Scoop, 195n3, 213, 217, 225n7
Slavery, 7, 9, 15, 20n11, 146, 168, 173, 174, 176, 177, 186, 188, 190, 191
 legacy of, 103
 modern forms of, 182
 profits of, 194
 See also Underground Railroad
Spencer, Scott, 218
Stanley, Gerald, 200, 213–220, 222
Stephens, Donald, 33
Sterilization, forced, 114, 180, 195n3
Stevenson, Garth, 92–94
Stone, Ken, 118–119
Stote, Karen, 180–181, 195n3
Strong, Gregory, 147
Sugars, Cynthia, 5–6, 19–20n6
Sunchild, Eleanore, 212, 215
Sunley, Christina, 4, 11, 109, 110, 112–113, 117–120, 124, 127, 129, 134–135, 135n1, 142
 Tricking of Freya, The, 4, 18, 109–135

T
Tanovich, David, 207
Thobani, Sunera, 71, 77
TIFF, *see* Toronto International Film Festival
Tombs, George, 190
Tootoosis, Jade, 216–217, 219, 220
Toronto International Film Festival (TIFF), 212–213
Torrance, Judy, 32, 48n8
Traister, Bryce, 6–7
Transnational, 7–8, 17
 contexts, 5
 studies, 2–6
Treaty of Paris, 147
Tricking of Freya, The (novel), *see under* Sunley, Christina
Trotsky, Leon, 85, 87, 88, 99–101
Trudeau, Justin, 169n5, 174, 175, 204, 210–211, 219
Trudel, Marcel, 190
Trump, Donald, 2, 20n10, 31, 174, 175, 179, 201, 210
Trump, Ivanka, 211
Tuck, Eve, 8

U
Underground Railroad, 143, 173, 176, 183, 185–192, 206
 and Canada, 181
 and Cleveland, 144
 legacy of, 168, 181
Underground Railroad, The (novel), *see under* Whitehead, Colson
United Church of Canada, 28, 30, 31, 34, 45, 48n6, 48n11
United Nations, 31, 211, 220

United Nations Declaration on the
  Rights of Indigenous People, 220
United Nations Permanent Forum on
  Indigenous Issues, 220

V
Viau, Robert, 61
Vietnam war, 2, 32, 122, 137n10
  (ch.5), 206
Violence, 27, 34, 37, 54, 71, 76,
    118, 119
  and Canada, 32, 48n8, 53, 55,
    213, 215
  colonial, 147, 213
  gun, 11, 200–203, 214–218, 221
  imperial, 214
  and Indigenous people, 2, 223
  racialized, 147
  state-sanctioned, 15, 70
  systemic, 55
  and the US, 9, 31, 32, 188, 202
Virtuosity, Canada's, xiii, 19, 28, 201,
    207, 221

W
Wakeham, Pauline, 55–56
Walks, Alan, 154–156, 160–161
Walls, Andrew, 30
War Measures Act, 94
War on Terror, 55, 72
Water crossings, 143, 144
Weekley, Carolyn, 40

Westall, Richard, 35
Whitehead, Colson, 4, 11, 18, 19, 176,
    177, 185–187, 189–192, 194
  Underground Railroad, The, 4, 18,
    176, 177, 183–194
Wilson-Raybould, Jody, 219
Women, 69, 98, 115, 119, 123,
    124, 127, 135, 174,
    178, 182–184
  Acadian, 69
  as caregivers, 68
  of colour, 77, 177, 179, 182,
    193, 195n3
  immigrant, 110
  Indigenous, 69, 73, 173, 180,
    185, 195n3
  and mental illness, 119, 120
  rights of, 43
  unwed white pregnant,
    113, 114
  See also Adoption, forced;
    Mothers, unwed
Wyile, Herb, 6, 7, 104

Y
Yang, K. Wayne, 8

Z
Zacharias, Robert, 4–5
Zangwill, Israel, 94
Ziemba, Rachel, 167
Ziemba, William, 167

Printed in the United States
by Baker & Taylor Publisher Services